Let Me Tell You How I Got SAVED

Charles Lewis Anthony

This is a work of non-fiction. The details and events are a recollection of the author's memory. Government names have been changed to protect the identities of the individuals, while nicknames remain the same.

CLF Publishing, LLC.
www.clfpublishing.org

Copyright © 2018 by Charles Lewis Anthony. All rights reserved. No portion of this book may be reproduced, stored in a retrieval system, or transmitted by any form or any means electronically, photocopied, recorded, or any other except for brief quotations in printed reviews, without the prior permission of the publisher.

All rights reserved. No portion of this book may be reproduced, stored in a retrieval system, or transmitted by any form or any means electronically, photocopied, recorded, or any other except for brief quotations in printed reviews, without the prior permission of the publisher.

Cover Design by Senir Design. Contact information- info@senirdesign.com.

ISBN #978-1-945102-71-4

Printed in the United States of America.

Foreword

Second chances may seem rare for most people. Who gives second chances anyway? It is ultimately up to you to have faith and trust in God to reverse the things that you believe have fallen apart in your life. Life may not seem wavering, but believing and trusting in God will help you to understand His promises. There is a future for your life, if you just put aside the things that are less important and give God your undivided attention. I say this because I have witnessed the life of this author, and he has gone through some drastic challenges and changes in his lifetime.

Deacon Charles Lewis Anthony has turned his life around from representing the streets and leaving his family and loved ones behind. He has suffered from the consequences of committing himself to a gang, serving and abusing the usage of drugs in the dirty streets of South L.A., to shifting 180 degrees to give that same energy to Christ, and has reaped the benefits of remaining faithful. He has been a true living witness of how God has reversed his life.

God hears you even when you think He is not listening. Do not give up, and remember that this life is not your own, and it's not always about you! Give God the honor and the praise for allowing you to be here today. Thank Him for the small things.

God's timing is not our timing, so patience is required. His blessings for you shall come to past. Be considerate and love one another. Even when you feel you are at your lowest point in life, or think that life's odds are against you, trust that God will even it out and provide for you. He is always on time! So, give it some thought today, pray, and watch how your life transitions.

Be blessed!
Maisha L. Jefferson

Preface

This book was written first and foremost to give our Heavenly Father all the glory for what He has done in my life! Hallelujah!!! Even though the book was written so all could enjoy, both saint and sinner, it was initially written for those who have not yet accepted Jesus Christ as the Lord and Savior of their life. Even those who may have cooled down their journey with the Lord, I pray something I have said or done in this book will rekindle a fire and draw you by His Spirit to fight the good fight of faith and continue to hold up the Blood-stained banner! This is my testimony!

I'd like to thank my mother Donna Marie Anthony for all her prayers and for never giving up on me when I was lost in the world.

I thank God for my beautiful wife, Christine Alicia Anthony for all of her love and support while I was writing this book.

May God bless our children: Vianté Anthony, K'Lynn Anthony, Tyler Wright, Charaiah Anthony, and Maegan Conway. Keep God first in your lives at all costs.

Shouts out to my dad, Kenneth Michael Anthony, Sr.; brother, Kenneth Michael Anthony, Jr.; sisters, Lakisha and Maisha Jefferson; and god-brothers, Wesley and Michael Crunk.

Photography by Kelly Brooks, with Shot by Kelly.

Much love to all of the homeboys and to the families of all the fallen soldiers taken too soon.

God bless you!

Chapter 1
64th Street

There was an uneasy feeling inside as I sat on the bathroom sink, looking into the mirror, into my own eyes. I was only three years old, but I knew there was something else to this living thing. As I sat there, just staring, I don't know if it was a voice or a thought, but it said I would not live. It said, eventually, I would die. Tears started to roll down my face as I sat there, just staring. The feeling became so overwhelming that the tears started flowing uncontrollably, and I started to sob. *What am I made for? How did I get here? What's after death?*

I guess my mother heard me crying and came to the bathroom. "What's wrong with you?" she asked, with a puzzled look on her face, holding the telephone receiver to her ear.

"I don't want to die!" I cried.

"Shut up, boy!" she said, as she slapped me and pulled me down off the sink. "Get your butt out of here!"

It was 1979, in South Central Los Angeles. 64th Street was our place of residence: my dad, my mom, my big brother Joseph Jr., and me. My dad was renting a one-bedroom apartment from his sister Briana and her husband Paul. Dad had a good job working for the city, but for some reason or another, we didn't have much. Joseph Jr. and I shared a fold-up rollaway bed that we slept on at opposite ends. That was the living room's only piece of furniture. Mama often complained to Dad that he should buy a couch and a coffee table at least, to make it feel like a home.

"This is not how I was raised, Joseph!" she cried. "What do you do with your paycheck? Just wait until I find me a job! You're going to see a change around here!"

"Shut up, woman!" Dad exploded. "You don't know what you're talking about! We don't need all that extra stuff!"

And, on and on they would argue until Dad would run out of words. Then, his hands started doing the talking. I'd be standing outside the closed bedroom door with Joseph Jr. calling for Mama, but the yelling and the crying would continue until it just died down. Sometimes, we would fall asleep by the door, tired from crying. Mama called the police a few times on the next day when she was released from her captivity and Dad was gone to work, but the cops said it was a domestic dispute, and they needed to straighten it out between themselves.

The violence continued…

One day, Mama taught Joseph Jr. how to dial 911, so he could save her from Daddy. "When you hear me crying, what are you going to do?" she asked.

"Call 911!" shouted Joseph Jr.

"That's right!" she said.

Mama took Joseph Jr. through a whole training course! She took him outside, so he could see the address of the apartment. She even walked him to the corner, so he could memorize the street signs. I wonder if she knew I was learning too, by just watching my brother go through boot camp. I was as sharp as a knife even though I was a year and a half younger. I had been learning my ABCs and 123s in little Joseph's preschool class while my mother volunteered. We were ready! Despite the fact that it was very confusing to be in between a war going on with two parties we both loved dearly, it seemed natural to be enlisted in Mama's army because we spent the majority of our time and training under her supervision.

"Ray! Ray! Raymond, put those marbles up, and let's go!" my mother shouted across the room.

"Oh, okay, Mama," I said as I filled my pail with Joseph Jr.'s and my marbles. Sometimes, we could play with those marbles for hours, but then it would be time to take a walk through the neighborhood to the local grocery store. My mother would speak to every neighbor as we went, and sometimes, they would visit for hours, talking about who knows what. It seemed as though she knew everybody! That could be a long trip depending on who was outside. "Looking good, Rachel," said Cleophus, with his chin on his chest.

"Ain't you supposed to be working?" Mama snapped with a smile still on her face.

"Check this out, I can fix these cars with my eyes closed and still have time to peek at you," Cleophus smirked.

"Leave me alone. I told you I was taken, oil man," Mama flirted.

"Is that whom you put that perfume on for?" Cleophus asked. Mama just continued to push the stroller past the auto body shop with that schoolgirl smile on her face. The grocery store was coming into view. I had my mind on those Neapolitan candies Mama usually gets for us as a treat, but Mama had something else in mind. In fact, she didn't go to shop for groceries at all. As soon as we entered the store, she immediately walked up to one of the women cashiers.

"Excuse me. I'm not trying to be rude, but I have something important to talk to you about," my mother said with a calm voice.

"Well, I don't get a break until another hour," proclaimed the cashier as if she was talking to the manager, who was twenty feet away.

"Okay, well here it goes," Mama reached into her purse and pulled out a small piece of paper. "My name is Rachel. You've seen me here before with my husband Joseph Watkins. I found your number in a pair of his pants, Sarah!" Mama said sternly, as she put the piece of paper next to the cashier's nametag. "I'm letting you know that he is married, and these are his two boys. If you have any decency that your parents raised you with, you will not continue to break up my family. You have a nice day," Mama said sarcastically, as she pushed me out of the store with Joseph Jr. trying to keep up with his little legs as he held onto the stroller. The cashier lady just watched us leave with her mouth open, a little embarrassed. I was wondering what happened to the Neapolitan candies, but I dared not ask and become the scapegoat onto which Mama's anger was released.

Being the granddaughter of a gospel preacher, Mama handled the situation quite well. It seemed that a humble spirit was seeping in, which unfortunately, had skipped her father. Her dad was a man whom neither Joseph nor I ever got to meet. Granddaddy Raymond, named after his dad and whose name I shared also, was a stern man, who was always spoken of as having a boiling hot, bad temper. He had gotten into an altercation with a young man when Mama was just a little girl.

The young man had owed two dollars to Granddaddy Raymond that he borrowed at the corner store. Granddad had obviously lost his patience while waiting for the two dollars to be paid back to him and went to confront the young man about it. Having the temper that he had, the conversation elevated into a fight, which, in turn, elevated into a stabbing. When the smoke cleared, Granddad had lost his life. Some say he died over two dollars, but anyone with any street smarts would say that the young man did not keep his word.

Chapter 2
The Big Fight

Joseph Jr. and I were awakened out of our sleep in the middle of the night to the hollering and screaming again that was coming from behind our parents' bedroom door. Only that time, it seemed a bit more heated. Along with the hollering and screaming, there came sounds of things breaking and furniture moving, then, of course, Mama's crying. We went running to the bedroom door joining in on the cries, knocking and calling for Mama. Then, a light seemed to go on in Joseph Jr.'s mind, and he remembered his telephone training. He ran to the phone and dialed 911. I was still knocking on the bedroom door, but I could hear little Joseph crying out, "He's hurting my mama! He's hurting my mama!"

After what seemed like an eternity, there were flashing red and blue lights in the driveway. A lot of the noise that came from the bedroom had died down, but Mama's crying was still constant. Then came the banging on the front door that sounded like when I banged and crashed my Tonka trucks against the door. The voice on the outside hollered, "Police, open up!" Little Joseph looked at me with a wide-eyed stare, as if he was remembering Mama's voice telling him not to open the door for anyone. After the second knock attempt, there was still no response from Mama and Daddy's room. Joseph Jr. went for the front door, yelling out, "I'm going to answer the door!"

Daddy came rushing out of the bedroom hollering, "Don't you open that door, boy!" But, it was too late! Little Joseph had already unlocked the door and turned the knob, and two officers came rushing in, telling Dad to freeze. They put handcuffs on him, and we looked up, seemingly in unison, to see Mama standing at the bedroom door. Her face was wet with tears, and her right eye was the color of the outside of a ripe avocado, and it was swollen to probably three times its normal size.

"You won't have to worry about this guy anymore, ma'am," one of the cops said in a deep baritone voice. "Just be smart, and don't let him into your house again." The officer grabbed Daddy by the back of his Afro and the handcuffs then proceeded to take him out of the apartment. The second officer started to ask Mama a whole bunch of questions, while the baritone-voiced officer came back in with a camera to take pictures of Mama's eye.

"Is this the first time this happened? How often does he hit you? Have either of you been drinking? Would you like to press charges?" The questions went on and on. It was like a really bad dream that I didn't understand. All I knew was Mickey and Minnie never acted that way, neither Donald nor Daisy. Even Popeye would beat up Bluto to protect Olive Oil, but he always loved Olive with all his heart. I just couldn't understand how two people who loved each other so much could hurt each other so badly.

The next day at preschool was a blur. I was walking around on fumes because of the ordeal at my home the night before. My "Jackson 5" Afro was flat in the back because I kept dozing off as I sat on my mat against the wall. I knew Mama was going to be mad because she always wanted to keep Joseph Jr. and my Afro nice and round. It seemed as though she was obsessed with our hair. She braided it every night and combed it out in the morning. She even carried a natural comb with the fist on the end just for emergencies! With the slightest dent in the side or "Afro-flare," she was running to the rescue with her comb. You would think it was her hair and we were just borrowing it.

"Wake up, Raymond!" shouted Ms. Ashley. "Come on, and pass out the graham crackers for me."

"Okay, Ms. Ashley...," I said with a yawn. My sleepiness must have been contagious because I had to wake up the girl next to me who had fallen asleep on my shoulder. She gave me a frown that seemed to say, "Why did you wake me up?" I was just as disappointed as she was. I guess the best sleep is when you're not supposed to be sleeping at all. Shortly after I broke the graham crackers on the dotted line and passed them out, Mama came into the classroom wearing her large dark sunglasses.

"Hello, Mrs. Watkins. Are you going to help me out today?" Ms. Ashley asked with a smile.

"Hey, Ms. Ashley. No, not today. I have some stuff to do," Mama said. She would usually jump at the opportunity to help, but that day, she was trying her hardest to not come any further into the class although the students were shouting, "Hi, Mrs. Watkins!" like popcorn.

"Raymond, get your coat, and let's go."

Mama was trying her hardest to camouflage that eye. She was doing a pretty good job, except for the bruising on the side of her face that the glasses could not cover. She didn't even notice my Afro until we got to the RTD bus stop.

"Boy, what you do to your hair?" Mama screamed astonishingly, as she dug into her purse for the fist comb. "You are four years old now! You are a big boy! I can't be following you around all the time making sure your hair is combed right! You need to be more careful and stop playing so ruff!" She went on and on, as she raked the comb through my hair. My hair wasn't as soft as it usually is in the morning, so with every stroke, my head was being snatched back and forth. If I had been in the dark, you could have probably seen the lightning-like static electricity popping.

When we arrived home, there were about fifteen young men from about seventeen to twenty-three years old, all wearing blue in the driveway. They were making their way upstairs to visit one of our neighbors, but they paused to watch Mama walk by.

"How you boys doing?" Mama broke the silence. She was only one year older than the eldest of them, but Mama had a very mature way about her that the adults called class.

"Alright, how you doing?" the eldest one that seemed like their leader responded.

"I hope y'all didn't come over here to start no trouble," Mama cut to the chase.

"Nah, we just visiting. You don't have to worry, pretty lady."

"Well, you know y'all not supposed to be over here, right?"

"We go where we want to go," one of the younger boys jumped in. "This is Eight Tray Gangsta Crip!"

"Yeah, cuzz!" they all started to chime in.

"Well, just be careful," Mama interrupted their testosterone party. "Me and my family have to live here."

"Don't even trip," the eldest one said as he started the gang up the stairs again.

At that time, our neighborhood was the territory of the L.A. Brimz. It extended from Aliso Village all the way to Florence Avenue, about a ten-mile stretch of Blood gangs. They were known as the Brimz because they wore brim hats and derbies. They also wore one pant leg cuffed up with the other down and their belt buckles to the back, while the Crips wore their belt buckles to the side. Mama knew that was a dangerous situation. Being that those Crips came all the way from 83rd Street, it was almost guaranteed they had guns. Thank God, no Bloods passed by and saw that sea of blue moving up the driveway! Their faces would have been turned up as if they were eating lemons and would have ultimately started a small war.

The color red was one of my favorite colors, so I naturally favored the Bloods more than the Crips. Plus, all the Bloods got along with each other, so they knew who their enemies were. On the other hand, the Crips were enemies with other Crips but friends with some Crips, and sometimes, they would call a truce or go to war with another Crip set on top of having to worry about the Bloods. It was 1980 and crazy!

A few days went by, and we were home from preschool. Mama had just made my favorite evening snack: peanut butter and jelly on crackers. I was ready to go outside, but I had to wait for Joseph Jr. to walk home from the elementary school. Because he was in the first grade then, Mama let him walk home with his friends. She had taken him on another one of her "Boot Camp obstacle courses," to teach him how to cross the street, looking to the left, then right, then to the left again. She warned him to never run across the street and, most importantly, to wait for the green light. Just when I was about to ask Mama for the tenth time if I could go outside, there was a knock at the door and Joseph Jr.'s signature shake of the doorknob. My countenance was immediately lifted with joy! "Mama, Joseph is here! Joseph is here! It's time to go outside!" I pulled her hand to help her walk to the door faster.

"Alright, alright," she said. Just as she opened the door, we were both shocked to see two Josephs!

"Daddy, Daddy!" I ran straight to him, and he picked me up and gave me a tight hug with a left to right rock, like he had been gone for years. "The policeman let you go?" I asked.

"Yeah, Ray! I missed y'all so much!" Daddy was happy to be free. Even though it was much more peaceful while Daddy was gone, we all missed him, even Mama, but she was trying her best not to show it.

"You are not supposed to be here," Mama said as she let them inside. "There is a restraining order on you to stay away."

"I know baby, but I have changed…" Daddy looked at Mama with puppy dog eyes. "I'm going to be different and treat my family better. Look! Look! Here's all my money. Do what you want to do." He got down on his knees and spread the cash out on the tile floor, but he kept his hands outstretched over it as he spoke, like a mother hen protecting her chicks.

"I don't want your money, Joseph," Mama said with a made-up mind. "It's more than your stinginess. You have some serious issues to work out with yourself. My cousins were ready to come out here from San Bernardino to do you some serious harm."

"Awe, baby! All families go through problems. I want to apologize for that." Daddy scooped his cash up and put it back in his pocket.

"No, Joseph! I'm not going to be your punching bag, and I didn't get married to share my husband with all the women in L.A.!"

"Well, how you gonna survive? You don't have no job!"

"You just provide for your sons!" Mama snapped. "Don't worry about me. I will figure out the rest! You can come and visit the boys and spend time with them, but you have to take your things and leave." Mama walked little Joseph and me outside to play. She stayed outside with us and let Daddy get his stuff together.

Chapter 3
Moving Forward

We didn't have much of anything, but Mama always said, "You make do with what you have." And that's what we did. Somehow, all of her neighbors started to help us out with fruit, vegetables, and bags of groceries. Mama seemed happier, and she smiled more. Most everyone on our street knew each other, so news spread fast. We were grateful for their kindness, but Mama kept saying she had to get on her own two feet. She explained her situation to the principal of my preschool Mrs. Tate and asked if she could work at the school full time.

Mrs. Tate liked Mama, but she couldn't hire her full-time. Instead, she said she would pay Mama under the table for a few hours more than she was already volunteering. Mama also went down to the welfare office and applied for assistance. She was able to pay the rent and shop for groceries! However, when we went grocery shopping, Mama didn't pay for the food with real money. She had a different kind of dollar called food stamps. They were weird looking, but we got all the food we needed! We even had cupcakes, cookies and stuff! We were so happy that we didn't know what to do! It was truly a new day!

Even after the divorce, Daddy still came by sometimes on the weekend and took Joseph Jr. and me different places to have fun. Sometimes, we'd go play miniature golf! That was lots of fun! There was a castle in front of the golf course filled with arcade games! Sometimes, Dad would take us to the beach, and Mama would be upset when we got home with sand in our Afros. Once, Dad bought an extravagant kite for us to fly, but we never could seem to keep it in the air. Maybe, it was because it was designed more like a satellite than a kite. We didn't care though, as long as we were having fun with Dad. Until one weekend, the mood changed. Dad brought us home with haircuts! Four years of growing the perfect Afro, five and a half for Joseph Jr. - gone. Mama had a natural fit! (Pun intended.) She yelled, and screamed, and complained, and even shed a few tears. That night, she immediately started the project over by braiding the two inches of hair we had left.

As we took our walks to the grocery store, I noticed Mama started slowing down more and more as we passed the auto body shop. Her conversations with Cleophus started getting longer and longer. It wasn't too long after that when Cleophus started showing up at our house on his motorcycle. Mama even introduced him to Daddy. Then, it seemed after that our weekend visits with Dad got fewer and wide spread apart. Dad was hurt by the news of the addition to his family, and any chances of reconciliation seemed to be lost.

And, he was right! Not long after that, Cleophus was living with us. Joseph Jr. and I had to share the living room at night with Cleophus' motorcycle that he put a sheet over. He said he didn't want anyone trying to steal it outside. I guess Mama didn't mind because Cleophus bought her a second hand component stereo set and a couch. One day, Mama told Joseph Jr. and me some interesting news while we were eating dinner.

She asked, "You guys want I little sister?"

"Uh, no!" we replied. I was wondering where she was going to sleep. With Joseph Jr. and I sharing a rollaway bed in the living room with a motorcycle three feet away, and Mama and Cleophus in the bedroom, it was starting to get real crowded in there.

"Well, you're going to have one," Mama said with a smile. "And, you're going to love her." And, that was the end of that.

After one of our weekends with Dad, as he was dropping us off, he asked Mama if he could use the restroom. She said, "Okay" and let him in, but as he came out of the restroom, Daddy slipped into the kitchen and into the refrigerator, while Mama was into her conversation on the phone in the bedroom. He fiddled around in the refrigerator, but when he came back out into the living room, he had not taken anything out of the refrigerator. He gave little Joseph and me a hug and said, "I'll see you boys soon." And, he left out of the apartment.

The next day after school, Mama's stepmother Darlene came to visit. As soon as she got to the door, Darlene began venting to Mama about my aunt and uncle, Suzette and James, who were only five and six years older than I was. While she listened very attentively about the bad behavior of her kid sister and brother, Joseph Jr. and I were tugging at her dress singing the national "Mama" song. "Mama, Mama? Mama? Mama, Mama? Mama?"

"What?"

"Can we have some orange juice?" She walked into the kitchen and poured us glasses of orange juice and offered Darlene a glass, but she declined and never missing a beat, continued with her rant. I began to sip my juice while little Joseph gulped his down. As we began to go back into the living room, Joseph Jr. began to stagger as if he just played a five-minute game of Ring-around-the-Rosie. As we got closer to Darlene, Joseph was about to collapse when she caught him.

"Something is wrong, Rachel! Take that glass away from Raymond!"

"Oh, my goodness!" Mama shouted as she snatched the glass out of my hands and poured it down the sink along with the remainder of the orange juice that was in the refrigerator. With Joseph Jr. still woozy sitting on Darlene's lap with his eyes half closed, she called my dad to take us to the hospital. After hearing the news, my dad was at the door in no time!

"How they doing?" he shouted as Mama opened the door. "Did you give them some milk?"

"No," Mama said clueless as though someone forgot to brief her on the milk. Daddy went and poured us both glasses of milk. He had to help Joseph Jr. hold the glass while he carried him out to the car.

"Come on, Raymond! Drink all the milk up and get in the car."

"Okay, Daddy." I took my cup of milk and drank it slowly on the way to the hospital.

"What did you do, Joseph?" Mama was crying hysterically. "Did you put something in that orange juice?"

"No!" Daddy snapped. "Why would you say something like that? Look, they're going to be alright! Just calm down and don't let Joseph Jr. fall asleep! We are almost there…"

The doctors had to do some serious work to Joseph Jr., while with me, they just pumped my stomach as I had only drank a small amount. I was hospitalized along with Joseph Jr. for the week. We stayed there just for observation. The nurse was sent to our room to ask Joseph Jr. and me a series of questions to see if we would tell the story in plain view. She was a very pretty lady with very pretty eyes that reminded me of my marbles back at home.

"So, tell me boys, what happened at home just before you came to the hospital? Did you have anything to drink?" The nurse smiled at us. She was so pretty!

"Orange juice!" we shouted in unison.

"And some milk!" I added.

"Did you guys eat anything?"

"No!" we chimed back. I was trying to be very cooperative in hopes of earning a hug.

"Did you have any medicine or pills?"

"Yeah, pills!" Joseph Jr. shouted. I was suddenly lost because I didn't remember any pills. All my hopes for a hug seemed to go out the door; maybe Joseph Jr. had his own plan.

"Okay. I'll be right back," the pretty nurse said to Mama. She left the room for a while and came back with a bottle of pills for a test. She wanted to allow us to try and open the bottle one at a time, starting with me. As she lifted me out of the bed, she gave me a big hug, and I was glad to hug her in return. She smelled of freshly picked flowers, and all I could think of was that my big brother was a genius.

"Okay, Raymond. Try and open this bottle the best way you know how."

"Alright," I said. I tried and tried, but I could not get the bottle open.

After about five minutes of watching me wrestle with the bottle to the floor, she said, "Okay, Raymond. That's enough. It's Joseph's turn." She picked me up and put me back into the bed, giving me a second hug. She gave Joseph Jr. the same treatment. Only that time, Joseph opened the bottle, and all the pills flew all over the floor. The nurse then explained that there were no pills involved and that if there were, Mama would have found all the pills on the floor in a similar way. So, the nurse proceeded to ask more and more questions.

We both pulled through fine and began to jump in the bed and play with the other children that were there. The best part was pushing the nurse's button whenever we wanted Jell-O brought to us. We were living like kings! The doctors were never able to determine what we had, being that they had no substance to test. They told Mama to keep a closer watch on us, and that it was okay for us to go home.

Chapter 4
Running Out of Space

It was springtime in 1981. I was then five years old. Mama was getting ready to have her baby, so Joseph Jr. and I had to stay with Aunt Helen until the baby came. We always had fun over Aunt Helen's house! There were always lots of family coming by, and they always made the best lunches for us children!

"Alright, children. Come and have a seat." Aunt Helen started handing out books to all the little cousins, like we were about to have class. It was a book of Bible stories for children. "Does everybody have a book?"

"Yes!" we all responded.

"It is very important to keep God first in your lives," she said. "Open up your book, and I'll read, and you can follow along."

Aunt Helen began to read stories of a man named David who became king. He killed a giant when he was just a teenager. She read other stories about a man named Jesus and how He was the Son of God sent to save the world from sin. Aunt Helen told us that God's name is Jehovah, and we can pray to Him anytime we want. It was a lot to take in. That was my first time hearing that stuff. That is not what they were teaching us in school.

When it was time for Joseph Jr. and me to go home, Aunt Helen let us take the books home that she had given us. With sincerity, Aunt Helen let me know that the information in the book was very important. I looked through the book from time to time, but I still really did not understand how the stories applied to me.

"Mama, we home! We back, Mama!" Joseph Jr. and I knocked on the door. What seemed like a month was only a week that we had been gone. Mama answered the door, telling us to be quiet.

"Y'all wake the baby up, and you both are going to get a whoopin'!" Mama snapped. She looked extremely tired. "Y'all can come in and see her. Just be quiet. Her name is Stephanie Marie Spinnard." I was the first into the bedroom! She was the prettiest baby I had ever seen with skin the color of dark chocolate. I gave her a kiss on the cheek, and to my surprise, she kind of tasted sweet, like sugar was on her face. "Get back, Ray!" Mama gave a stern whisper. "You can't be all in her face." I climbed down off the bed, so Aunt Helen and Joseph Jr. could see the new bundle of joy. The way everybody was whispering, I knew things were going to be different around there.

The collection began! Mama was obsessed with baby supplies. There wasn't a gadget, feeding utensil, or toy that Mama didn't buy or planned on getting. She finally had her real live baby doll to dress up and play in her hair. The space in the one-bedroom apartment was getting tighter and tighter. At least Cleophus got rid of the motorcycle. He said he wanted to stop risking his life on it, so he could live to see his daughter grow up. So, he went and bought a new 1976 225 Buick. He called it a "Deuce and a Quarter."

Mama seemed to arrange everything so it wasn't in the way. I think she realized she was running out of places to put things. Even though she would mention to Joseph Jr. and me that everything has its own place when we forgot to pick up our toys, well, it seemed she hadn't learned her lesson because the next spring, we were welcoming to the world Ashley Latrice Spinnard, the new baby of the family!

We were now six people in the one-bedroom apartment. The only good thing about the situation was Mama no longer hesitated when Joseph Jr. and I asked to go outside and play. She didn't even come outside to watch us. She just said not to go too far. Sometimes, we would be down the street, and when it started getting dark, Mama just yelled out our names, and we knew it was time to go home. Sometimes, we would be at one of our friend's house, and Mama would call their parents and tell them to send us home. Either way, once we got word from Mama, that ended our fun for the evening. We didn't have much money, but Mama always made sure we had what we needed. She even made sure we had what we wanted at Christmas time. Somehow, everything worked out just fine.

Chapter 5

Revival

The baby girls were growing fast. I began to see the same thing take place with Stephanie and Ashley that was going on with Joseph Jr. and me. Whenever Joseph's clothes got too small for him, they became my clothes, and Stephanie's clothes became Ashley's clothes. Mama didn't let anything go to waste. She also used cloth diapers, so she could wash them out and reuse them to save money. Mama was very good at stretching a dollar from today to next week.

It was 1983, and President Ronald Reagan signed a proclamation on February 3, making 1983 the year of the Bible. That must have sparked a revival because it seemed like everyone started going to church and inviting other people to go also. One of our neighbors, Roberta Fisher, even invited Mama to her church.

"You should come, Rachel," Roberta said with joy. "The Spirit be moving up in there! God is making a way for His children! Whatever you're worried about, cast your cares upon Him, and He will work it out!"

"It sounds good!" Mama said. "But, I have all these kids, and Cleophus is not going to take us. He has to go to work." Cleophus had just started a new job driving garbage trucks, and he was determined to present himself as a good worker, which he says starts with being on time and with good attendance.

"Is that what's stopping you?" Roberta jumped in. "I got plenty of room in my car! Be ready at 10AM girl!"

"Okay," Mama said unsure. "I guess everybody needs a little Jesus in their lives."

"You better know it!" replied Roberta.

When Sunday morning came, Mama woke us all up early, like it was time to go to school. Only we didn't get dressed in our school clothes. Instead, Mama pulled out of the closet some of the clothes we wore for Easter. She was always dressing us for Easter, but we never went to church. It was usually a trip to Disneyland, the Orange County fair, or some other fun place. I started thinking, if church called for us to wear our Easter clothes, it must be fun! I couldn't wait to get there!

Mama got us all dressed and groomed and had us sitting on the couch waiting. Joseph Jr. must have had the same thoughts of fun times I was having because he kept getting up and dancing like James Brown.

"Sit your butt down, boy!" Mama popped him with the natural comb. Stephanie, Ashley, and I laughed at him and greeted him back to the couch.

"And, don't sit all the way back on that couch, Joseph and Ray! I am not about to keep combing y'all hair all morning!" We both knew she was serious about those Afros, so we sat on the edge of the couch. After the incident with Daddy and the barbershop, Mama was determined to win! She braided our hair every night religiously and combed it out in the morning. At that point, Joseph's and my Afro were probably twice the size they were before! We looked like two dancing microphones.

"Rachel, you ready?" Roberta yelled from outside, as she came down the stairs.

"Come on, y'all. Let's go." Mama released us from the couch. "Yeah, we ready, girl! Just waiting on you."

"Okay. Let's go, so we can get a good parking space."

We all piled in the car ready to go. The suspense was eating Joseph Jr. and me alive. The girls were only one and two years old, so they really didn't understand the connection yet. I wondered how come we hadn't gone to this church thing before. The whole drive there, which was not that far compared to Disneyland or the OC fair, Joseph Jr. and I stared out the window, hoping to notice some of the tall rides as we pulled up. Roberta pulled into the parking lot of a big building with a cross on it. Just as I thought to myself, *How come we are stopping?*, Joseph shouted out, "Who are we picking up here?"

"Nobody, Joseph Jr. This is the church," Roberta said.

"But, where are all the rides?" I asked.

"Yeah?" asked Joseph Jr.

"There are no rides here, boys. This is where we come to worship God and give Him thanks for all the things He has done for us," Roberta said. Immediately, my excitement turned to curiosity as I thought about the things Aunt Helen had told us and the book she had given us with all the pretty pictures of heaven. *This might be an interesting day after all.*

As we went inside the church, an usher dressed in white with white gloves on led us to the front where there was enough room for all of us to sit. All the people were singing and lifting their hands to God. Remembering what Aunt Helen had told us, it started to make sense. She had said, "You can't see God because He is a spirit, and He is everywhere, so you have to have faith and know He will never leave you nor forsake you." She had also said that those who worship Him must worship Him in spirit and in truth. I was amazed at how everyone knew the song that was being sung, even other people who were just walking in! They seemed to fall right in place as they joined in worship, reciting every word of the song.

It started to bother me that my family was the only ones not singing. Roberta had left us and joined the choir in the stands. It was too exciting to be still, so I joined in with the clapping. Then, after a few times of them repeating the chorus, I joined in with what I had memorized. Roberta, in the choir stands, had started screaming and shouting and jumping around! The ladies next to her started to hold her down, and others fanned her with a fan, but the song went on. They sang the same song three times in a row, but the words that stood out to me were, "Peace, Be Still."

There were no mascots in costumes at church. There were no cotton candy or candy apples, and surely, there were no rides, but that day I had a different type of fun that I cannot explain. I knew there is some type of connection with people and God, and even though we do bad things, God, for some reason, still loves us. I was yet seven years old, but something was telling me I was created for a purpose by a master creator. I knew I was different from the animals. That's for sure. There were so many things I wanted to know, but for some reason, I wasn't able to articulate the question without getting sent out of the room.

Chapter 6
Finding Uncle James

After that wonderful experience at church, there was always something coming up, so we could not return with Roberta. One week, Mama's stepmother Darlene came by and wanted us to go with her looking for her son, which was my uncle James. James was thirteen years old and was running away from home to avoid the strict rules and punishments that were given by his mother. My mother always told him and their younger sister Aunt Suzette that if their father were still alive, they wouldn't be so disobedient. James and Suzette respected my mother as their older sister. That's why Darlene came by to get her to talk to James. She said he would only run if she went looking for him alone. So, Mama agreed and gathered us all into Darlene's station wagon for a manhunt in Inglewood.

It didn't take us long after reaching Inglewood, where Darlene lived, to see Uncle James walking down one of the side streets.

"James!" Mama hollered out the car window. James turned around and stopped in his tracks with a perplexed look on his face. He recognized the station wagon but was shocked to see his big sister getting out of it.

"Where you been, boy? Get in this car!" Darlene exploded.

"Let me talk to him," Mama said as she got out the car. Mama counseled James on the sidewalk for about thirty minutes. The whole time, we kids were stuck in the station wagon with Darlene acting like a pit bull on a chain. She couldn't wait to get ahold of James! She pulled a belt out of her purse and laid it on her lap waiting for the okay from Mama. In my mind, I was telling James to run! I had witnessed a whooping that his sister Suzette received, and it was not nice! Tethered to the upper kitchen cabinet by a belt around the neck, while unsuccessfully dodging the second swinging belt… crucial! She looked like a disgruntled cat on a leash! I could only imagine that James most likely got worse treatment because he was a boy. That would explain why he was on the lamb!

"Wait till he gets home! He gonna wish he never ran away," Darlene was ranting to no one in particular. "Children, obey your parents that you may live long upon the earth," she said. "That's the Word of God!" Just as the sermon started to close, Mama came walking back to Darlene's window, but James remained on the sidewalk awaiting his verdict.

"Okay, Darlene, James is going to apologize to you for all the things he did and for upsetting you, but he is not coming home unless you promise not to whoop him." Mama took a step back and waited for Darlene's response. Knowing the temper of Darlene, I guess Mama was expecting her to jump out of the car and chase James down! James might have thought the same thing because he was surely prepared to run. Darlene waited about thirty seconds then took a deep breath. "He think he's slick, but I'll give him that! I'll compromise today."

"Alright, James. It's alright!" Mama turned and hollered to James. James came walking to the car with a sigh of relief, grateful for his "not guilty" verdict and got into the backseat with the rest of us children.

"Sorry, Mama," James said convincingly.

"I accept your apology." Darlene turned to James with the swiftness of an eagle! "But the next time you do something, anything, I'm going to get you for the old and for the new! Do you understand?" She had a look on her face that could straighten a crooked nail! To Darlene and Mama's surprise, all of us children responded in unison, "Yes, ma'am…"

Mama immediately started laughing hysterically. Then, we all started laughing! Even Darlene smiled and slowly started to chuckle. The thick air was cut, and we had a nice ride home. As Darlene drove off, headed back to Inglewood, we all knew it wouldn't be long for James to receive that "old and the new" because he was always getting into some kind of mischief. From fighting with Suzette to burning down the backyard tree, Darlene could count on him to keep his end of the deal, and you can best believe, Darlene would keep her promise also.

Chapter 7
The Best Lesson of School

The next day, I was walking home with one of my classmates by the name of Curtis, who I also walked to school with in the morning, if he was ready to go. That day, however, was a little different. We had extra company from another kid named Brian, who was more Curtis' friend than mine because they both lived on the same street, and I lived around the corner. We walked along the way towards our homes while playing what we call "The Dozens." It was a series of "Yo Mama" jokes that went back-and-forth, until you either ran out of jokes or someone got mad. Usually, the latter would happen right after the former took place automatically. Being that we knew each other, often times the jokes were really true, but it was fun, so we engaged with joy.

Brian started in at Curtis, "Yo Mama so short, she had to show her ID to the gate monitor before leaving our school!"

"Ha ha!" We all laughed. It was true. Curtis' mom was really short, just a few inches taller than us first graders.

"Yo Mama so fat, they told her she wasn't allowed in the school until after breakfast!" Curtis struck back.

Then, Brian switched to me. "Yo Mama's Afro is so big, everybody walks close to her when it rains!"

"Ha ha ha!" We all laughed.

"Your Mama is so ugly, the police passed by your house and told you to keep that big dog on a leash!" I snapped back.

"Ha ha ha!" Curtis and I laughed, but Brian only smiled, a small smile showing his feelings were getting stepped on. So, I switched to Curtis.

"Your Mama stinks so bad, city workers keep coming to your house because of neighbors' complaints of a sewage break!"

"Ha ha ha!" Brian and I laughed.

"Well, stop coming to my house then! Nobody asked you to come to my house!" Curtis was hurt.

"Ha ha ha!" Brian and I laughed louder.

"Tell Yo Mama that toilet perfume ain't cool! Neither is that butt-flavored toothpaste!" I instigated.

Brian and I were laughing so hard, we had tears in our eyes! Little did I notice, Curtis had tears also, but he had tears of shame that quickly turned to rage… He charged at me, swinging his fists wildly! The first right to my left jaw let me know the game was over. I jumped back with rabbit-like reflexes into defense mode! In between Curtis' wild swings, I gave him a left jab and a right uppercut to the chin. That was something my big brother would practice on me, and all I could do was tell Mama, but that day it was real life! The punches must have dazed him because he switched to wrestling mode and tried to grab me. I twisted his arm and put my forearm into his neck as he came at me with his head down. The twist allowed me to fall on top of him, giving him several blows to the stomach before I quickly jumped to my feet.

As I jumped up, I saw Brian in my peripheral view out of the corner of my eye coming at me with his fists balled up and raised! I quickly turned and gave him a three-piece combination that made him back off! It all happened so fast. I hadn't realized the large crowd of kids who formed a circle around us yelling, "Fight, Fight, Fight!" As I pushed through the crowd and walked home, I thought to myself, *Not bad for my first fight. I think I just discovered one of my skills! Too bad I had to lose a friend in the process though.*

Sometimes, the best lessons in school are not in the books at all. Don't get me wrong. I loved reading, writing, and arithmetic. Math was my favorite! The numbers seemed to open a new door in my mind. Adding and stacking them, breaking down and subtracting them! I was a construction worker with numbers! Then, reading and writing came next. Once I figured out how to sound out the words, reading became fluent. I could dive right into a story, and it felt like I was an eyewitness at the scene. It was my idea of time travel. I'd jump into a book and leave this place. Writing became a powerful tool because then the story was my own, and I had the ability to bring the reader into my mind like I owned my very own amusement park. It took me a while to realize that to know what a person is thinking is very valuable. You could save someone's life, but to know why a person thinks the way he/she does is priceless. You could save the person and possibly save a generation.

At school, that day was show and tell! Show and tell was always exciting, plus you got a break from school work! Always a plus! Mrs. Sparks, my first grade teacher, had a friend who owned a 35-pound turtle! It was huge! We were all excited to meet and pet the turtle. Mrs. Sparks instructed the class to push back all the desks in the classroom. Then, we sat in Indian style in a large circle on the floor.

"Okay, class. We're going to put the turtle inside the circle, and when he comes by you, you may touch him gently!" announced Mrs. Sparks. She made sure she emphasized the word "gently." Last week, Shirley brought her pet rabbit named Puff Puff. Reginald grabbed Puff Puff so hard that the rabbit screamed. It was very educational because the entire class discovered that rabbits have the ability to scream. Everyone was laughing and smiling, except for Shirley, who ran over and took Puff Puff out Reginald's grasp, with tears in her eyes.

The turtle walked slowly around the inside of our circle. Each child got a chance to pet him. Some rubbed its shell, while the braver students rubbed its feet and pet the top of its head. I think we were all wondering, in the back of our minds, if Reginald could also make the turtle scream. That would have been cool! Just three more students, and it would be my turn to pet Mr. Turtle, but all of a sudden, something seemingly huge blew into my eye! I started rubbing and squinting my eyes. My eyes started to tear up something fierce, but I couldn't get whatever it was in there out. I was so involved with my eye that when I finally got it under control, the turtle was three children past me. I had missed my turn to shake Mr. Turtle's hand. On top of that, whatever was in my eye came back with a vengeance!

"Okay, class, line up for recess!" shouted Mrs. Sparks. "Except for you, Raymond. I want to speak to you for a moment."

"Alright," I said with my head down, still rubbing my eye. As I sat back into Indian style on the floor, Mrs. Sparks instructed the line leaders to lead the class to the play area. After the last student went out the class, she came and also sat in Indian style, right in front of me.

"Raymond, are you okay?"

"No." By that time, my face was wet with tears again from rubbing my eye.

"I noticed you didn't even pet the turtle when he walked past you. Why all the tears?"

"My eye, something is in my eye," I said with a muffled voice, head down, still rubbing my eye.

"Oh, no! You poor, baby!" she said with a very sad whine. She scooted closer to me. At that time, I thought she was about to help me out and blow into my eye like Mama had done before, but she put her arms around me and began to sniffle.

"I know just how you feel… It hurts so bad." Mrs. Sparks began to cry. "We just don't know when it's our time to go. That's why we have to love each other as much as we can with the little time we have." Mrs. Sparks was freaking me out. Why did she just start crying out of the thin air? I didn't know! I just enjoyed the hug while I tried to get my eye straightened out.

"I'm sorry for your loss, Raymond," she continued. "I was the same way when my father passed away. I would cry just at the thought of him. I know you will miss your dad very much."

Then, it dawned on me. She thought when I said, "Something was in my eye," that I said, "My daddy died" instead. My goodness!

"It's okay to cry. Take all the time you need," she said, as she rocked back-and-forth with her hugs and rubs on my back.

WOW! I wanted to tell her what I had actually said, but that was too good! I couldn't pass up the special treatment! The only time I got that was from Grandmama when I was about to leave her house. I decided to ride it out and see where it would go. Plus, I didn't want to embarrass her after she cried for nothing, conjuring up feelings about her dad. I should have been the one consoling her. So, I did the best next thing. I hugged her back.

We sat hugging in the middle of the floor the entire recess break, and the rest of the day, I sat in the back of the class doing nothing. Just when I thought it couldn't get any better, lunchtime came. Not only did I hang out with Mrs. Sparks again, but she bought me lunch from the teachers' lounge! Everyone knows the teachers' food is ten times better than the students'. I was in ecstasy! Another first grade teacher who taught next door, Mrs. Blinn, even stopped by to give me more hugs and consoling words. I was in too deep!

Later that same evening, I was playing marbles in the living room after dinner with my brother. I had forgotten all about the day's fiasco when suddenly the phone rang.

"Hello," Mama answered. "Oh, how are you, Mrs. Sparks?" Time seemed to freeze. Joseph Jr. was still talking about the marbles, but I didn't hear anything he said. I had already ripped my ear off and thrown it over by my mother.

"Is everything okay, Mrs. Sparks?" Mama continued in the sweetest voice. "Parent conference is not until a couple of months, right?" I knew then I was about to be in big trouble! "His daddy died? I must be taking it hard?" Mama's voice got deeper and louder. "That boy's daddy ain't dead! I just talked to him today! I'm very sorry, Mrs. Sparks! I will deal with Raymond, and he will be apologizing to you tomorrow! Okay, bye. Raymond, come here!"

I walked slowly towards her. That's when I remembered Aunt Helen saying, "Your sins will find you out."

"Yes, Mama?"

POW!!! She slapped me so hard, I saw a flash of light, and it felt like her hand never left my face! "Why did you lie to your teacher and tell her your daddy died?"

"I didn't," I said honestly.

"Oh, now you want to lie to me?"

"No, Mama!" She was about to come towards me, so I started explaining what happened as fast as I could. "She thought I said that, but I didn't say that!"

"I don't care! You should have straightened it out before now! No TV for you for two weeks, and you are going to apologize to her tomorrow! Do you understand?"

"Yes, Mama."

The next day, it was a long walk to school. I didn't want to face Mrs. Sparks after what happened. How could I explain what I did? She would probably hate me forever. Well, I had no money to leave the state, so I had to face my problem. As soon as class started, she told everyone to read their storybooks silently. Then, she asked, "Raymond, can I see you outside?" I walked out into the hallway.

"I am very sorry for what I did, Mrs. Sparks. By the time I knew what you thought I said, you were already hugging me and crying."

"That is no excuse, young man! You had many opportunities to come clean. Do you know what you did to my emotions?"

"I know. I'm sorry."

"Okay. I accept your apology, but don't ever do anything like that again! If the shoe was on the other foot, you would understand."

"Yes, ma'am," I said with sorrow. I was about to go back into class when she grabbed my arm.

"Just for kicks, what did you actually say yesterday?"

"Something was in my eye."

"Ha ha ha!" Mrs. Sparks started to laugh. I smiled and laughed with her. "That is something!" She gave me a hug, and we went back into class.

Chapter 8
94th Street

Mama and Cleophus finally came to the conclusion that the one-bedroom apartment was getting entirely too small for six people. So, they found a three-bedroom apartment for us on 94th Street between Hoover and Figueroa Street. It was an extremely large complex of about thirty-five apartment units. The apartments we were leaving were only four units. It was a drastic change of our environment. Not only that, but we were used to seeing a majority of the color red every day being in the Blood's territory, but after the move, we were smack dab in the heart of the 94 Hoover Crips neighborhood, who at the time were really tight with the Main Street Crips, who are often hanging out in the complex as well.

All we saw was blue! Even the apartments were blue. Mama didn't like it, but Cleophus convinced her that it would only be temporary until we found something better. Joseph Jr. and I both pleaded with Mama to not change our school. So, she compromised with us and bought us bus passes to catch the bus and finish out the school year, but next year, we would have to change schools.

For the first week in the new apartment, Mama didn't let Joseph Jr. and me play outside. Every time we would ask, "Mama, can we play outside?" She would say, "No, y'all play inside. These kids are too bad."

But, it was the adults who actually made the place a war zone. There was a fight almost every day! Sometimes, entire families were against other families! Mama would watch the live theatrics from inside the screen door, and we children would sneak a peek on either side of her. The fights were crucial and educational at the same time. I started studying the different fighting styles the different fighters had. Some swung wildly, trying to hit anything moving, but other fighters swung with precision and landed their punches every time like a game of connect the dots. One day, a fight was about to break out between two ladies when one ran upstairs to her apartment and came back outside with Vaseline caked on her face and neck to prevent scratches. There were tricks to the trade.

Even though there were knock-down, drag-out fights, not long after the fight was over, they would most of the time make peace with each other. They loved each other with the strangest type of love. I guess that was one of the rules of being from the same gang. No matter how bloody they got, they never held a grudge. Sometimes, they gave each other hugs. It was during the rival gang fights when Mama told us to lie on the floor because that's when the gunshots began! There were lots of gunfights and drive-by shootings. We could even hear other gunfights that were happening around the corner and on other streets. It was like the 4th of July every night! Joseph Jr. and I would lie on the floor and guess what kind of gun just went off.

Clacka! Clacka! Clacka! "Awe, man! That was a 38-revolver!" we'd say.

Boom! Boom! "Oh, that was a 12-gauge!" I'd say.

POW! POW! POW! "That's a 22-automatic!"

Lah! Lah! Lah! Lah! Lah! Lah! Lah! "Ha, that was a 9mm," Joseph Jr. would shout out, not realizing that potentially someone may have just been killed.

Joseph Jr. and I would have in-depth conversations about the gangs and which ones we liked and disliked. We both agreed that the Blood gangs were the best because all the Bloods got along fine with other Blood gangs. The Bloods seemed like they had more money, and they were clean most of the time. It was harder to be a Blood because the Crips outnumbered them, so it took more courage and street smarts to be a Blood. On the other hand, the Crip gangs killed other Crip gangs all the time. They seemed to always be at war with each other and the Bloods at the same time. Sometimes, the feuds would cease, but it was hard to tell who were their allies and who were the enemies at any given time. They didn't dress as clean as the Bloods. I guess because the Crips' color was blue, they wore their clothes a few times more before they washed them. There were also a few Crip gangs that used to be the Blood gangs. So, a lot of Crips seemed like followers and not leaders.

It was 1983, and gang violence was rampant in L.A. The news stations had stopped putting a lot of the gang violence on the news, which freed up a lot of airtime for other issues. The most notorious gangs in Los Angeles that kept ringing a bell at that time was the Villain Blood Gang located on the east side of L.A. and then L.A. Brims on the west side. The Villains name said it all, but the L.A. Brims were well known for their brim hats. Of the Crip gangs, it was the East Coast Crips and the Hoover Crip Gang that were the two of the largest Crip gangs in L.A. Joseph Jr. and I came to the conclusion that if we ever joined a gang, it would be a Blood gang. Our uncle James had already joined the Center Park Blood Gang in Inglewood, so the Blood gang was already in the family.

Speaking of Uncle James, his mother Darlene called my mother and told her James had been arrested for breaking into the elementary school. Because he was fourteen years old, the police told Darlene she could come down to the station and pick James up because he was a juvenile. He would be allowed to go home free to show up for his court date, but Darlene told the police to keep James because he was too much for her to handle. She was fed up... So, they kept James in juvenile hall. I guess she meant what she said about the "old and new punishments."

"Ahhh!" Someone was screaming outside! I looked at the clock as I turned over in my bed, and it read 1:28AM.

"Ahhh! Help! Ahhh! Help!" The screaming and shouting continued. I slid out of bed and walked to the living room rubbing my eyes wondering, *Why are they fighting so early?* As I began to look up, I noticed my mother was already at the front door with the lights off. She had the door cracked open just enough to peek through.

"Who's fighting now?" I asked.

"Shhh!" Mama turned around startled by my voice. "Be quiet. They are beating a man with a bat!" she whispered. The screams continued, and Mama closed the door before Stephanie and Ashley woke up. "Go back to bed, Raymond," Mama said as she walked back to her room with tears in her eyes. The police never showed up, nor did anyone dare to call them. Everyone seemed to just turn a blind eye in those types of situations.

The next day, Mama found out from some of the neighbors that the man was an undercover police officer. He managed to crawl down the street after they stopped beating him with the bat. Someone called an ambulance for him, but unfortunately, the man died when the paramedics finally arrived. Those kinds of incidents became normal. No one called the police, ever. If they didn't come on their own, the law was in the hands of the gangs. Sometimes, their crimes were perks for the kids in the neighborhood. For example, when they robbed the ice cream and fruit trucks, they would take all the money and then give all the merchandise to the kids. Free ice cream! Can't argue with that! While everyone ate ice cream, the older kids would take the hot ice from the coolers of the trucks and put it in bottles of water. Then, we all waited patiently from a distance and watched them explode! That was fun in the ghetto.

It took about a week for Mama to let us play outside. She was super paranoid of the neighborhood, yet she bought us bus passes and taught us to catch the bus to school by ourselves. All we did was go to school and come home, until the weekend came… Mama was standing at the door, watching all of the children playing. There were about seven girls taking turns playing "Double Dutch" jump rope. Mama stared at them for a while, reminiscing on her own childhood. She had a look on her face as if she wanted to holler out, "I'm jumping next!"

There were around fifteen boys running back and forth, here and there, all over the place. They were playing "Cops and Robbers," but only a few actually had toy guns. The others improvised! Some had hair combs. One boy had a piece of an old curtain rod. Another had a red toy guitar. Others had sticks, plastic baseball bats, and other toys that their imaginations immediately transformed into guns. One of the boys who had the red toy guitar noticed my mom watching them as he was running past and stopped. He asked a question that would change my and Joseph Jr.'s lives.

"Can your boys come outside and play with us?"

"Oh, no!" Mama replied. "Y'all too bad!"

"We are not that bad. We're just having fun," the boy responded in his defense. He looked to be about nine or ten years old.

"What is your name, young man?" Mama asked.

"I'm Jeffery Bonk, and that's my little brother Philip Bonk," he pointed to an eight-year-old who carried a plastic shovel as a gun. "We live next door to you."

"I guess I can let them come out and play...," Mama said incidentally.

"Let them boys outside, girl, before they tear up that house!" a woman shouted, as she walked toward Mama. "Hi, how are you doing? I'm Claudia Bonk, and these are my two boys." Mrs. Bonk was a little older than Mama, but she had a personality that made everybody's day fun.

"Hi, I'm Rachel Watkins," Mama laughed. "I just want to make sure they are safe."

"They alright," Mrs. Bonk said.

"And make sure they bring a gun!" Jeffery shouted.

He was too late because Joseph Jr. and I were already standing behind Mama with our toy guns, which we had gotten last Christmas. It was a cop set that also came with a small plastic billy club and plastic handcuffs. Mama laughed as she turned and saw us ready to be released from prison.

"Y'all go ahead outside." Mama unblocked the doorway, so we could pass through.

"Sometimes, you just have to let boys be boys," Mrs. Bonk said. "It's good for them. Being that they are made from frogs and snails and puppy dog tails. They are not like girls, who are made from sugar and spice and everything nice."

"Yeah, you're right about that," Mama agreed.

Chapter 9

Freedom

As Jeffrey introduced Joseph Jr. and me to the other boys, I noticed some of them didn't go by their real names, but by nicknames. There was Junebug, Woonty, and Bunbun. Then, there was Squeaky, who had twelve fingers and twelve toes. We found out that a lot of the fights that were going on were usually involving a member of Squeaky's family. They had a huge family of six children, aunts, uncles, and cousins all in one apartment. If you had a disagreement with one of them, you had better be prepared to fight the whole family because they all came outside and jumped into the scuffle. That usually ended up in family brawls. May the best family win! There was another boy in the bunch whose nickname was Belly! They called him Belly because his stomach was the size of a basketball. It looked as if he had a tumor, but Belly didn't seem to be in any pain. He played just as rough as all the others.

Besides "Cops & Robbers" and "Rock Wars," we also played "Hide & Seek" around the large apartment complex. The game was intensified when the girls were included. It became "Hide & Go Get It." Boys against girls and vice versa. You were allowed to touch the girl you found in places that were different from your own, if you know what I mean. Those who were a little older were more experienced, but I was happy with just the kissing and touching. I was amazed at how much softer the girls were than my own body. From that point on, I looked at girls with a whole new perspective. I wanted one for myself.

Yet and still, I didn't know how to make that happen. Nevertheless, the seeds of lust were planted, and they began to grow immediately.

Once Mama got to know a few more neighbors, she began to loosen the reins on us boys a little more. On the weekends, we went to the gas stations with some of the other boys to earn money, pumping gas. I was a quick learner, and it was fun. We always ended the day by rewarding ourselves with a 32oz mystery-mix fountain soda and a pocket full of candy. We were working boys. When summertime came around, all the schools gave the children free lunches during the week. Now, there were three schools in our vicinity: Bret Hart Jr. High, Manchester Elementary, and 96th Street Elementary. It was our goal to get a lunch from all three, but most of the time, we only made it to two of them before they stopped giving out lunches. Yet and still, we went home with full stomachs, searching for the next adventure.

Sometimes, the apartment manager, Eugene, would throw candy out the upstairs window of the apartments that he had converted into a candy store. Well, maybe I should just say store because he sold everything from there, from candy to bleach! Eugene's store really came in handy for tenants because sometimes he would let them run up a credit tab when they didn't have money. He also gave away money and food along with free candy that he threw out the window to all the tenants below who were scrambling to catch it. It was fun for the whole complex. Everybody loved Eugene, and the gang members never robbed him. They seemed to forget about their tough guy personas and joined in all the fun. Even though their main goal was to catch the balled up dollar bills, after the smoke cleared, the hard core gangsters had pockets full of candy like the rest of us kids.

Chapter 10
Fun with Uncle James

Uncle James finally called! We hadn't heard from him in quite some time. He told Mama the juvenile detention camp the court had transferred him to was going to start him on a weekend-release program. He would be allowed to go home on Friday nights and stay until Sunday night. Being that his mother did not want him at her house, Mama said he could come to ours. I could only imagine the feelings of rejection Uncle James must have felt. For some odd reason, he never showed any emotion about it, nor did he bring up the subject at all. He was always happy at our house! If it bothered him, we could never tell the difference.

The first time Uncle James came for the weekend, we had a blast! Aunt Suzette came to spend the weekend with us. She was only thirteen, but her mother let her catch the bus by herself.

Pow!! Uncle James socked Joseph Jr. in the hipbone, and Joseph immediately fell to the floor in pain!

"That's how you quickly disable your opponent if you are in a fight," Uncle James declared.

Pow!! He gave me the same treatment, and I fell to the floor in paralyzing pain.

"Don't be demonstrating on them!" Mama said.

"Yeah, how would you like it if we socked you up?" Aunt Suzette jumped in.

"They're not hurt," Uncle James defended himself. "I know how to sock them safely." While he was talking, Joseph Jr. had recovered and jumped on Uncle James' back! I limped to join in with blows to Uncle James' stomach.

"Yeah, that's right! Get him, y'all!" Aunt Suzette shouted as she grabbed Uncle James and put him in a headlock. Mama also joined in the fun, trying to take him down!

"Y'all can't handle me!" Uncle James shouted as he tossed Aunt Suzette and Mama around with Joseph Jr. still on his back and me holding onto one of his legs! We couldn't take him down! He was too strong! We wrestled and played around for about thirty minutes until Aunt Suzette banged her head on the wall.

"Oh, uh, uh! I quit!" she yelled. Everybody broke out laughing.

"You only got us because there's no room in here!" Mama shouted. "Next week, we are taking it to the park!"

"No problem!" Uncle James agreed. "Choose your battlefield."

We were exhausted. Uncle James seemed to have reserve tanks of energy. "I love it," he said. "This just gives me practice for the enemies behind those walls." He took out a pair of shower shoes out of his bag that had the initials C. P. B. written on them.

"Whose name does that stand for?" I asked curiously because his name began with a J.

"That's my hood. It stands for Center Park Bloods!" Uncle James said proudly. "I'm walking to my neighborhood tomorrow. You want to come with me?"

"Yeah," I said.

The next day, we walked all the way to Inglewood and back. We stayed on the busy streets because we had to walk through many enemy territories to get there. We started down Hoover Street, which is kind of busy, but a very narrow street. Uncle James didn't mind because he said we would enter into Denver Lane Blood territory as we got close to Imperial Highway. Once we got to Imperial, we walked down

Imperial Highway all the way to the city of Inglewood. The busier the street, the better for us is what Uncle James explained. The Hoover Crip Gang was a very large gang, but they were more likely to bring trouble on the back streets because that is where they hung out and patrolled their hood the most.

After making it out of the apartment complex, the rest of the way was a breeze. It really should have been our demise, but because Mama was always the people person, she gave the gang members a forewarning that Uncle James was her brother and to leave him alone. They seemed to honor her request as we walked past them. No one asked him what set he was from. They just gave him a stare as they looked down their noses at him.

As we reached Inglewood, Uncle James seemed to relax a little more. He started to notice familiar faces and ran into quite a few people he knew. We went to the high school playground where some of the gang was hanging out. Those were the teenagers around Uncle James' age. They were all glad to see him, but we couldn't stay long because we had to walk back home because there were no older homeboys around with a car. We had to make it back before it got dark because after the sun went down, busy street or not, it was easy for the both of us to become a statistic in the streets of L.A. Thank God, we made it back home without any incidents.

Sunday evening, Uncle James had to go back to the juvenile youth camp. We were all feeling down because he had to leave. Even Uncle James was a little sad, but he encouraged everyone and said, "Don't worry. When they let me go free, I'm going to get a good job, and everybody can come visit me at my nice house!"

The week didn't go by fast enough. I looked forward to Friday evening when Uncle James would show up again. Mama and Aunt Suzette also contemplated how they would take him down in the wrestling match at the park. They were seriously determined to conquer him.

"Okay, Suzette," Mama strategized. "Since I'm the strongest, you can grab him by the legs, and I will tackle him down."

"Yeah," Aunt Suzette agreed. "Then, I'll get him on his stomach and pull his chin back!"

"Wait, Suzette. We don't want to kill him!"

"Oh, okay," Aunt Suzette relented, as they both broke out laughing.

Friday finally came! It was a nice hot summer day. No one was arguing or fighting outside that day. It was going to be a great day! So, I thought… Until a U-Haul truck pulled up outside with Mrs. Bonk driving. Jeffery and Philip were moving away! That was very unexpected! I was really going to miss them. We had a lot of fun and laughs together, especially when Mrs. Bonk asked Mama to braid Jeffery's and Philip's hair the same way she French braided Joseph Jr.'s and mine at night. They both had some rough hair! Philip made it through with his shoulders hunched with every stroke of the comb. It was funny! When Jeffery's turn came, it only took a few strokes and the comb broke! Hilarious! I was really going to miss those dudes.

As the day grew later into the evening, we were waiting for Uncle James to show up at the door. Mama and Aunt Suzette were ready to go to the park with their sweat pants on. When it had gotten later than usual for Uncle James to show up, Mama started to worry.

"I wonder what's taking him so long!" Mama said. "He doesn't usually take this long to get here. I hope nothing happened. Come on, Suzette. Let's walk to the bus stop, and maybe, we will see him coming."

"Alright," Aunt Suzette agreed.

Just as they walked to the door, to all of our surprise, there was a knock at the door. Mama and Aunt Suzette looked at each other with anticipation in their eyes as Mama opened the door.

"James! What happened to you?" Mama shouted as Uncle James stood in the doorway with blood on his face. "Come on in here!" Mama immediately jumped into nurse mode, grabbing a towel and wetting it to clean his wounds.

"They tried to jump me, but I was handling them," Uncle James said as he sat in a chair, preparing to receive his special treatment.

"Who jumped you?" Aunt Suzette asked.

"Like about five Hoover Crips," Uncle James said very calmly, like that happened every day. "They couldn't fight though. One of them hit me over the head with a bottle. That was the best lick they got."

"I guess what you told them about you being his sister doesn't count around the corner, huh, Rachel?" Aunt Suzette threw in a little of her sarcasm. Mama just glanced at her as she continued to check Uncle James' head for glass.

"No, those were some different dudes," Uncle James interrupted. "I've never seen them around here before. Are we still going to the park?"

"No, we not going to the park!" Mama looked at Uncle James in disbelief. "Even though there's no glass in the cut, you need to heal. We'll go next week."

"I'm alright," Uncle James insisted.

"Boy!" Aunt Suzette exclaimed.

At that moment, I knew Uncle James was a little crazy! I also couldn't help but think about the time Curtis and Brian tried to double team me. That's when I knew my skills ran in the family. Uncle James had five opponents compared to my two, and the only wounds he had were a rather small cut from the glass on his head and several small cuts on his knuckles from hitting them.

Mama used to take us downtown to the theatres to the Bruce Lee movies. Joseph Jr. and I would come out of the theatre acting like we knew karate. Bruce Lee would beat up a bunch of dudes and leave the fight with only a scratch or two. He was a legend of his time! To see that type of fight in person would be awesome! I couldn't wait to see Uncle James in action!

The next Friday rolled around, and Uncle James made it home without incident… Thank God! We were all on pins and needles until he knocked on the door. I think Mama was the most nervous after she insisted on meeting him at the bus stop, and Uncle James insisted even more for her not to. He explained that not only would his reputation be ruined, but his life would be in danger even more so if the gang members saw him being walked home by his big sister. It would be a sign of weakness. Being that there were members of the same Hoover set in the youth camp he was in, news would travel fast. The "word on the street" could either make you stronger, or ruin your life once it hit the system inside the institutions. Uncle James said he'd rather live with the consequences that come with being in a gang. That was the life he had chosen.

That same evening, we all went to the park as promised. Manchester Park was a nice-sized park with lots of grass. Enough room to tackle Uncle James down and no room for Aunt Suzette's excuses of bumping her head on the wall. It was pretty much a repeat of part one in the apartment. We could not get him on the ground no matter how hard we tried! Joseph Jr. and I grabbed his legs, Aunt Suzette jumped on his back, Mama tried to tackle him, and even Stephanie and Ashley added their little pushes, but yet and still, he just shook us off and danced out of our grasps. He was stronger than we contemplated. We had tons of fun though!

The next week came, and we all waited for Uncle James to show up at the door on Friday evening. We all couldn't wait to have more fun! Aunt Suzette was now living with us permanently because she wasn't getting along with her mother. Aunt Suzette was over our house most weekends lately anyway, so it was almost natural for her to show up with the rest of her belongings. At age thirteen, Aunt Suzette was experiencing her own version of the treatment Darlene had given to Uncle James. We waited and waited, and again Uncle James did not show up. Mama and Aunt Suzette walked to the bus stop to see if they saw him coming, but even after they watched five buses pass them by, they came back home without Uncle James.

"Oh, my Lord. What could have happened now?" Mama was super worried.

"Nothing seems to be going on in the neighborhood, so maybe he never left the institution," Aunt Suzette said.

"Yeah, you're probably right," Mama said with a sigh of relief. "I'll call down there in the morning and find out what's going on." Mama called the next morning and was able to speak with one of the counselors at the youth camp. The counselor explained Uncle James had lost his privilege to come home on the weekend due to fighting. It was a very sad day... No more weekends with Uncle James.

Chapter 11
Manchester Elementary

Once our summer vacation was over, it was time to go back to school. Only that school year, Joseph Jr. and I would be starting our new school, Manchester Elementary. We were excited to see what new things they had and different activities they did, because Manchester was a bigger school than 68th Street School. Joseph Jr. was starting fourth grade, and I was starting second grade. That meant we would only see each other before and after school because our classes took lunch and recess at different times. So, when we walked out of the cafeteria after finishing our breakfast, we parted our separate ways.

The administrative office had mailed our room numbers home, so Mama told me I had to find Room 12. Each teacher had a sign held up on the playground with their room numbers posted, so the students could find them and line up accordingly. All of the classrooms were positioned in numeric order, so it was easy to find. When I reached number 12, there was a short and pretty black lady holding the number 12 above her head! She had a black and grey afro (which everyone called salt and pepper) with a part on the side.

"Good morning," I said. "My name is Raymond Watkins, and I'm supposed to be in your class."

"Good morning, Raymond," she said, with a smile and a look that seemed to say she was impressed with me. Maybe, she liked my afro. "I'm Ms. Ascot. Go ahead and line up in the back of the boys' line."

"Okay," I said. As I moved to the back of the line, I thought to myself, "It's going to be a great year!" The first student I met was the boy in line in front of me whose afro was bigger than mine! I was intrigued. You don't find Mama's results of obsession too often in others. As I stood behind him, I looked closely, and I could still see the parts on his scalp from his mother braiding the hair in unison with my mother in separate homes. He turned around as I tapped him on the shoulder.

"Braids every night, huh?" I asked.

"Even on Sundays!" he said. Then, we both broke out laughing.

"Especially on Sundays," I concluded.

"What's up, man? I'm Timothy," he shook my hand.

"What's up, Timothy? I'm Raymond," I said.

Timothy became my tour guide of the school slash information kiosk, being that he had been attending Manchester since kindergarten. He told me the main activity of the playground was kickball, which I loved! That's what we mostly played at 68th Street Elementary School. Every week, our class activity changed on the playground. We had Four Square one week, Tetherball another week, or even Handball, and the girls always loved jumping rope. No matter which activity we had, the boys were always waiting to get back to kickball.

The ball used was a hard soccer ball. The goal was always to kick a homerun, which was seldom accomplished because we only had the strength of a second grader. But, if you had clumsy outfielders on the opposite team, anything was possible. It was because of that game that Mama had to keep buying Joseph Jr. and me new shoes, but she didn't know that. She just kept saying, "You guys are too hard on these shoes!"

Timothy also gave me the heads up on the principal, Mr. Green. He said to never go to his office because he was super mean! He also gave swats to the students who were sent to him. He had a large paddle hanging on the wall of his office with the word CORRECTION posted over it. The paddle seemed to be custom made with a hand grip and holes in it to cut through the wind in the process of a swat. That was enough for me to stay out of trouble! I never even saw the color of the paint on the walls of the principal's office.

By the time we were in the third grade, Timothy and I were best buddies. We were the two kids with the biggest Afros in the third grade. Anyone could distinctly determine who we were from across the kickball field. A few other classmates stood out while kicking the ball also. Tyree, for example, had a red Afro! Who could miss that? Keanan stood out because he was the brother with no Afro. Then, of course, there was Curtis, who also had a red Afro, but it was only two and a half inches thick. Curtis was kicking homeruns in the second grade, but now that we were in third grade, Curtis came back to school kicking the ball over the fence! He set the bar!

There was a girl in my third grade class who I instantly fell in love with by the name of Kattie. She had smooth, dark chocolate skin and long black hair down her back. Who knew, she may have even tasted like chocolate, but I would never know. I didn't know how to tell her how I felt about her. Even though her house was along the way as I walked to school, and sometimes, she and her little sister would walk just feet away from me and my big brother, yet and still, I had nothing to say but hi. I don't know what was wrong with me. The moment I was out of her presence, I would be fine. I could debate, tell jokes, and even sing, but there was something about that girl that took the words out of my mouth and threw them in the trash.

It didn't help much when my eye doctor told my mother I would need glasses in order to see the chalkboard more clearly. I knew how cruel kids could be towards students wearing prescription eyeglasses, and I didn't like the idea one bit. Mama explained I only needed to wear them to see the chalkboard, and then, I could take them off. That was easy for her to say. I had a reputation to uphold! I didn't want to go from cool kid to nerd in 8.6 seconds. I hated the glasses and refused to put them on! I'd decided if I needed to see the chalkboard clearly, I would just act like I needed something off the teacher's desk and walk up to the board with a quick glance. It worked for me.

Those glasses stayed brand new in their case, sitting comfortably in my desk. That was until parent/teacher conference rolled around, and my mother asked the teacher if I had been wearing my glasses. The teacher had no idea I even wore glasses, and I was in for a beating when I got home. So naturally, I was beat into submission and agreed to wear the magnifying windows on my face. I reluctantly put them on periodically during class for about a week, just so the teacher would form a memory of seeing them. Then, they went back inside their case, inside my desk, and stayed there.

One day, we had a "rainy day schedule"! I loved those days because the whole class was allowed to take their lunches back to their classroom. Just the privilege of eating at my desk made me feel like a king. Then, after lunch, I'd play a few games of checkers with Timothy. Some of the other students were upset because we had kickball that week on the playground, and they weren't sure if the rain was for one day, or if we would be "rained in" all week. Me, I didn't mind. It was the walk home from school that I failed to prepare for. Instead of putting on the hood of my coat, I let my Afro fill up with rainwater on the way home. Big mistake! When I got home, I shook out all the water onto the living room floor carpet. By the time I looked up, Mama was charging towards me with her whooping belt! She wore me out, on sight!

Maybe I was wrong, but all of those whoopings were starting to build up tension. I was getting whoopings left and right. I was starting to think maybe I was her stress reliever. I even got whoopings for the things that Stephanie and Ashley did!

One day, there was a fight going on outside with multiple neighbors involved. Mama was watching through the front door, so I grabbed a chair and pushed it underneath the kitchen window. Unfortunately, I climbed up in the chair too fast, and when I stood up straight, my forehead cracked the kitchen window.

Yep, I got whoopings for accidents also. I remember Cleophus telling me one day that it was better to give than to receive. You see, that was the problem. I was receiving all the whoopings with no one to give any to. Until one day, walking home from school, Marcus, one of my classmates, was teasing Amber about her weird-shaped glasses.

"You look like an alien cat," heckled Marcus. "I'm going to call you space cat!"

"Ha! Ha! Ha!" All the children laughed around us as Marcus continued to spit out more jokes. I was the only one not laughing and Amber, of course, who didn't seem to think the jokes were funny. That was the very reason I didn't want to wear my glasses! I didn't want to be teased. I was used to playing The Dozens back and forth, but nobody ever had anything on me to push my buttons until then. It didn't help that Marcus was known for having an arsenal of jokes in his memory bank and was very quick witted. Just when it seemed he was running out of Amber jokes, he turned in my direction.

"Hey, he wears glasses, too!"

Bing, bing, bing! That's all it took! I was on him like white on rice! He didn't have a chance! Before he knew it, I had him on the grass, taking out my frustrations on his face! My adrenaline was racing, while everyone was chanting, Fight! Fight! Fight!

I welled on him for about thirty seconds, until some older kids pulled me off him. It felt good... *I don't think Marcus will be mentioning my glasses anymore or anybody else's for that matter.* The discovery of more fighting skills intrigued me and made me feel like some sort of superhero whose powers grew stronger and stronger! On the other hand, I also realized that just like Granddaddy Raymond and Uncle James, I also had a bad temper that once ignited I couldn't control. I definitely didn't want to get killed over two dollars like Granddaddy Raymond, and Mama always told Uncle James (who was well known in the streets for having great hands in fights) that he couldn't whip everybody. One day, he would meet his match. So, as I thought on those things as I walked home, I made a decision to try not to get upset with those I consider friends.

Chapter 12

Back to Church

One Sunday morning, Mama was up early cooking breakfast. She looked outside and saw a big blue and white church bus pull up in front of the apartments. She went out to the bus to ask questions as a few of the neighbors' children got on board with nice clothes on that we only wore on Easter Sunday. She found out that the bus came for pick up every Sunday morning around 8:30AM for whosoever wanted to go to church.

"Y'all going to church next week!" Mama hollered out as she came back inside. "Brother Johnson will be picking y'all up bright and early! I didn't even know they came by here every Sunday."

Well, now we all know. This should be interesting. A new church... I was anxious to see if it was exciting as that holiness church Roberta took us to. There was a holy presence in that place. You just knew it was time to worship God. I wanted to experience that again.

The next Sunday morning came around, and Mama cooked breakfast and got us all dressed up. Mama knew how to get us up and at 'em when it was time to go somewhere. She would cook breakfast first and then wake us up. The smell of buttermilk pancakes, bacon, and eggs would fill every room! Getting dressed first before we ate was the rule, so naturally, we got a move on!

At dinner time, I was usually the last at the table. Throwing lima beans on the floor or taking liver to the bathroom and flushing it down the toilet was my technique. Stephanie and Ashley even beat me eating. Breakfast, on the other hand, was my favorite meal! She couldn't get too weird with breakfast, so it was always good! Mama heard the roaring of the engine outside as a church bus pulled up...

"Alright, y'all! Finished or not, it's time to go. I'll see you guys when you get back." All four of us filed out of the apartment still chewing. Ashley was upset because Mama wouldn't let her take her orange juice with her. "You are not taking my cup to church, little girl," Mama told her. "And y'all keep an eye on your sisters, Joseph and Ray," Mama hollered after us.

"Alright," we replied.

The church was huge! As soon as we pulled up to the church with the title, "Church of Christ" on the front, they separated us according to age groups for Sunday school classes. Sunday school was fun and interesting. It was very similar to school. Instead of learning reading, writing and arithmetic, we learned about God and His son Jesus instead. The teacher was very good at explaining the scriptures out of the Bible and relating them to today's society. I liked to learn new things, so I was all ears.

Brother Clark explained the bad things we did were sin, and we were made enemies of God because of them, but God still loves us, and He had a plan to get rid of all of our sins. He sent His son Jesus to die for us and to be raised back to life again to be our Savior. He explained sins had to be washed away with the blood of Jesus, and if we believe it by faith, we can be saved and have eternal life. It sounded like a good plan to me! I loved it! I finally had an answer to that voice in my head that kept telling me I was going to die. I didn't want to die! I wanted to live forever, and Brother Clark told me that believing in the finished work of Jesus the Christ was the way to do it!

After Sunday school, Brother Clark instructed the class to proceed to the kitchen for nutrition time. That place was getting better and better! I had no idea where the kitchen was in the huge church, but the way the children were filing out of their different classrooms and seeming to merge into one line like working ants, it was pretty easy to follow the flow of traffic. Along the way, I met back up with Joseph Jr., who was already holding hands with Stephanie and Ashley on each side of him.

"How was the class with the ten-year-olds?" I asked Joseph Jr.

"It was alright. They talked about being able to live forever," Joseph Jr. said in a slightly melancholy tone.

"Did y'all have fun in class?" I asked Stephanie and Ashley.

"Yeah!" they both exclaimed. "We sang a lot of songs," Ashley shouted.

"Oh, okay," I said, as we grabbed our snacks and sat down in the large kitchen area that was downstairs from the church area. Some of the mothers served a choice of cookies or cake and chocolate milk or punch to drink. Everyone seemed to be satisfied and didn't complain. I casually picked the conversation back up with Joseph Jr.

"Yeah, we talked about the same thing in my class. Do you think it's real what they are saying?"

"It must be. They all believe it, and they are teaching it in every class," Joseph Jr. said.

"What about you? Do you believe it?" I asked.

"Yeah, I guess so… You?" Joseph replied.

"Yeah, man. I think they're right," I said.

"I hope so," Joseph said. "I hope so…"

"Yeah, me too," I said.

After everyone finished their snacks, there was another separation happening that nobody explained. They just seemed to do it naturally. Only that time it wasn't every age group to themselves, but the adults faded off in one direction, and the youth from seventeen and under faded off into the other direction. Joseph Jr. and I followed suit with our sisters into a sanctuary that was small compared to the adult sanctuary, but it was bigger than the entire property of most storefront churches. They even had their own ministers in there. One of them shouted out as we made our way to the pews, "Welcome to Jr. Worship!"

We found out later how different the church was from the holiness church we visited with Roberta. I noticed there was no music in the church. Oh, we sang songs, but without any musical instruments. It was different. The minister mentioned in his sermon that although there were many other Christian churches, they believed if you didn't belong to the Church of Christ, you wouldn't be able to go to heaven. That seemed strange to me because I knew I felt the presence of God in that holiness church, and I didn't feel the same way there. *How could all those Christian churches who claim to be Christian, not be Christians?* Yes, that church was indeed different. Despite it all, I did learn something very important: Any time someone makes it their business to come against another person or group of people and organizations just out of thin air, beware. They themselves are usually the problem.

Chapter 13
37th Place

"I got it! I got it! Thank you, Jesus!" Mama was shouting and smiling from ear to ear, as she waved a letter over her head.

"You got what?" Cleophus asked perplexed. "Calm down and tell us, so we all can celebrate."

"The Section 8 papers I applied for a year ago for low-income rent!" Mama replied. "We can move now!"

"Oh, wow! That is a blessing!" Cleophus started smiling also. "Now, I can spend less time shopping for TVs."

That was something we all agreed on. Our apartment had been broken into on three different occasions, and on every instance, a television was stolen, twice from Joseph and my room, and once from Cleophus and Mama's room. Come to find out, one of the neighbor's sons had started smoking crack cocaine. Before, he had been a gentleman and a stand up big brother to his siblings, but he had allowed a terrible addiction to transform him into a thief and a robber in order to supply drug money for his habit.

But that young man was not the only victim of circumstance. The Black community was being eaten alive by the monster drug. Families were breaking up left and right. People were going to jail for drug-related crimes. But the worst was the Black businesses in the community that inadvertently fell victim, like the Mom and Pop shops and restaurants that were Black owned. The drug was slowly destroying the Black community as a whole. If Los Angeles was affected in such a devastating downfall of production and moral well-being, I could only imagine what it looked like across the country.

I thank God my parents never fell victim to that monster drug. It wasn't hard at school to see that the children suffered the most. You automatically assumed the parents of certain students were on drugs by their continuous poor upkeep of appearance or the blatant hunger at lunchtime, as if that was all there was to eat until tomorrow. And, you were usually right.

Cleophus and Mama immediately started searching for apartments for rent. We needed a three bedroom, which we already had, but applying the Section 8 voucher to the application could lower the rent by up to two thirds of the cost. It wasn't long before they found one! Mama didn't waste no time! Mama started packing the day she received the voucher, so we were ready to go. She even gave the church bus driver, Brother Johnson, the new address to pick us up for church. It was a three-bedroom apartment on 37th Place, between Vermont and Normandie. Right down the street was USC, and next to the campus was the coliseum, where the Raiders played football, and the L.A. Sports Arena, where the Clippers played basketball.

Joseph Jr. and I were looking at the graffiti on the neighborhood walls to find out which gang was in the area. We kept seeing F.T.B. but didn't know what it stood for. I knew though that just by having a B in the initials and it wasn't crossed out, that it was a Blood neighborhood. It wasn't the Villians like Joseph Jr. wanted or the Center Park Bloods in Inglewood that I was gravitating to because of Uncle James, but we were both satisfied to be back in Blood territory. A couple more years on 94th Street and we would've been Hoover Crips.

The first day in our new apartment felt good! There was a feeling of peace that we didn't have on 94th Street. The apartment complex wasn't as congested. There were only six units in the building. I started hanging up my clothes in the closet and helping Joseph Jr. move the dresser where we wanted it before we put our clothes inside. Then, it would have been too heavy for us to lift, and we didn't want Mama to have to help us. All of a sudden, I heard noises coming from outside our bedroom window. I looked out the window, and there were a few kids running around and playing in the back of the building.

"Hey, y'all just moved in?" one of the boys asked, as he noticed me in the window.

"Yep," I replied.

"What's your name?" he asked.

"Ray, what's yours?"

"Ben," he said.

"Oh, okay. I'll see you when I come outside," I said.

"Alright," he said.

After I finished unpacking my clothes out of the boxes and into my dresser drawers, I went outside to take a break. The second person I met was Clayron, who was throwing a ball in the air to himself in front of our door.

"Hey, what's up? I'm Clayron."

"I'm Ray."

"Come on. Let me show you where everybody is at," said Clayron.

"Alright," I said. As we started to walk down the street, I asked Clayron, "Hey, what does F.T.B. stand for?"

"Fruit Town Brim," said Clayron. "From Aliso Village to Florence, it's all Brimz! This is the Fruit Towns though. I guess they call them that because we got all kinds of fruit trees in the neighborhood. By the time summer gets here, you will get a taste of the fruit! Strawberries, apples, Mau berries, peaches, oranges, lemons, grapes, plums, apricots, and loquats, just to name a few."

"Ha," I laughed with anticipation.

"But, we eat mostly loquats. Bags of them!" Clayron made it clear as we started to walk through the yard of an abandoned, two-story, baby blue house. "This is the clubhouse."

"Oh, okay," I said, looking up at the huge house. "It's the biggest clubhouse I've ever seen!"

"Yeah, and the best we've ever had. So, enjoy it while it lasts because when they sell the house, we have to find another spot to flip."

"To flip?" I asked.

"Yeah, to flip…" Clayron repeated as we entered into the backyard. There were about fifteen boys back there, all taking turns jumping off an old refrigerator that was turned onto its side, jumping onto two stacks of four mattresses, one stack in front of the other. They were all like miniature gymnasts and acrobats, ranging from eight to twelve years of age. They did back flips, front flips, back twists, front twists, double back flips, and combined back flips with a tuck and a twist! I was amazed!

"Aye, everybody! This is Ray!" Clayron interrupted.

"What's up, Ray?" everybody echoed my way.

"I'm Demandre," one of the boys said. "Do you know how to flip?" he asked.

"I don't know. I've never tried it, but I'm about to find out!" I climbed onto the refrigerator and ran full speed, jumping onto the first stack of mattresses and doing a front flip with a tuck high in the air and landed on my feet. "Yeah, I can flip." I jumped off the mattress smiling, proud of my accomplishment.

"We got a natural, y'all!" Demandre shouted. "We're playing H.O.R.S.E. Do you want to play?"

"What's that?" I asked.

"You have to do the same flip as the person in front of you, but if you mess up, you get a letter of H.O.R.S.E. until you spell the whole word, and then, you are out of the game. If the person in front of you messes up, then you get to start with your own flip," Demandre explained.

"Oh, okay, but hold on. Let me go and get my brother. He might want to play, too," I said, as I started toward the front yard of the clubhouse.

"Alright. Hurry up," Demandre said.

I was excited! That was going to be fun! I went and got Joseph Jr. out of the apartment, and we both went back to the clubhouse as I explained to him the game of H.O.R.S.E. As it turned out, Joseph Jr. was even better at flipping than I was. I ended up receiving all five letters of H.O.R.S.E. and was out of the game.

As the game ended, Joseph Jr. and I learned everybody's name. Just like 94th Street, most of them had nicknames they had earned or was an acknowledgement of a characteristic of themselves, such as Darrell or Dookie, who got his name after trying to hop over the school fence and soiled his pants in the process. How about Demandre, who they called "Hook" on account of the shape of his head. Then, you had "Ethi" which was short for "Ethiopian" was what they called Larry, not because he was an Ethiopian but because he was so skinny, he looked like one. I had an unconscious habit of letting my bottom lip hang open whenever I stood idle. Unfortunately, Darrell "Dookie" immediately noticed that about me and yelled out, "Open Mouth."

"Ha, ha," everybody laughed, and the name stuck. Then, there was Jared, who was dark skinned as a crow, so the nickname was applied. Ben also was there, who I had met from my bedroom window. They called him "Beak" because of a scare he had gotten in Mississippi between his nose and top lip when he was younger by running into a nail. Sooner or later, everybody earned a nickname, and if you were around at the time they received their nickname, it said a lot about your street credentials and respect. Of course, as we got older the names changed into more gangster nicknames and for some, more devious.

Besides the flipping, the mattresses were not the only thing in the clubhouse backyard. There was a large pile of bike parts from various bikes. If someone needed a bike (which everybody had one), all he needed to do was come and put one together. There were even cans of spray paint, just in case you didn't like the color. Next to the pile of bike parts was a large wooden cage about half the size of a single car garage. I had noticed earlier the flock of colorful pigeons that continued to fly back and forth over our heads. It had to be about fifty to a hundred birds.

Every now and then after one of the boys completed his flip on the mattress, he would look up and clap his hands at the birds, and they would begin to flip in the air as well. The birds lived there. They were an extension of the boys. I began to like the birds as well and in turn hate cats because they were always trying to get themselves a pigeon meal.

As the sun went down, everyone broke out into a game of The Dozens, while calling in all the birds. Little by little, the crowd was getting smaller, as each boy heard the distinctive call of his parents, calling him into the house. Sure enough, Mama yelled out, "Joseph and Ray!" and we knew the night had officially come to an end!

The next day was Sunday, and after Brother Johnson dropped us off from going to church, I was ready to go explore with the gang. I went inside our apartment and quickly changed into my play clothes because there was no way Mama would allow us to play in our church clothes, and school clothes were even worse! So, I threw on my Tough Skin jeans with the patches on the knees. Those jeans were built for playing outside!

"You coming outside, man?" I asked Joseph Jr.

"Naw, I'm about to watch the Three Stooges and then the Little Rascals on TV," he said.

"We are the Little Rascals, and the rest of the gang is waiting outside," I said.

"I'll probably come out there later," said Joseph Jr.

"Alright," I said, as I walked out the front door. It was a beautiful day in January 1985. Although winter was still wagging her tail, she was usually friendly in California. It was definitely more comfortable because Mama had finally taken Joseph Jr. and me to the barbershop to cut the Afros off for good. Times were changing in L.A. The Afro was fading out, and the Jheri Curl was coming in. You either got a Jheri Curl or a baldhead. We took the baldhead while my mother chose the Jheri Curl for herself. That was the new style in L.A., and I'm sure other states found out what we were doing out here and followed suit. I loved Los Angeles, despite all the negativity that comes with it. Not only is the weather superb, but the people had a freedom in their spirit that makes the state's name ring bells. Yes, Sacramento is the capitol of California, but they should have voted for Los Angeles.

Having made my way down the street, I saw Clayron heading to the clubhouse.

"Hey, Clayron!" I shouted.

"What's up, Ray?" Clayron smiled, as he turned and saw me coming. Clayron was a year older than I was but a little antisocial. But, he had good reason. He couldn't handle yesterday's sundown game of "The Dozens." The jokes just got way too real for him, and no doubt, boundaries were crossed that shouldn't have been. The problem with The Dozens, especially amongst children, was the more hurtful the joke, the better the game. Come to find out, Clayron's little sister, Jeanette, who was eight years old, was molested in the alley by a grown man. Subsequently, Jeanette started to develop the body of a grown woman before it was time. One of the boys hollered out, as the game escalated, "Hey, Clayron! Let me touch your sister and see what gets bigger!" Clayron snapped! That was the last straw! Game over! Clayron immediately jumped on him like a kangaroo fresh out of his cage! Four of the boys had to pull them apart.

I could tell that sort of thing happened often for Clayron by the way he listened to people talk. He stayed ready to defend his sister and the rest of his family. He was already a ticking time bomb. Someone just had to simply push his buttons. Because I was a fresh face on the block, he seemed to trust me more. Thank God that once informed, I was wise enough not to tamper with the quagmire of his emotions. That was the travesty of "The Dozens." You found out the hard way everyone's boundaries, but once found, it was up to you to cross that line. No doubt, everyone had a line.

"Where are you headed to?" I asked Clayron.

"I'm about to climb this tree in the front yard of the clubhouse. I want to see if I can make it to the top," said Clayron. "You want to climb up with me?"

"Alright, let's go," I said. The paper tree in the front yard of the clubhouse seemed to be about thirty feet tall, but it was no match for the huge pomegranate tree I used to climb on 94th Street. As we began to climb the tree, Clayron surprisingly began to talk about the incident that happened the night before.

"Do you think I was wrong for going off last night?"

"No," I said. "You have to defend your little sister. That's a big brother's job. I have two little sisters."

"Good," he said. "Because I don't regret it. Don't ever talk about Darrell's grandmother. You know, the one we call "Dookie" right?"

"Yeah," I said.

"He is the coolest dude on the block and the best at everything: flipping, running, swimming, bike tricks, you name it, but talk about his grandmother, who's resting in peace, and you will soon find out that he's the best at fighting also," Clayron said.

As Clayron went on giving the rundown on the neighborhood kids' emotions, I noticed Black Robert, out the corner of my eye, walk through the front yard and head to the back where everyone was flipping on the mattresses and feeding the rolling pigeons. They called him Black Robert not only because he was dark skinned but also to distinguish him from the other Robert who lived down the street who was called Fat Robert for obvious reasons. He didn't say anything as he passed by, but he glanced up at Clayron and me in the paper tree, as if to listen in on Clayron's synopsis. I didn't think anything of it until a few minutes later when the gang came to the front yard with Ben leading the way.

"Aye, what's up, Ray?" Ben hollered out with a frown on his face. "You out here talking about my mother?"

"Naw, man!" I responded in shock as I made my way down the tree. "I don't even know your mother." Immediately, I knew the conspiracy was conjured up by Black Robert to see if I knew how to fight. Ben, being my age and size, was the perfect match for the duel. I felt myself putting on the same frown that Ben had as I jumped to the ground, but it was intended for Black Robert. Being that Ben was not about to change his mind about the situation, I kept my eyes on him. He was determined to fight me. I was angry at Black Robert, but he was too big for me to fight. He was already in the eighth grade, as he was five years older than I was.

"Black Robert said you was talking about my mother, so you're about to fight!" Ben steamed as he approached me. In an instant, I switched my anger towards Ben for the fact that he was believing Black Robert. He swung and hit me in the jaw, and like two pit bulls off the chain, we locked up! Punching, swinging, and tussling with each other.

We both grabbed one another in a headlock and fell to the ground wrestling and punching with our one free hand.

"Get him, Ben. Get him!" the crowd roared. Because I was the new kid on the block, I didn't expect to have any fans. I simply held my own in defense mode. As the older boys (including Black Robert) pulled us apart and the smoke cleared, everyone walked away nodding their heads in approval. I had passed the test. Later, Ben and I would miraculously become best friends.

Chapter 14
Lenicia B. Weems Elementary

The next day, Mama didn't hesitate with changing our schools. It seemed like she wanted to cut all ties and get as far away from 94th Street as possible, unlike moving from 64th Street where we were allowed to catch the public transportation bus to finish out the school year. We even visited some of the people that lived on 64th Street to this day, but 94th Street was a stepping stone that Mama wanted to cast in the sea of forgetfulness. Our new school was right around the corner. There were no long walks like Manchester Elementary or bus rides like 68th Street School. The name of the school was Lenicia B. Weems Elementary School. It was named after one of their former principals who passed away.

The enrollment process wasn't as long and drawn out as I thought it would be. That was due to the fact that Mama had gone prepared as always. Thinking ahead, she stayed up late the night before, looking for Joseph's and my medical shot record and birth certificate. Mama prided herself on preparation. It was the key to utilizing the time at hand. She always had us to set out our clothes at night for the next day, so we didn't waste time in the morning daydreaming in the closet. We were always on time and usually got the award for perfect attendance, except for my first grade year when Joseph Jr. caught the chickenpox and was out of school for two whole weeks. Then as soon as he got well, it was my turn to play connect the dots on my skin as I itched and scratched for the following two weeks.

"Alright, y'all be good, okay," Mama said, as she walked back into the lobby of the attendance office where Joseph Jr. and I were waiting.

"Alright, Mama," we both said.

"This nice lady is going to walk you to your new classes," she said, beckoning to the office worker next to her.

"Alright, Mama." We knew she had to get home to relieve Cleophus of watching Stephanie and Ashley. It was very seldom that Cleophus stayed home during the daytime. If he did, it was because of an emergency like today or he was super sick with the flu. He never let losing his job at the maintenance company stop him from making money. He still had enough skills to survive with fixing cars and motorcycles that he never had to punch a clock again.

When I got to my new classroom, I was immediately put on the spot. "Attention, class," announced Mrs. Douglas, my new third grade teacher. "We have a new student joining our class today! His name is Raymond Watkins! Can everyone welcome Raymond today by saying, "Hello, Raymond"?

"Hello, Raymond," the class shouted in unison. Mrs. Douglas was a blonde-haired white lady full of joy. She kept large jars of candy on her desk that I assumed were for students with correct answers. As she continued to speak and almost bounce around, I had to change my assumption: The jars of candy were for her, and she reluctantly shared with the students for the sake of hospitality. After she showed me where the closet was to hang up my coat, she took me to my new desk.

"Make yourself at home, Raymond. There are pencils and crayons for you inside your desk," she said.

"Thank you, ma'am," I said, as she smiled and walked back to the front of the classroom.

As I started to check out the contents of my desk, I heard a familiar voice. "Aye, I thought your name is Ray." I looked up and saw sitting at the desk across from me was Ben.

"Aye, what's up, man?" I gave a loud whisper. "My name is Ray. It's short for Raymond." I was glad to see someone I knew in a room full of strangers.

"Oh, okay," Ben said. "That's kinda like my name. Ben is short for Benjamin."

"Yeah, that's pretty cool," I said. It was like the fight we had had never happened. Maybe he was used to dudes not fighting back and was glad to get a challenge for a change. Although I know the peer pressure was thick, we both had to walk through it. Somehow, it made us better. Whatever the case, I was glad he had his head on straight. I guess he realized Black Robert was playing a trick on him. When the class went out to the playground for recess, I got a chance to talk more with Ben.

"Who's the best at kickball here?" I asked.

"Kickball? We don't play kickball here. We play sock ball," Ben said.

"What? You guys don't play kickball?" My whole world was crushed. Kickball was always the highlight of the day at Manchester Elementary. To be able to kick the ball over the fence almost made you royalty! I had never done it, but I was confident that next year, in the fourth grade, would give me strength. That new school just took my dreams and threw them on the floor to be walked on like the resume of an unqualified applicant. At least Mama would save money on buying new shoes so fast. Thanks a lot, Weems!

As we made our way to the sock ball area, one of the students threw in the ball, and we sorted out the teams. They even used a totally different ball for this sport! It was a large rubber handball, and the goal was to sock it as hard as you could to get a homerun. As everyone got situated, out of the corner of my eye, I saw two old friends, Kevin and Terrell, walking towards me.

"What's up, Ray!" They both smiled. "They got you over here, too?" Terrell asked. They had both left Manchester Elementary a month apart.

"Yeah, man!" I said, shaking each of their hands. "What's up with this sock ball stuff?"

"I know what you mean, man," Kevin said. "It's pretty cool though once you get used to it."

"Yeah, but nobody ever socks it over the fence, so there is no champ," Terrell said.

"What? Are you serious?" It was unreal to me.

"Yeah, if it ever goes over the fence, it's because of a foul ball. Never socked to the other side of the playground," said Terrell.

"Have fun though, man. You'll like it," Kevin said. "We have to get back to our area before we get in trouble. We'll be seeing you around."

"Alright," I said. "At least I got my B-DOGGS! What's up, Tyrell? You know you out of bounds now, right?" I said half-jokingly, knowing that Terrell's whole family was from Neighborhood 40s Crip Gang.

"It's still 40s, cuzz!" Terrell smiled as he and Kevin walked back to their play area.

"Ha! Be careful," I laughed and went ahead and tried to enjoy the new game called sock ball, which turned out not to be so bad. As we lined up to go back to class, I noticed just across the street were about twenty-five Bloods with red on, hanging out at what seemed like one of their homeboy's house. I remembered meeting a few of them in the back of the clubhouse. More cars were pulling up to the house, and the crowd was getting bigger. Then, Ben gave me a nudge and said they had just come from a funeral. Right away, I knew they were from Fruit Town Brims, and the first thought that came to my mind was, Terrell must be getting picked up from school.

Chapter 15
Best Bud Ben

One week, the play area for our class was Four Square. Guess what? Four square was super boring! Whenever our class would have a boring activity, we would always play our favorite game, "Grab the Biggest Butt"! Chasing the girls all over the playground as if they were living chocolate bunnies and eating them alive was the goal. Ben and I were always the first to kick off the game; then, a few of the boys would join us. The girls seemed to like it as well, as they ran slowly, while giggling and laughing. The fact that they never slapped our busy hands away was very encouraging. It was far better than Four Square.

As a young boy, I was raised not to use profanity. Those types of words just didn't come out of my mouth. Maybe, it was because my mother didn't use curse words. It wasn't that we didn't hear them because Cleophus cursed like a professional. Even Joseph Jr. had let a few choice words come out of his mouth on a few occasions, but he didn't get whoopings on sight like I did, so I stopped bothering to tell on him. Whatever the case was, there was a strong urge for me to use curse words. I know it seems strange. I guess most people just grow up using profanity as naturally as they learned to speak their native language, but I remember making a rational decision that that was what I wanted to do. Sure enough, as soon as I made that decision, the foulest of words flowed in my vocabulary so naturally as if I had been saying them my whole life.

Being that Ben and I were in the same class and we lived in the same apartment building, we began to grow closer and closer. We found we had a lot in common. Besides chasing the girls around, we also liked to save our money that we made from hustling on the weekends. Ben introduced me to Chase. Chase was an older gentleman who lived down the street from us, who worked at the college. He had a big house with lots of shrubs all around the yard. The first boys on the block who made it to Chase's house on Saturday morning had the privilege of working for him. Ben and I would be up bright and early washing Chase's car and cleaning up the fallen leaves around the yard. It was the quickest $10 made on a Saturday.

Then, Joseph Jr. and I had become little professionals at pumping gas on the weekends while living on 94th Street, but the boys on 37th Place had a different hustle that everybody could join in. There was the 32nd Market on the other side of the college. We would all walk to the market, sometimes ten to fifteen deep. The market was perfect for the hustling youth because there were bars on the outside of the exits that prevented the customers from taking their baskets to their cars. So, for a single mom or elderly person, we were a lifesaver.

Now, there were two exits from the market that led out to the parking lot: one on the west end and another on the east end of the building. I usually stayed and worked the west end because on the east end about 100 feet away was the ice cream shop. One thing I had learned while pumping gas is that you celebrated after the job was finished for the day, and with the ice cream shop being in plain sight, temptation would send some of the boys home as broke as they came. We all split up, half on one side and half on the other. The flow of customers exiting the market was much more fluid than pumping gas. It was enough for everybody to leave happy.

Most of the customers paid about $.50 to one dollar or two dollars to five dollars if they were generous, but I will never forget this one elderly white lady. She had a big job, maybe fifteen or twenty full bags in and under her shopping cart. Although most customers would have you watch the cart while they pulled their cars up to the bars, she had only parked about thirty feet away and suggested to just carry them to the car. No problem. Most elderly women were a little more generous than the elderly men who also helped with the job, so I went back and forth and gladly carried all the bags to the car, all the while thinking of adding at least a couple more dollars to my earnings for the day.

As I brought the last two bags to the trunk of the car and closed it, I said, "All done, ma'am," as I approached her on the driver's side of the car.

Then, she said, with the biggest smile ever, "Thank you very much, young man," as she placed one penny in my hand. God bless her heart and fill it with love, in Jesus' name, Amen.

Chapter 16
Summertime Reunited

Everybody loved 37th Place, young and old. Maybe it was because we had the best ideas that drew kids from the whole neighborhood to come and hang with us. When summer time came around, there was unlimited fun to be had. Some of it was even invented! We usually started our day grabbing the summertime free lunches at the school and the church. Then, we made sure we stopped by Mrs. Wimbly's house, who always gave us each a handful of candy. After that, the rest of the day was usually an adventure that went into the history books of our childhood.

One of our pastimes was going to the Swim Stadium at Exposition Park, next to the L.A. Coliseum. The price of admission was only $.50, but if you had an empty Coke can or a Kool-Aid package, you could get in free! That was where I learned to swim and was privileged to wade in the deeper parts of the pool. On the other hand, a few others, including Joseph Jr., stayed in the one feet of water, either refusing or unable to learn how to swim, which in their case was a wise decision being that in four feet and up, you had to be aware of the stealth dunkers on the prowl. We had big fun!

Sometimes, the day of swimming was cut short if one of the boys from another neighborhood said something out of line to one of us, like the time when we were playing Marco Polo. Darrell, who is in six grade, had bumped into another kid who was about his same age. Because it was an accident, Darrell said, "Excuse me. That was my fault."

"I know it was your fault, cuzz," said the boy. "Next time, look where you are going!"

Why did he say that? Darrell snapped and immediately grabbed the boy by the neck with his left hand while punching his face with his right. The lifeguards had to jump in the pool and pull them apart. Darrell was kicked out of the pool, so that meant we were all kicked out because our crew stayed together. As we all got out of the pool, about fifteen of us, Darrell looked back at the boy that he used as a punching bag and told him, "Just so you know, I'm not your cousin, Blood!"

The boy's eyes got as big as golf balls, but he dared not say anything else to Darrell, seeing how many of us there were. We usually stopped at the corner store on our way back to the block, but just in case our snacks were not enough, raiding the fruit trees was always a good plan. There was indeed enough variety of fruit in the neighborhood to make an outstanding fruit salad, but while the juicy loquats were still in season, they would always remain the favorite choice. Then, back to the clubhouse we went, headquarters!

The fun never stopped on the 7 Block. We would even have spontaneous block parties! Especially in the summer when Demandre's older brother Boogie would bring his DJ equipment outside with Rock Daddy rapping on the mic; they'd rock the neighborhood! Hip-hop was alive and well and not just on the East Coast. Here on the West Coast, we had our own style. The idea was to "Keep It Gangsta," but before long, someone would go in an alley somewhere and find an old piece of linoleum or a cardboard box. That's when the pop-locking and break dancing began! Time to see who could get down! Too fresh!

The contest would go on for hours, as we took our turn on the makeshift dance floor, showing off our skills. Then, someone would grab the microphone and start a freestyle rap. As the sun started to set, if we weren't already playing football in the street or basketball on the school playground, we usually ended up playing one of our games we had invented. One of them was "No Touch Cement"! The object of the game was to get away from the predator without touching any cement. The only exception was if you walked on your hands. Being that most of us had the skills of a gymnast, it was basically a game of tag on steroids! We could jump and flip off brick walls, walk on top of fences, hang from apartment staircases, and even walk on a pair of upside down crutches as if they were stilts, anything to avoid getting caught, and if you happened to touch cement, you were automatically "It"!

Another game we so cleverly constructed was "The Belt Game"! That game evolved from the fact that we all got whoopings from our parents, and I probably got the most from my mother. Anyway, that was our opportunity to relieve some stress and give someone a whipping instead of getting one for a change. The game was to hide the chosen belt and whoever found it could whoop everybody until they made it back to the safe base. You'd better run fast, because the whooper was coming full speed, screaming, "Who's your daddy?"

We knew almost everyone in our neighborhood, especially if they were eighteen and under. All of our parents had each other's numbers, so there was no problem if we spent the night over one another's house. We were all like family. One day, the family was extended as I was walking down the street headed to the clubhouse when I heard a familiar voice call my name, "Ray!"

As I turned around to see who it was, low and behold, riding his bike was Jeffery Bonk from 94th Street!

"Hey, what's up, man?" I was ecstatic. "What's going on? What you doing over here?" I asked.

"We just moved in across street," he said smiling. "What neighborhood is this?"

"This is the Fruit Town Brims," I said.

"Oh, okay. We just moved from the East Side Blood Stone Piru's. I've been bangin' with them," Jeffery explained. "They call me G-Nutt!"

"Oh, okay. It's still BLOOD Love!" I said. "Where is Philip? Joseph Jr. and my mother will be happy to see y'all and Mrs. Bonk."

"Yeah, they are in the house unpacking. It's good to know y'all are in the neighborhood," Jeffery said.

"Yep. Aye, let me take you to the clubhouse, so you can see everybody," I said.

It was good to see Jeffery again! When he and his family had moved from 94th Street, the fun had changed. From Mrs. Bonk on down to Jeffery and Philip, they were all natural comedians who could make you laugh until your stomach hurt! Jeffery was also a natural big brother to everybody who was his friend. He had a huge heart that he wore on his sleeve, but if you were his enemy, he was like a vicious pit bull that had been released off the chain! Jeffery was a type of friend you wanted to have around during good or bad times.

We also found out Jeffery had another skill that he discovered since he had moved from 94th Street. Jeffery was a skilled rapper who should've been on the radio. He also wrote my first rap, which I recited every chance I could get. I had skills in beat boxing for the rappers, but after that first rap, I was hooked!

Come to find out, when Jeffery saw Darrell, it was another reunion. Darrell had lived on 94th Street before also, but he had moved to 37th Place just before Joseph Jr. and I had moved to 94th Street, so we had just missed him. What a coincidence. We were all together on 37th Place!

Sometimes, the family would grow unexpectedly, like one day when we were all playing outside. Joseph Jr. and I were playing with our Hot Wheels racetrack in front of our door as Stephanie and Ashley played with a few of the girls that lived in our building. All of a sudden, there came a strange face. A boy, whom we had never met in the neighborhood, came flying through the apartment yard on skates and accidentally ran into and knocked down Stephanie, who started crying. Neither one of us actually saw the collision, which I'm sure was an accident, but at the cry of distress coming from our little sister, we immediately jumped into protection mode.

First, Joseph Jr. jumped on the boy, hemming him against a brick wall with body blows. As I joined in, giving him his issue, the boy's skates were no longer on his feet. As Joseph Jr. decided to pick one of them up and use it as a weapon, the boy went running down the street. We later found out that the boy's name was Edward, who later received the nickname Frog. He had just moved in with his cousin Simon down the street. Who would have known that after the smoke cleared, Joseph Jr. and Edward would become best friends, just as Ben and I had.

Chapter 17

Conformed

1985 was all the way live! But, '86 was a mystery mix! It was a year of transformation as I began to walk away from the light into exceeding darkness. The church bus began to show up on Sunday mornings less and less as Mama would stick her head out the door and give a release wave to Brother Johnson, yelling, "They woke up too late!"

Brother Johnson would still show up every other week to see if we would be ready for Sunday school, until one day, he stopped showing up. I didn't know it then, but it was the beginning of a vicious spiritual attack of evil upon my life, ultimately trying to destroy my soul. The songs that we sang in Sunday school and church, like "Yes, Jesus Loves Me" and "Jesus in the morning, noon time, and sundown" were still in my heart. Yet and still, despite the fact I still remembered John 3:16, *"For God so loved the world, that he gave His only begotten Son, that whosoever believe in him should not perish, but have everlasting life"*... I still found myself slipping into darkness.

Besides the bi-annual whooping I would receive for not wearing my glasses in class, I was getting into more and more trouble at home, from pestering my sisters, Stephanie and Ashley, to debating with my mother when I knew I was right, but in her eyes, I was giving her "back talk," and there was zero tolerance for that. Although not verbally stated, my behavior was slowly labeling me as the "bad seed" of the family. My sisters noticed the trend and quickly took advantage of it. Anytime they would get into trouble or break something, all they had to say was, "Ray did it!" I was beginning to believe my mother just enjoyed whooping me.

I mean seriously! I felt like the piñata of the family! Every time I turned around, I was getting my issue of "the belt." A big one was falling asleep, "Ready Road"! That was her saying for sleeping in your clothes like you're about to jump up and hit the road. If it was my week to wash the dishes and I fell asleep, that was double trouble. I got whipped out of the bed and received another week of washing dishes. I did that one so much that I just became the dish boy. Maybe that's why I analyze dishes so much. I actually became good at it. Maybe some of the punishment was beneficial, but from moving too slowly when she called me, to getting a second cup of Kool-Aid, some of that stuff could have been talked out, but I was getting "beat into next week"! Maybe in her mind, it was some kind of callisthenic exercise or a stress reliever. In any sort, I was not happy being part of her gym equipment.

One day, Jeffery and I were coming back to the block after "joy riding" on the maintenance golf carts in the college parking lots. The fun only ended after Jeffery hit a parked car. Someone must have called it in because before we could get off the campus grounds, we were surrounded by USC security! We were taken to the campus station, where they called my mother who came and picked us both up. Jeffery had told the officer I had nothing to do with it, and we had just met up. He took the whole blame and the officers even told my mother the same story! But she didn't buy it by a longshot! As she walked us home, Mama said, "I'm going to whoop both of y'all!" Jeffrey took off running through the neighborhood and disappeared. I got the whooping for both of us, while Jeffery and the gang watched through my bedroom window.

Usually, the whooping came with a punishment or restriction, which I got a lot of also. No playing outside and no television. One day, Mrs. Bonk saw me looking out the window at all the fun that was going on and offered my mother money to bail me out, but it never happened. I had to serve my time. After being set free of one of my sentences, I found out my buddy Ben was going to live with his dad. Although we would be attending different schools, we still managed to keep in touch with family events and birthday parties.

Times when I wasn't on punishment or school was in, I was getting more involved with the gang lifestyle. I loved it! I had started wearing my belt buckle to the back, which was how the Blood Gang wore theirs. The Crips, on the other hand, wore their buckles to the side.

One day, about four of us were fooling around in the alley when Demandre suggested I get put on the hood, meaning I had to fight somebody. I agreed because I only knew two or three Center Park Boys, and that was including my uncle James, and I didn't know anybody from the Villian Blood Gang. All my friends were from Fruit Town Brims. That was a big decision at ten years old, but I already knew the answer. It was Brim Gang!

I got down with Larry for about five minutes fighting, and it was on. The big homies started calling me Spike, suggesting I kind of resembled the actor/director Spike Lee. Even Jeffery later decided Fruit Town was home. Although he had love for the 30s Pirus, the 30s Brims were family.

There was a bond between us that no one could break. Blood brothers for real. Sometimes, we seemed closer than our own relatives. Our crew was so tight that we even got together before the school year began in order to agree on what kind of school clothes we would get for the coming year, so we could all wear the same style. One year, we got all colors of khaki pants, except for blue of course, with suede steel toe boots, which we called "CK stompers"! The next year, we all got different colors of Levi jeans and Levi jackets with fur inside. The following year was corduroy Levis and then cross cords with silk shirts.

We were styling! If our parents didn't buy our school clothes, then we made a way somehow. We were hustlers.

We did everything together. If one of us got into a fight with an enemy, we all fought. Never back down or show signs of weakness. It was not a good look to have mud on your name because news traveled fast in the streets. Even if you were locked up in jail, word would hit the streets even faster, be it bad or good. So, it was best to stay hard. We were the Fruit Towns! Apples, peaches, and plums! Where the trees grow tall and the fruit grow strong!

The big homeboys were doing their own thing, staying gangstered up, keeping the hood tight, and making money. They already had their reputations, so all they had to do was maintain them. We, on the other hand, were the younger generation, wild and making a name for ourselves. First, you had the OG's or original gangsters. Most of them had been around since the hood began in the late 60s and early 70s when they were gladiators, who evolved and branched off from the Black Panthers.

Then, you had the second generation, the Baby Gangsta Brimz or BGBs, who were mostly between eighteen and twenty-five years of age at the time. Darrell, who was now called Lil Loko, Lil T-Bone, Lil D-Mack and a few others decided we had to have our own generation. That's when the TGBs began, the Tiny Gangsta Brimz, some of the most notorious gang members on the west side of L.A. Buckwheat, one of the Neighborhood 20s Bloods hung out with us so much, he decided to be a Brim also. The big homie changed his name to Lil Killa Jess.

Chapter 18

Finding Talent

Even though I was getting deeply involved in the street life and had even started smoking marijuana, believe it or not, I still completed my assignments and homework for school. I was good at it! I enjoyed figuring things out. It was fun to me. My teachers must have noticed something in me because they began to pick me to participate in spelling bees and speech recitals. One year, I memorized the entire Dr. Martin Luther King Jr.'s "I Have a Dream" speech to recite for a Black History Month program. That was pretty cool!

In the fall of 1988, I began junior high school at James A. Foshay. It was a new world to me. Despite the fact that Foshay Jr. High was majority Crips, I became pretty popular almost instantly. Being that Joseph Jr., Edward, and a few other homeboys were already there in the ninth grade, they introduced me to most of the ninth grade class and even a little bit of the eighth grade. Joseph Jr. was very popular! Everybody knew him, and all the girls wanted to hang around him. So, I was Joseph's little brother. A large amount of the six graders who graduated with me from Weems also went to Foshay and were then in the seventh grade with me. It wasn't too hard to find friends.

There were a few downfalls for some of the seventh graders who were called "Scrubs." They weren't allowed to walk across the "ninth grade lawn" or else risk getting jumped by the ninth graders. There was also a thorn bush across the street from the school that we walked by. The bush was the only thing that belonged to the seventh graders because they got thrown in it by the ninth graders. It was the "seventh grade bush." A few other hazing or to make it plain -bullying tactics- were done, but I managed to escape all those things being "Joseph's little brother."

The fact that we had six classes to attend in one day was a challenge for me, but once I got the rhythm going and stopped having to carry around my list of classes, I was doing just fine. The cool thing was that two of the classes were allowed to be electives. Electives were classes that the students themselves were able to choose from according to any skill that they had or wanted to learn. I chose art class because I like drawing things, and the second was band.

When I saw that one of the choices of electives could be band, it was a no-brainer. I had been wanting to play an instrument, but I didn't know which one yet. The band director gave everyone instructions to walk around the room and take a look at all of the instruments to decide which one favored us if we hadn't picked one already. I began to roam around the room. There were many to choose from laid out around the room, but what caught my attention was sitting behind a glass window in a small room off to the side. It was a drum set. I imagined myself playing some cool combinations like a professional jazz drummer, synchronizing beats released from the diverse sounds of the set.

Ting, ting, ting, boom, tat, tat..., tat, boom, tat, ting, ting, boom, tat, tat, boom, boom, tat, boom, boom, boom! My mind was made up. I was going to learn to play those drums! When it was time for everyone to present to the class which instrument they had chosen, I was the first to jump up and announce the drum set. Unfortunately, the instructor explained there was a complicated issue with the drums and that teaching them required more time than was available during class while teaching the remainder of the class the other instruments. He said I could either practice after school or at the end of the class, but it would have to be on my own free time. Of course, I was highly disappointed, as were the three or four others who had drum sets on their minds.

Why didn't he say that before he told us to choose an instrument? How come the perfectly good drum set sat in the class where students come to learn instruments? I felt denied by a very bad attempt of a copout. He just didn't want to teach is what I felt. I decided that the roadblock was not going to stop my goal. I was going to learn two instruments because that was the case at hand. I already knew that after school was out of the question. The streets were crying too loudly after 3:00PM to even barely get regular homework done, but I was determined to fit the drums in somewhere. So, I grabbed a flute and sat down.

Chapter 19
Taking the Bitter with the Sweet

After all the letters were sent back and forth to El Paso Robles Youth Center, Uncle James was finally coming home! It had been four long years in the system. Now, they were releasing him at the age of eighteen. Mama had gone to pick him up from the bus station. The whole time, Joseph Jr. and I kept peeking out the window to see if they had shown up yet. Finally, while we were watching TV with the volume on low, we heard Mama's car door slam shut. We jumped up to peek out the window again, and sure enough, it was Uncle James outside carrying a box of his belongings. He had bulked up to twice the size in muscle since we had last seen him, and his hair had grown long with braids.

"Let's hide, so we can jump on him!" Joseph Jr. said.

"Alright," I said.

"They must be sleep," Mama said, as they walked through the door. It didn't take long before we couldn't stand the suspense any longer and jumped out yelling, "Surprise! Welcome home!" We all laughed and hugged Uncle James who seemed overwhelmed.

"Thanks, y'all," Uncle James said. "It's been a long time since I've had real joy!"

The family was back together again! Only Aunt Suzette had gone to live with Aunt Rose in San Bernardino, California. As soon as she got word, she was on her way to L.A. to see her brother. More love and laughter were shared as we celebrated with Mama's homemade tacos.

We were all amazed how Uncle James could put them away. I believe he ate about eight or nine tacos with everything on them! He had the appetite of a horse! The next morning was the same thing but with pancakes! His stack looked like a scene from a cartoon. Mama didn't mind at all. She kept pouring them in the skillet, happy that her baby brother was free.

Later that day, it was inevitable that we would resume the wrestling match we had begun four years ago. Aunt Suzette kicked it off! She was determined to get Uncle James down, but he was too strong for her. He didn't even bend as she jumped on his back. In fact, he carried her around like a backpack as we all jumped in and tried to help her take him down. Once again, our attempts were futile, but we had fun trying!

Since Mama had gotten a job at the college and had gotten off welfare, she was a dedicated workaholic. She had no more time to watch daytime soap operas and then discuss them on the phone with other women who did the same thing. She had a new attitude with confidence that things were going to get done on time. So, that evening she didn't cut Uncle James any slack.

"Okay, listen up little brother," Mama told Uncle James. "I know you're fresh out, and you want to catch up with your homeboys, but you have to stay out of trouble if you want to stay free. Because you don't have a job yet, I am giving you a job. Your job will be to wake up every morning and look for a job. I get off work at 5PM, so I don't want you to come home until then. The weekends are your off days. Can you handle that?" Mama finished her speech.

"Yeah, I can handle it," Uncle James smiled. "That was my plan already, anyway."

"That's good," Mama said.

"But tonight, I'm hitting the streets," Uncle James said.

"Alright now. You be careful out there," Mama said.

"I will," Uncle James said. He made a phone call. "Aye, I'm out! Come scoop me up!"

About thirty minutes later, three cars full of gang members pulled up in front of the apartment building with the bass of their music vibrating the windows in the apartment. There was no need to blow the horn; Uncle James knew that was for him.

"I'll be back later, y'all," Uncle James said as he made his way out the door.

"Be careful," Mama repeated.

After we finished eating dinner and, of course, I did my job cleaning up the kitchen and putting the food away, everybody took their baths and laid out the next day's clothes. Mama usually allowed us to watch TV for a little while before she made that final announcement, "Alright, time to go to bed, y'all." As the time passed, it was getting closer to the end of the program we were watching, and that mental alarm clock of "bedtime" was about to ring. Suddenly, there came that bass again that vibrated the windows, but that time at a slightly lower volume. We all knew that it was Uncle James coming back from Inglewood. Mama looked up with a sign of relief from worrying about her little brother, but she played it cool and waited until he knocked before opening the door.

"Did you have fun?" Mama asked with a hint of sarcasm.

Uncle James replied, "Uh, yeah. Big fun."

"You stink, Uncle James!" Little Ashley shouted and covered her nose. She was right! The smell of alcohol lit up the living room as he came in. Uncle James just smiled at Ashley and made his way to the bedroom Joseph Jr. and I shared, trying his best to maintain his composure. There were about fifteen minutes left in the movie, after which Mama gave the final call for lights out. As I turned off the TV and made my way to the bedroom, I noticed even in the hallway that the smell of alcohol was even stronger along with a sour smell. I slowed down in the hallway and looked back at Joseph Jr. with a frown of repulsion. Joseph Jr. went in the room first and turned on the light.

"Whoa!" Joseph Jr. shouted.

As I went into the room, low and behold, Uncle James was on the floor, knocked out on his back, covered with pink vomit all over his chest and face as if he had turned into a vomit fountain in his sleep. Mama came into the room, asking what happened. When she saw the sight of Uncle James, she released a long descending whistle.

"James! James! Get up and clean that stuff up!" Mama shouted.

Uncle James began to stir from the sound of Mama's voice, smearing the vomit on his chest with his hand.

"Ha!" We all laughed.

"Don't you know you are supposed to eat before you drink alcohol?" Mama asked.

"I had some Ritz crackers," he replied, as he got up.

"Well, that explains the white chunks! Can't hang with the big doggs, huh?" Mama joked.

"Can't hang with that Cysco!" Uncle James replied. "That stuff is lethal!" he added, as he made his way to the bathroom.

Lah! Lah! Lah! Lah! Lah! Gunshots rang out in the night. It wasn't unusual to hear that familiar ring, even in the Fruit Towns. It wasn't as bad as 94th Street, which was every night, but it was 1989, and the streets were wild everywhere. It was normal, unfortunately. Joseph Jr. and I settled down on our knees on the sides of our bed to prepare to recite one of the two prayers Mama had taught us.

"Now I lay me down to sleep. I pray the Lord my soul to keep. If I should die before I awake, I pray the Lord my soul to take. Lord, please bless and watch over my family and friends, in Jesus' name, Amen!"

The second prayer was, "Jesus wept!" That's it, short and sweet before every meal. Mama definitely taught us that it was very important to give thanks to God for all He had blessed us with, and it truly was a blessing. Thinking back on the days of peanut butter and jelly on crackers after coming home from preschool, which I thought was a treat, but unknowingly was all we had, the Lord had brought us a mighty long way!

The next day was a breeze! School was stress-free and smooth flowing! Nothing was able to steal my joy! I was too excited that Uncle James was finally free! It was celebration time! Until… On the way home from school, I saw the block packed. Everyone was hanging out. Normally, that wouldn't be unusual except that everybody was around the corner on 37th Drive. Usually, if the block was packed like that on a normal hang out, it would be on my street, 37th Place. That's how I knew something was wrong.

As I approached the crowd, the first person I spoke to was Demandre, who was looking really sad. Then, I knew for a fact something was wrong if he was sad, who we had given the name "Insane." He began to explain that Al-Dogg had gotten killed the night before. He said someone went up to his car and shot him while he was parked in front of his house sitting in the car. As he continued to give me the rundown, the anger in his voice began to build up more and more. I was in shock! I proceeded to drift off into a daze. I was looking at Insane while he was talking, but my mind was back in the bedroom the night before to just before I said my prayers and the gunshots had rang out.

I thought about all the "what if's" that maybe could have prevented the tragic outcome, such as if I could have patrolled the neighborhood, then I would have seen the enemy coming. What if I would have run around the corner last night when I heard the shots? Then maybe, I could've called the ambulance quicker. How about- what if I said my prayers ten minutes earlier and asked God to protect my friends? Then,

Al-Dogg would still be alive. The truth is, it was too late for the "what if's." Al-Dogg was gone. I didn't realize it, but I had already walked away from Insane during my daydream. Everything was a blur. Al-Dogg was about four or five years older than I was, but he was still my peer and the first one to get killed.

Al-Dogg's murder sparked a mini war in the community, with back and forth retaliation. Then, I understood why the gunshots on 94th Street rang out every night because they stayed at war constantly. As the year progressed, the gang life was more real than ever. Thus, it began my collection of incomplete dreams, which were funeral obituaries of young men who the majority didn't make it to see the age of twenty or twenty-five. However, some were shot and were blessed to escape death, such as Lil J-Rock, who was shot seventeen times with a .9mm and lived to tell the story. Even G-Nutt and Lil T-bone were shot together with a 12-gauge shotgun. Thank God the shooter was far back enough for the buck shots to spread a little, lessening the impact of the blast. They both lived to talk about it and still have a few buck shots in their backs today.

Others didn't make it and joined the box of incomplete dreams, such as Baby Snake, who was the same age as Joseph Jr., fifteen. Then, there was Lil C.K., who was my age but really didn't count, and I didn't get his obituary because he decided he would turn 40s Crip and leave the neighborhood. He claimed the homies weren't showing any love. He even came to the neighborhood and announced his plans. He got himself killed right in the 40s not too long after. Then, there were others like the homeboys Too Chilly, Looney Lon, Suga Bear, and Red Cap, who got the next thing close to death, which was a lifetime prison sentence.

We all knew the consequences of the lifestyle we had chosen, but the deception is that we never thought the buck would stop on us. It was as if we were playing Russian Roulette every day with a feeling of being invincible, when in fact, we didn't even know we were walking around blind.

I was sitting in my room playing with a .22 caliber Dillinger that the homie Les Dogg let me keep for a while when the phone rang. My mother had gone grocery shopping and took the girls with her, Joseph Jr. was outside playing somewhere, Uncle James was most likely in Inglewood, and Cleophus was probably on the east side somewhere underneath a car. So, unfortunately, I had to answer the phone. The phone rang twice. *Maybe, they will figure out no one is home and hang up*, I thought. Then, I could finish practicing how to walk with the gun tucked in my waistband without it falling. The phone rang a third time… I snatched the receiver up like it stole something.

"Hello!" I snapped.

"Hello, may I speak to Kim?" a small sweet female voice asked.

"Um, I think you have the wrong number," I said in a much calmer voice.

"Are you sure? Is this 731-6022?" she asked in disbelief.

"Yeah, but no Kim lives here. She gave you the wrong number."

"Oh, okay. I'm sorry about that," she digressed.

"No problem, but wait a minute. What's up with you though? What's your name?"

"Kiesha," she said with a softer tone that made me think she was blushing. Come to find out, she was thirteen years old just like me. The Mack of the Year Award definitely went to me that day because in the course of one phone call, I managed to not only invite her to my house, but I convinced her to skip school and come over the next day. I didn't even know that girl, and she didn't know me from a broom against the wall.

The next morning, I was in creep mode, like a professional cat burglar. I told Kiesha to leave her house as if she was going to school but instead to head over to my place. Instructing her not to call until 9AM was very important. That would give me enough time to get back home after everybody had left for the day. I had stayed up most of the night going over my plan with careful precision. The scenario of meeting her for the first time also played over and over in my mind. My main goal was not to say or do anything stupid that would ruin my chances of getting to know her a little more, learning from my past mistakes. The last girl that had liked me at school was a disaster on my part. Even though I had walked her home a few times and we had shared a kiss in the park, I hadn't figured out how to direct my spontaneity in a productive way.

One day at lunch, right after the bell rang to send us back to class, I saw her walking with her friends, wearing pink stretch pants. As I watched her from behind, I got a wild idea that giving her a wedgy would be funny. So, I did it. Guess what? It wasn't funny. She gave me a look without words that told me whatever plans I had with her were a wrap. Back to the drawing board. That's why I had to be very careful with Kiesha, because I knew if I got too comfortable and stopped thinking, I could ruin a potentially good thing with one of my so-called conversation pieces.

The plan began very well as I proceeded with my normal routine of walking to school with Joseph Jr. We usually knocked on various girls' doors that Joseph Jr. knew, so we could walk them to school along the way. Even though our dad no longer came around, Joseph Jr. had a natural ability of being a gentleman. Little did he know, he was also teaching me.

As we reached the school, there was enough time for everyone to go to their lockers and exchange books before the first period class began at 8AM. I put my books away in my locker from last night's homework; then, instead of going to class, I slid back out of the side door. Then, I headed to Hamburger Dan's to kill a little time to make sure Mama and everybody was gone about their day. I even gave them a little grace period just in case they had forgotten something and needed to double back to the apartment. The plan was working beautifully!

No sooner than I returned home, I began to straighten up the place. Not so much cleaning but removing embarrassing baby pictures that were hanging on the walls that Mama thought were adorable. It was ten minutes past nine, and I was beginning to lose all patience. I thought about walking to the bus stop to meet her, but I didn't want to miss her call on the way, which could cause her to leave and go back home. *Maybe if I hurry down to the bus stop, I can catch her getting off the bus or standing at the phone booth trying to call me. Okay, I'll run down there.* As soon as I started towards the front door, the phone rang.

"Hello," I said, hoping to hear that sweet voice.

"Hi, this is Kiesha," she replied.

"Good morning, Kiesha. Please tell me you're down the street."

"Yes, I am," she replied with that sweet soft voice. I had an instant grin on my face like the Kool-Aid man.

"Oh, okay. I'm about to come meet you," I said.

"Okay, bye." She seemed just as excited as I was. I hung up the phone and was out the front door, cheesing. *This girl better be pretty*, I thought. The suspense of seeing how she looked was intense. Then, I thought, *But, what if she's ugly? Okay, she's never seen me before either, so if she's ugly, I could just keep walking like it isn't me. Cool, that's the plan.* I knew the closest payphone was at the gas station on Vermont, but before I could reach the corner, I saw a slim, chocolate girl with long braids approaching me. She wore lip gloss just as I like girls to wear, and she had perfect brand new breasts the size of cantaloupes. Wow! I wanted to jump up and down for joy, but I kept my cool. That sweet soft voice didn't lie.

"Kiesha?" I asked as I got closer to her.

"Yes, and you're Raymond," she smiled. "Not bad."

"Not bad yourself," I replied, shaking her hand and looking her up and down. We started to walk towards the apartment. "Did you have any trouble on the bus?" I asked.

"No, I was only hoping that you didn't stand me up," she said.

"You and me both," I said with relief. "Don't tell anybody, but I was about to run to the bus stop to meet you." She laughed and put her hand on my chest. I laughed with her, but I knew she was performing a subtle check for muscles. Good thing I did my push-ups the night before with Uncle James. My yoke check was tight, and the look she gave affirmed it.

Everything was definitely going according to plan. There weren't even any adults passing by or peeking outside that could potentially tell my mother I was ditching school that day with a strange girl in her house. I slowly picked up the pace a little bit just in case. As we made it inside, I asked her, "Would you like something to drink?"

"No, thank you," she said. "But, I would like to use your restroom."

"Oh, okay." I showed her to the restroom and went to my room to spray a little more of that Adidas cologne on me to make sure it was working. Then, I checked the mirror to make sure no eggs or bacon were in my teeth from the morning's breakfast sandwich. I had just gotten a fresh haircut the other day, so my lineup was smooth. As I reached for my brush to agitate my waves a little bit, I heard the bathroom door open. I rushed to the bedroom door, so she could see where I was.

"Is that your room?" Kiesha asked.

"Yeah, you want to check it out?" I invited her in.

"Yeah, let me see how messy you are," she said jokingly, with a smile. She had the cutest smile with those nice lips and that lip gloss that made them look juicy. As she passed me in the doorway, I could smell her perfume. It was a sweet intoxicating smell like flowers mixed

Let Me Tell You How I Got Saved

with banana pudding that made me want to follow her around with my eyes closed giving long, slow inhales.

"I'm surprised," she said.

"Surprised at what?" I asked, snapping out of my daze.

"At how clean your room is," she said. "Most boys' rooms are disaster areas! Clothes everywhere, dirty dishes on the dresser, and all kinds of candy wrappers and stuff on the floor," she looked like she was having a flashback of a bad day.

"I don't know whose house you went to, but Moms is not having that here," I explained. "Her motto is that everything has a place, and she has designated my brother and me to be superintendents over the items positioned in this room. Failure to do so can be detrimental, if you know what I mean."

"You're funny," she giggled, walking closer to me. "Smart and funny." Her chocolate skin started to look edible to me. I couldn't take it any longer! I went in for the kiss, wrapping my arms across her back, pulling her closer. She was very susceptible and feminine, melting into my arms as I kissed her like that was where she belonged. My plan for the day had gone perfectly up to that point. That was as far as I had ever gone with a girl, besides grinding on top of our clothes.

As things started to get hot and heavy, my plan evolved into an exciting game of impromptu experiences. I proceeded to lift up her shirt, and to my surprise instead of refraining, she lifted her arms to help me take it off! I was super excited! That was far better than experimenting with myself in the bathroom. What happened next as we both ended up without a stitch of clothing exceeded any of my nocturnal emissions by far. Although I was new at that, I seemed to be a natural. Everything was flowing smoothly with no mistakes or embarrassments. For some reason, I did expect her to ask me how come my eyes were so wide, but I failed to prepare an answer. Thank God, she didn't ask me.

At the end of our rendezvous, I walked her to the bus stop as she made her way back to her side of town. I went home and tried to collect my thoughts on the whole matter. Besides the fact that her name was Kiesha who lived on the east side and was thirteen years old, I realized I had no clue who the girl was. I had just lost my virginity to a girl who had the wrong number.

Chapter 20
Strongholds

Things were really starting to look up for Uncle James! He had not only found a job as a dishwasher with free soul food lunches, but also a second job at night as a maintenance man. God is good! Uncle James didn't waste any time finding his own place to stay. Although he loved living with us, he said that a man should always have his own castle. That way, you don't have to deal with the politics of someone else's kingdom. That was very true, but until I got old enough to move out also, I had to deal with "the politics."

The summer of 1989 was hot! Not only the heat from the sun, but the heat from the LAPD was scorching. Demandre's brother Boogie had made a go-cart for Demandre the year before that was custom-built to look like a Nissan truck with a camper on the back that actually lifted up on hinges. Even though all the little homies in the neighborhood were paired up with their own go-cart teams, Demandre's go cart was the ride of choice. We all shared the go-cart, and Demandre didn't mind taking turns with us all. It even had headlights and a real car stereo powered by a car battery that would've put some of the big homies' stereo systems to shame.

That year, Insane put a motor on his go-cart that stepped up the game a notch. He was teammates on the Nissan truck with Lil T-Bone, and it was often too much fun and not enough time for everybody to ride. Naturally, everybody wanted their own, so we could all ride together. Some got themselves motorized mini bikes and dirt bikes through the five-finger discount. Clayron, who was my teammate on our red Baron, had moved out of the neighborhood, but all was not lost. We also kept a few Honda Elite scooters around the neighborhood that everybody shared that were taken from the college. Whoever did not have their own mini bike or go cart at the time would ride the Honda scooters. No more pushing with manpower. We were now working with gas!

One day, I went outside, and everybody seemed to be gone. I figured they must have been somewhere riding, probably through the college or in the 20s. Then came the homie Keis, mobbing down the street like Run DMC. He had on an Adidas jumpsuit with the sneakers to match. I don't think he owned anything that wasn't Adidas.

"What's up, Ray?" he said as he approached me.

"What's up, man! Where everybody at?" I asked.

"You already know. They all riding out, probably in the 20s somewhere," he said.

"Yep," I replied.

"Where is Joseph Jr.?" Keis asked. "Is he in the house?"

"Yeah," I said.

"Oh, okay. I'm about to go ask Ms. Watkins for a sandwich," he said.

"Good luck! I'm about to go find one of those scooters," I said.

I headed to the backyard of Insane's house, next to the old clubhouse. I figured someone would be back there tending to the birdcage or something. It was unusual to see the hood so dry, but I knew the homies couldn't be too far. They were somewhere having some big fun. That was for sure. The birdcage was locked up, and no feed was on the ground. Not a soul was in sight.

"Man! It's a ghost town today!" I said out loud to myself, as I started to head through the alley.

"Hey, Spike! Where are you going?" someone shouted. It was Lil Killa Jess on the side of the house, smoking a joint.

"Trying to find one of those scooters," I said. "Where is everybody?"

"They boned out earlier," he said." They probably in the Doves at the park. I know where two of the scooters are. We can go get them in a minute."

"Where? Who got the scooters?" *I hit the jackpot! We about to have some fun now!*

"The Littles got 'em," he said.

"Is that right? Oh, okay," I answered myself.

The Littles were three of our Hispanic homeboys who were brothers. We called them "The Littles" because none of them were over five feet tall. I helped Lil Killa finish his joint before we headed to the scooters.

"Knock, knock!" Lil Killa shouted through the screen door of the house. It looked like a family party was going on. I could smell the different Spanish dishes as they walked to and fro inside the house with plates of food.

"What's up, Blood?" Lil Third came to the door.

"Soowoop business," Lil Killa replied.

"Where are the scooters?" I asked.

"They are in the backyard. Go around to the back, and I'll open the gate," Lil Third said. "Y'all want some of this food?"

"Man, you know we want some of that food!" I said.

"Yeah, hook us up!" Lil Killa replied. We went around back to the scooters. Lil Third came and opened the gate for us empty-handed. The smell of the Mexican dishes was causing the hunger munchies to kick in from that joint earlier. "What happened to the plates?" Lil Killa didn't hesitate.

"I got my sister in there hooking them up," said Lil Third already looking like he ate too much.

"What's the occasion?" I asked.

"Oh, it's a little get together for my cousin. He got a promotion on his job," Lil Third said.

"Here you go, guys," his sister came out through the back door with two nice and hefty plates of enchiladas, refried beans, Spanish rice, and a nice garden salad.

"Thanks a lot. We appreciate it," Lil Killa and I said, as we gladly took the plates with our bloodshot red eyes. Lil Tim Stacks and D-Dan came out with toothpicks in their mouths looking stuffed, and we all talked and laughed a little bit while we ate before jumping on the scooters.

"Alright, Blood! Good looking out!" I shouted to the Littles, as I rode one of the scooters out the back gate.

"Yeah, that was bool! On the B!" Lil Killa said as he rolled the other scooter out.

"No problem, Blood! Y'all be bareful out there," replied Lil Third. That was our Blood language that to the outsiders may have seemed weird, but it sounded like the portrayal of Langston Hughes. The idea was to change all words that begin with the letter 'C' into a 'B.' And even some 'S' words, such as 'six' became 'bix.' That also was a symbol of our disdain and hatred towards the Crip Gang. For example, "I was eating a bowl of Baptain Brunch Bereal! On Bloods!"

Putting everything on the Bloods was another one of our fingerprints. It gave assurance to the listener that you were definitely telling the truth, but it also depended on the person saying it and how much loyalty they had to the Blood gang. For the most part, we were all liars, cutthroats, and thieves. So, accepting the promise was at your own risk. Amongst us true homeboys who grew up together, there was honor amongst thieves, and our word was our bond. Unfortunately, there were definitely speckled cattle betwixt and between the herd. So, you had to know the difference. Those were the ones who lied and blew up the B, then later would say, "Oh, well. The B already has two holes in it." Watch those dudes! Your life may depend upon it.

The scooters were running just fine! Despite the fact that we didn't have the keys to them, all the homeboys treated them as if though they were our own. Once, we had to buy a can of Fix-a-Flat to inflate one of the tires, but other than that, we just made sure gas was in the tanks, and it was time to ride. The Littles must have gassed them up the night before because we both had full tanks. We smashed through the neighborhood headed towards the 20s park. There was almost a guarantee that the homies would be over there with their go-carts and mini bikes. If not at the park, they would most likely be around the corner from there at Lil Loko's girlfriend's house. She had a little sister, and the rest of the homies were in competition for a chance at her. They were pretty black girls who looked to be mixed with Asian. Beautiful!

The park was dry except for a few Neighborhood 20s Bloods that were hanging out. Lil Killa and I stopped for a little while to ask if the homies had been passing through there. They told us they hadn't been riding by all day. Our stay got extended a little longer when the blunts started going into rotation. The goal was to get as high as we could without falling asleep and to stay high all day. My high was gone from the joint Lil Killa had earlier, so it was definitely time for more medicine. I was cool and laid-back when I was high. As I was always but even more so when I was high. Some people got the giggles and laughs at everything even if it wasn't funny.

For me, on the other hand, my senses seemed to be more keen like a canine. Food smelled and tasted better! If I were talking to a girl, I could convince her that water wasn't wet, and she would choose me instead of the other guys. Every now and then, a rap session would kick off, and we would all go around the circle taking turns rapping a freestyle flow. If I were high enough, especially after Chronic, I could flow a whole album for you freestyle! That was our pastime: trying to escape reality. We chopped up some more game with the Doves before Lil Killa and I went half on another sack of weed to take with us. By that time, the sun was easing its way to the west towards Venice Beach.

As we jumped on the scooters, I had to tell myself to pay attention to the road. I was so high and feeling so good, it felt like I was in a dream. Kind of like when you were taking a leak in the morning, and it feels so good but you have to make sure you're really awake and not half asleep, peeing in the bed. Looks like I wasn't the only one discombobulated. I noticed Lil Killa almost losing his balance as he tried to start his scooter, but he played it off like he was looking for something in his pockets when he gained his composure.

Before we headed back to the hood, we took a spin around the corner from the park just to make sure none of the homies were at Lil Loko's girlfriend's house. Nope, the whole block was a ghost town. We doubled back and headed towards the hood. On some blocks, we were able to get top speed on the scooters before having to stop for traffic. Smashing up Budlong, hitting a left on Jefferson, and then a right on Catalina. Then, it seemed like out of nowhere a helicopter came down flashing its spotlight on us! I don't know about Lil Killa, but my high was gone immediately! We continued smashing down Catalina as the chopper circled around us. As we got to 36th Street, we hit the corner and jumped off the scooters using the trees and an apartment building as cover.

The police chopper circled around again, and as soon as the apartment building blocked its view, Lil Killa took off running across the street to the homey Drak's house. I didn't want to risk the police seeing me and then following me straight to Drak's house. I knew it was time to split up. I waited for another circle around the building, and I took off running down Catalina, hopping over the side gate to the house on 36th Place that everybody said Sammy Davis Jr. used to live in. That house had a lot of shrubs and trees in the backyard plus a canopy to keep me covered. I was just hoping and praying that the chopper didn't see me when I ran from under the trees.

I stayed in the backyard for about thirty minutes, listening to the police cars speed past when they finally slowed up. When I felt it was safe to come out of hiding, I waited a little while longer before I came out of the yard and ran home. It was another one of those nights where my mother didn't ask any questions. She was just glad I had made it home. From the look on my face, she could tell it could have been worse.

The next day, I found out why we couldn't find the TGB's. A bunch of them had gone with Insane over to his grandfather's house, who was a gospel preacher. They all had a good time until the pastor called home with disappointing news. Insane was in trouble with his parents something crucial! His mother was making a public demand to round up all the little homies on account of the pastor calling her to report that the church's offering money was missing from his house. It was alleged that Insane had found the money and split it up with the homies. By the time his mom had gathered them all up, they had gone out and bought Nintendo's and brand new clothes.

Yeah, Insane was in some major trouble on the home front. Although he was one cat to be admired for his flipping skills and bike tricks, that was one day, I was glad I wasn't him. My mother would have killed me! I guess the good thing about it was that he was in trouble with family and not the police. A few of the Tiny Gangstas had already started going to juvenile hall spending their summer vacations doing push-ups and fighting Crips. The homie Biz managed to escape "the halls" one time and hit the block with a giant boom box radio like everything was cool. He, Lil T-Bone, and I were hanging out with the radio blasting as it sat on the ground. Biz walked off somewhere around the corner and never came back. Little T-Bone left also. I ended up taking the boom box to my house and immediately upgraded the single speaker tape deck Joseph Jr. and I had been sharing.

"Awe, man!" shouted Joseph Jr. at the sight of the stereo. "Where did you get that from?"

"Don't even trip," I replied. "Sounds good, huh?"

"Yeah, man," Joseph checked it out.

The stereo had detachable speakers with long speaker wires, which allowed you to place the speakers on opposite sides of the room if you chose to. You could also add more speakers if you liked.

I tried not to get too attached to it just in case Biz came asking for his radio. Then, I would have to humbly give it back. Unfortunately, Biz didn't make it back. The homies found out he had gotten locked up again and was facing about ten to fifteen years in jail. It happened like that sometimes. A few of the homies would end up spending most, if not all, of their twenties in institutions. That was one of the consequences of doing the things that gang members do, and some things were never talked about.

Summer was ending, and fall was beginning, and along with fall came school. It was the beginning of the eighth grade for me and time to shine on my own without the shade of my big brother's umbrella. I started walking to school some days with the homie Red Flagg when he was ready to go, who had just started the seventh grade. Flagg was about a year and a half younger than I was, but in hood years, he was my senior being that both his parents were OG's from the hood. You can say he was literally born a Fruit Town Brim.

We would go through the hallways mobbing like we didn't care that it was a Crip school. As we passed through, we could hear them whispering, "There they go," but they wouldn't flex unless they were in a crowd. All it took was one instigator to kick it off, and generations of built up hate would explode.

At times, they tried to run us out of the school to no avail or should I say their big homies who were high school age or older tried to. They would post up in front of the school at the end of the day about ten deep waiting on us. Then, we would make a phone call to our big homies, who would pull up in their cars with pistols, demanding they let the little homies up out of there.

Despite the danger, I never switched schools; I just worked around it. All the Crips at the school knew who I was, and I knew who they were and didn't care. Aside from the gang banging, we were all the same, just separated by some colors and some streets. Some of them were actually cool, and a few, believe it or not, had saved my life in street situations because of respect. We all knew each other's first and last names.

Over the summer, it seemed everyone had experienced a growth spurt but me. I was friendlier with the ground than I was with the sky, still standing at 5'4" tall. Maybe my spurt was coming later, so I thought. What did change were my eyes. They had gotten a little more blurry probably due to the fact that I'd rather squint my eyes than put on my glasses. Mama surprised me at the optometrist's office and allowed me to pick out my own frames. I was ecstatic! I picked out the nicest gold, wire rimmed frames I could find. Far away from where they stock those plastic contraptions that might as well have had the words NERD SECTION posted about the display case. I looked good in my new frames! Plus, I could see further than twenty feet in front of me. It changed my life! I wanted to wear them all the time.

To my surprise, when I wore them to school, I was getting compliments instead of the nerd jokes that other students had gotten in the past. Maybe, they only did that in elementary school. Whatever the case, I was comfortable with my new pair of eyeglasses and was prepared to fight to defend them. I had made up my mind that I would rather have the blessing of eyesight than to walk around blind thinking I was cool.

When I learned the girls approved of my new look, I was on a mission to conquer the entire eighth grade female class. Ever since that little fling I had with Kiesha, my hormones seemed to be racing on steroids. I wanted all the pretty girls! I wanted to try them out like 31 flavors, but the goal was to get as many virgins as possible. Just so she would remember me for the rest of her life as being her first. I was a father's worst nightmare.

There was one girl by the name of Trisha who was so fine. I couldn't help but to smile at her whenever she was in my presence. Trisha already had a boyfriend, but she opened up a door when she started smiling back and flirting with me. She would walk past and make noises, like "Mmmm," like she wanted to taste me, and I was more than willing to give her a sample. Trisha wanted me bad. It was all over her face, but she didn't want to risk getting caught by her boyfriend. I wanted her also, so I made her my own personal project. She was a part of my homework assignment. I studied her closely.

One day, her boyfriend didn't come to school, so I decided to walk her home and maybe change her mind about cheating along the way. The only problem was that Trisha lived right down the street from Denker Park, right in the heart of the Harlem Crips neighborhood. There were plenty of stories about dudes getting shot, robbed, or jumped just because they risked their lives going to the wrong neighborhoods to see a female. That was them. I was different. Nothing would happen to me… So, I thought. Trisha and I walked down Denker Avenue in front of the park and turned right onto 35th Place, as we laughed and talked about how much we liked one another.

Unfortunately for me, she was still scared of her boyfriend finding out she had cheated. She had mentioned he would probably kill her if he found out, which started me to thinking maybe he was already beating her up on a regular basis. As we passed the side of the park, I noticed a group of Crips on the opposite side of the field, hanging out and talking loud amongst each other. Every other word that came out of their mouth was "cuzz," which was burning my ears off, but I stayed focused on Trisha and our conversation.

"You know you want to be with me, Trisha. Why don't you follow your heart?"

"I do, but I'm scared," she said as we arrived to her house in the middle of the block.

"Don't be scared of that dude," I said. "Let me worry about him."

"Well, if it's meant to be between me and you, then it will happen. Okay," she replied.

"Sounds good," I said. She was a hard nut to crack. At least the outer layer began to peel away.

"Thank you for walking me home. I really enjoyed your company," Trisha smiled. "I have to go before my daddy comes out here," she said, glancing at the man looking at us through the curtains in the window.

"Oh, okay. I'll see you at school tomorrow," I smiled back at her and waved at the man in the window who just stared at me like a statue.

"Bye, Raymond," Trisha said as she went in the house. Just as I came out of her yard, before continuing up the block towards Normandie Avenue, I looked behind me towards the park to see if the coast was clear. To my surprise, there were about five Crips on the sidewalk by the park, and I could see one pointing at me as if to say, "There he goes right there!"

They immediately started climbing into a small car, and I took off, running in the opposite direction towards the hood. As I got to Normandie Avenue, I didn't wait for traffic at all. I just ran across the busy street, dodging cars, then continuing on 35th Street. As I looked

113

over my shoulder, I could see they were sitting across Normandie, waiting for the traffic to break. So I broke, straight through somebody's yard and hopped their back fence. I ended up on 36th Street, after going through a couple more yards.

Although I was in the hood, I wasn't safe yet, but I didn't see the small car, so I slowed down a little. Maybe, they gave up and went back to their hood. I hopped over the two parking lot gates of Weems Elementary and jogged across the playground to the other fence on the 37th Street side. As I started climbing the fence, I heard gunshots behind me and bullets whizzing past my head! Swiftly, I climbed over the top of the fence when one of the bullets skinned my left shoulder. I jumped down and ran through another yard as fast as I could!

The next street was my block, 37th Place. Quickly, I ran to our apartment building and into my apartment. I went to my room, trying to catch my breath while looking at the hole in my shirt. Taking off my shirt, I noticed a small cut that burned, but I was okay. I guess the stories I had heard were true. Don't get caught slipping! Especially for a female! Yeah, whatever, because if Trisha had told me the next day that her dad was out of town and to come help her with her bra clip, I would go back over there in a heartbeat. She was too fine!

My youthful lusts were not the only thing that had a hold on me, so it seemed. I began to hear that voice again that had told me I was going to die when I was three years old. Only there were many other voices along with it, all whispering different things at the same time. It was as if every negative activity I was involved in was assigned a voice, and they were all trying to speak at once.

Sitting in class, most of the time, I would finish my assignments before the time was up. Then, I would work on homework assignments, so I wouldn't have to take so many books home. However, if all assignments were complete, and I was sitting idly, I would find myself for some reason drawing pentagrams in a circle with the numbers 666 above, in the palm of my hand, with an ink pen. I didn't know why I was doing that. I couldn't remember too much of anything about church, except for a few Sunday school songs and John 3:16. At times, when the voices in my head would start to get too loud, I would begin to sing to myself one of those songs, such as "Yes, Jesus Loves Me." Then, they would calm down. *Who could I talk to without being called crazy or forced to take some medication that from what I heard would probably make me crazier?*

I didn't want to end up like the homie Lunatik who was trying to cope with the fact that his father had been recently arrested when authorities found four of their family members dead underneath their house. Maybe that's what happens when you answer the voices. I just chose to deal with it on my own. If anyone asked me what I believe in, without hesitation, I would have told them I was a Christian, but if they had followed me around, it was evident I was doing the devil's work.

One evening, the voices started to haunt me again as I was getting out of the shower. It was like having ten to twenty people whispering in my ear at once, and each of them was trying to tell me something different. That time, instead of singing a Sunday school song or quoting John 3:16, I stared into the bathroom mirror and tried to make some sense of what they were trying to say. Big mistake. All of a sudden, it seemed as though the multitude of voices began to mesh into one. It seemed to be whispering, "No hope. No hope." I started to sink into a great state of depression and sadness. As I stared into my own eyes, I began to believe the words I was hearing in my head. "No hope." There was no hope. There was nothing I could think of to give me the will to see the next day.

Before I knew it, I was opening a bottle of pain relievers that I took out of the medicine cabinet. I ended up taking about eight or nine of the pills and went to bed with no hope. After I woke up the next morning without any problems, I thanked God for another day. Then, I came to a conclusion that there was a purpose for me being alive. I didn't know exactly what it was, but I knew it was something more to this thing called life. I made up in my mind that it would be better to live and find out the outcome than to die and miss the show.

"Aye, Spike. What's brackin'?" shouted the homie Cowboy as I was returning home from school.

"What's up, Blood?" I said as we shook hands with only our middle and ring fingers in order to simultaneously throw up the Brim gang sign. Cowboy was already in the eleventh grade, attending Manual Arts High School. He was the kid brother of Black Robert and the cousin of Red Flagg, but we never used the word cousin because it sounded too much like cuzz. All the bloods simply said, "Relative."

"You made it to see another Fruit Friday, huh?"

"On Brimz!" I responded. "What's all these clothes doing outside?" There were jeans, shirts, and shoes scattered all in front of the apartment all cut up into rags.

"Oh, Lil Loko and Flagg started cutting up each other's clothes with scissors," Cowboy said. "Don't ask me why."

"That's burnt out. Now, they gotta hustle hard and buy more clothes," I said. Cowboy lived in the apartment above mine, and his bedroom window faced the street. I looked up as a pair of cut up red All Stars came flying down out of the window. "Awe, stall! They're still up there doing it?"

"Yeah, they're at war with each other's clothes!"

"Ha!" We both laughed.

Lil Loko was living with them for a while because of an argument he had had with his parents. The protest against each other's clothes was funny, but I knew in my gut it was the streets to be pitied because Red Flagg and Lil Loko needed a new wardrobe, and it was the streets that were going to pay for them.

After I put my books inside and went back out, I noticed a crowd starting to accumulate in front of the apartments. Homeboys and homegirls were coming from far and wide. Every hood had a hood holiday on the day pertaining to the street they represented. Because I was from 37th Place, my block celebrated on March 7, the third month and seventh day. The Fruit Towns were a little special though. Although it was barely winter, we had hood holidays every Friday. It was Fruit Friday. Fruit Fridays were mostly for the hood to come together amongst themselves since we didn't have the meetings anymore on Saturdays at Weems Elementary lunch tables. The third month seventh day was when we really did it big with other Blood hoods coming to celebrate with us, and we did the same with them on their days.

Outside, it was a gathering of the criminal mind. As there are many facets of a criminal mind, there are the same facets sectioned off in a gang. As they say, "Birds of a feather flock together." Even though some birds still strayed into other flocks, they were usually distinguished by one. Some of the flocks were the Gangstas, Killers, Dope Dealers, Gamblers, Pimps, Robbers, Thieves, Con Artists, and Extortionists just to name a few.

If I had to label myself, I'd have to say I was amongst the gangsters and gamblers. That was how my mind state and profession in the game was explained. The gangstas didn't speak much of their agenda. They moved in silence. They kept the street code and honor amongst thieves. The gangstas could very well be the staple of every other flock, the base if you will. Although some were not gangstas at all. Then, there was the gambler. The gamblers had little to no fear of taking risk. Mostly in games of chance, such as crap games with dice, dominoes, and card games, involving money wagers, they were skilled in speculation and were usually pretty accurate.

The gamblers were easily detected because they were usually involved in a game of chance of some sort or trying to start one. Most gamblers had other forms of obtaining income, but it was the gambling that either catapulted or stagnated their wellbeing. A true gambler could survive off gambling alone.

Naturally, a dice game conjured up after K-Luv walked up shaking a pair of dice in his hand hollering out, "What they hitting for?" I immediately jumped in the "Teedle Lee." Les Dogg won the Teedle Lee, so the dice were on him. We started out shooting five-dollar fades and then side bets for five dollars. As the game progressed, D.G. hollered out, "Shoot $10!" That would change the net worth of the game and narrow the players down to only the serious gamblers. Those with two and fews would eventually fade out after they'd pieced up with each other a few times trying to bounce back. I was able to hold my ground as the dice landed on me. I had a nice streak, hitting sevens and elevens on the roll out. I was rolling my points, sometimes hitting them in the door. I started increasing my winnings with side bets also, as the streak was in my favor. I bet the 6 or 8, the 9 or 5, and the 10 or 4.

Gamblers would try to throw your concentration off with the "come a new" bet. That bet gave you a brand new set point besides the one you already had. Because math was one of my favorite subjects, it didn't bother me. I hit the "come a new" bet also. When I finally crapped out, I had cleaned up enough to survive the game when K.O. hollered out, "Shoot $20!"

I caught another fade, and then, the dice were back in my hands. I caught another streak, but not as long as the last one. Before I knew it, the dice were on Money Sacks, as he hollered out, "Shoot $40!" That was kind of steep for me, but I tried to hold it down. Who knew, maybe it was my day to break up the game. I caught a few fades but the confidence wasn't there. I decided to back off before I was left with just enough for coffee cakes at school. The game was left to the Ballers. D.G. ended up breaking the game up after hours had gone by, and the sun had set. He collected the last of his winnings and counted up the blood money. Yeah, I know for a fact it was blood money because some of my blood was on it. I had snapped my finger so much and so hard on the rollout that my middle finger has split wide open.

"Aye, Spike. You going to the Ponderosa?" Cowboy asked.

"For what? What's over there?" I asked.

The Ponderosa was an apartment building around the corner on 37th Drive. It had an enclosed courtyard in the center of the building closed off from the streets. The Ponderosa was a good place to hang out because you didn't have to worry about any drive-by shootings.

"D.G. is about to go to the store and get some brews for everybody. We all meeting at the Ponderosa," Cowboy explained.

"Is that right?" I responded.

"Yeah, I think I'm going to take my first drink tonight," Cowboy said with confidence as if the timing was perfect.

"Yeah, why not? Me too," I said.

I had already been smoking weed for a couple of years by then. Being that I was in eighth grade, it was time to take it up a notch. We hung around for a few minutes to give D.G. enough time to drive to the store before we faded off from the rest of the crowd and mobbed around the corner. I knew when Cowboy said the drinks were for everybody, I know he meant only the Tiny Gangstas. It was a TGB thang!

When we got to the Ponderosa, the homies were already going inside and getting comfortable. Les Dogg and D.G. came in and set up two bags each of St. Ides 40oz beers on the ground, and we all grabbed one. The initial taste as I cracked open the 40oz was nerve jolting and nasty, but as I continued to take swigs, it became refreshing and relaxing. The taste didn't seem so bad anymore. It was like a craving was building up when in fact it should have been repulsive. While I was going through my own experience, about three quarters of my way through the bottle, I noticed Cowboy leaning against the wall. The buzz was hitting him hard!

I could remember the Drug Abuse Resistance Education (D.A.R.E.) class that we had in the sixth grade. It came to mind how the officer talked about a person's tolerance to alcohol depended on his/her weight. That puzzled me, because Cowboy was probably about thirty pounds heavier than I was. Nevertheless, I opened my eyes a little wider to pay attention to my surroundings just to make sure I was maintaining my composure. It was a pivotal moment in my life, and I had yet to realize the importance of the door I had just opened. You could say it was somewhat bittersweet because it was fun to drink socially, but later it would definitely become a stronghold in my life.

Chapter 21
Time to Roll

I was tired of walking around the hood and riding bikes and scooters. If I wanted to go someplace away from the hood, I would have to get on the bus, and buses in L.A. were not the safest place to be. So, I decided to teach myself how to drive cars with one of the G-Rides that was around the neighborhood. A G-Ride was a stolen car that was usually used in some type of criminal activity or stripped down and sold for parts. Sometimes, they were even used for an occasional joy ride, but that day I was going to utilize one for educational purposes.

I knew there was one in the hood just sitting on Catalina Street, waiting for someone to drive it. It was an old Delta '88. A long four-door car that was probably too big for me to drive for the first time, but I didn't care. I was my own instructor anyway, and so far, I had everything I needed, including a flathead screwdriver to start the engine and my brownie gloves to prevent fingerprints. I jumped into the G-Ride ready to roll. My feet were nowhere near the gas pedal, so I scooted the seat up all the way. I remembered how to start it from watching the homeboys I had rode with before.

The steering column was already popped, so all I had to do was start it with the screwdriver. I did my trick with the screwdriver, and the engine turned but didn't turnover. I hit it again, and the engine roared as the radio came on, playing Eric B and Rakim- "Check Out My Melody." I threw the gear in drive and took off like someone was chasing me.

Pumped up, I forgot I was supposed to stop at the stop sign at 37th Street, but I slowed down and came to a stop at the next one on 36th Place and made a left. It wasn't until I had made a right on Budlong, that I remembered I should be signaling my turns with the blinkers. Okay. I got it. I eased off the gas a little, attempting to get comfortable with the car. *A natural!* I thought. That was easy to say, but I hadn't gone backwards yet or attempted to park. Nevertheless, I was doing pretty good going forward. I made a right on 35th Street and another left on Walton Avenue, expecting to pass by a few of the homies that were hanging out. The hood was dry without a soul in sight. I didn't want to turn onto Jefferson with its busy traffic. I wasn't ready for that yet, so I turned right through the alley and went through to Catalina Street. Bad mistake…

Bam!! I hit a telephone pole and got the car stuck at an angle that I couldn't get out of. I always wondered why the city put the wooden pole right in the alley, decreasing the width of driving space. It didn't matter at that point. The only thing that mattered was making the right decision before the police showed up. Either I was going to spend twenty minutes trying to figure out the correct way to get the car back straight or abandon ship before it was too late and go find another G-Ride. It was not a puzzle! I chose the latter. As I was getting out of the car, I saw the big homie Monkey Hustle walking up.

"What in the world you got going on, man?" he said looking at the condition of the car.

"I got stuck, Blood! Can you get it out real quick?" I asked.

"That's 'cause you can't drive!" He laughed.

"Blood, you gonna get it out or not? Hurry up before one-time comes." I had no patience.

"Yeah, give me those gloves," he said.

"Go ahead," I said, handing over the gloves. He seemed to pull the car out of the alley with no problem! I had a lot of practice to do.

"Here, young blood," he said as he handed the brownie gloves back to me. "Next time, stay out of the alley until you get some skills."

"Good looking out," I said as I jumped back in the G-Ride and smashed off. I knew I needed to learn a few more skills before I could claim to know how to drive, but it was only my first lesson, and I was hooked! I decided that was my new hobby. I had to get it down packed. That day was enough to digest for one lesson, so I parked the G-Ride back on Catalina Street.

The next morning, I had big plans to drive the car to school. Then after school, I was going to practice a little more. I also wanted to show off a little as I passed by the other students walking to school, but when I got outside and walked to Catalina Street, the car was gone! Someone took it! Hot and heated wasn't enough to describe the way I felt as I walked to school with my flathead screwdriver and brownie gloves in my back pocket.

All day, all I could think of was driving. It seemed like 3:00PM took years to come. I would have left school early, but I had worked so hard on my homework and wanted to find out the grade it would get me. As soon as school let out, I was out the door. No socializing and no extra books because I had completed my homework for the night during class. I was on a mission! I knew one of the homies had probably used the G-Ride for something else, so I was hoping that whoever had it had brought it back already.

"Soowoop!" I heard somebody holler out as I strolled through the hood. It was Big Yak on his beach cruiser. I knew it had to either be Yak or Lil T-Bone hollering out, "Soowoop," because neither knew how to whistle. Who knew that later the "Soowoop" call would become the distinct "Blood Call" of the Damus?

"What's hatnin, Blood?" I asked as Yak got closer on his bike.

"What's hatnin? What you 'bout to do?" he asked.

"I'm looking for that "G" that was on Batalina," I replied. "Where is it?"

"What you need the 'G' for? What, you about to go CK? You need the heat?" Yak asked.

"If I do go, I'm not taking that Dillinger," I said as we both laughed. Everybody knew Yak had that two shot Dillinger in his sock with a pocket full of bullets.

"I don't know who got that 'G.' I haven't b'd it," Yak said as he rode the bike in circles in the street.

"Alright, I'm about to go bee if it's on the drive," I said.

"Alright, be bareful, Blood," he said as he rolled off on the beach cruiser.

"Yeah, be bareful," I replied.

I made my way to the drive to no avail. The G-Ride was nowhere to be found. *Maybe, it's on the seven street... No. Maybe, it's on the six... No. Maybe, it's on 35th... No. Maybe it's by the projects... No.* I went all through the hood except for across the railroad tracks on 38th, Rolland Curtis Place, and Leighton Avenue. My guess was that the police had found it and had it towed. Whatever the case, it was getting late and was time to have a drink with the big homies back on 37th Place. Sure enough, one of the homies told me that's exactly what happened. The police had got it.

After all of the walking through the hood that I had done, it was time to chill. A drink was well deserved, and the cognac was already on the ground, right next to the busted bag of ice and several cans of pineapple juice. Usually, Hennessey was the cognac of choice for its smooth taste, but on some rare occasions "white" was the poison of the day, being vodka or gin. Be it dark or white, the rule was never to mix the two, unless you wanted to give it all back onto the curb, turning your stomach inside out. Of course, everyone learned the hard way, including me. What more could you expect of a lifestyle that was indicative of rebellion and being hardheaded? There will be many travesties.

The night was getting late, and homies were still pulling up putting more bottles on the ground. With my screwdriver and brownie gloves still in my back pocket, I couldn't stop thinking about driving. The conversations were remedial, and the dice game wasn't appealing. I decided to take my third cup of Hennessey and fade off from the crowd. What better time than then to go and get my own G-Ride? I had spotted a nice one earlier while mobbing through the hood that might be a good candidate for the cause. It wasn't a Delta '88, but it would do just the same.

There it was, just waiting for me, and the street was quiet as a mouse. I looked around and checked my surroundings before I quickly popped the back corner window and got into the car. Immediately, I began cracking open the side of the steering column to bypass the ignition switch. Then came the hard part, breaking loose the steering wheel lock. I tried and I tried with all my might until I was sweating, but I couldn't seem to break it loose. Just when I started to give up before someone noticed my unsuccessful antics, I looked up and low and behold coming down the street again to the rescue was Monkey Hustle!

I opened the driver's door and yelled out in a loud whisper, "Hey, Blood! Come here!"

"What you doing, youngsta?" he said, walking towards the car.

"You know what I'm doing… Hop in and help me pop the steering wheel," I said.

"Hurry up, youngsta! You always into something…" he said, as he jumped into the passenger seat and close the door softly. Quickly, he pulled the top of the steering wheel towards himself as I helped pushed in the same direction until it broke loose. Then, we reversed the process as he pushed and I pulled until it popped again, freeing the steering wheel to turn freely. "... and next time, do your pushups," he said, getting out of the car.

"On Brims. I did my push-ups, but good looking out though." I jimmied the screwdriver into the neck of the steering column and lifted it. Jer, jer, jer, JROOM! "Yeah! It's on now!" I said to myself. "I'm about to paint the town red!" I took off and hit the corner with no brakes, screeching the tires. Whosever car that was, they were probably looking out the window by then, but oh well! It was too late! I was gone!

I began cruising around, trying to get the feel of the car. It was light traffic at that time of night because it was getting late. That was a plus for me, so I could practice my skills. The L.A. lights were beautiful at night! Especially that night because my Hennessey buzz gave each light a halo around it. I imagined myself as a movie star, cruising around without a care in the world. Heading west, I ended up in the Jungles in the Black Pee Stone's hood. I figured I'd grab a beer and cruise back to the hood. In the Jungles, there was always someone selling beers out of their apartment after the stores had closed. The B-Doggs loved it!

I definitely loved it because no one ever asked how old I was or to see my ID. I was in and out, no problem. It was a good thing because I couldn't wait to jump back into the car and drive some more. I felt like it was Christmas morning, and that car was on the top of my gift list. I was addicted to driving! It was time to head back to the house. Despite the fact that I wanted to keep cruising around, it was almost 2:00AM, and I didn't want to be the target for the police to pull me over being the only car on the road. As soon as they would have seen an eighth grader go by with his back super straight to look over the steering wheel, it would have been a wrap. As I made it back to the hood, I decided to park the car in an alley, so it didn't end up missing like the last one did. I sat in the car and finished the beer before I went inside.

The next morning after I got dressed for school, I went into the kitchen to begin making my specialty: the bacon, scrambled eggs, and cheese on toast sandwich.

"Good morning," my mother said as she took a seat at the kitchen table.

"Good morning," I replied back while scrambling my eggs. I tried not to look at her, knowing she was leading up to asking me where I had been the night before.

"Ray, let me ask you a question," she began.

"Yeah," I said.

"Why do you do the things that you do?"

"What do you mean?" I was stalling.

"You know exactly what I mean," she said. "With the drinking, smoking, gambling, and Lord knows what else you be up to. Then, you went and got an earring in your ear without my permission. You know I don't like that. I mean, just tell me, what am I doing wrong?"

"You're not doing anything wrong," I replied.

"Then, what is it then?" Mama asked with her hands out and palms up.

"I just want to do my thing, like the big boys," I replied.

"Like the big boys?" she snapped. "The big boys are going to jail or getting shot and killed! The big boys have to look over their shoulder all day and every day! The big boys have to sleep with one eye open! Is that the kind of life you want to live?"

"That's not going to happen to me," I said as I walked past her out the front door for school with my bacon and egg sandwich in hand and a flathead screwdriver in my back pocket. It was a beautiful day, and I wasn't about to let her ruin it. It was time to roll!

I made my way to the G-Ride parked in the alley behind our second clubhouse because someone had bought the two-story house. That one was only one level, but it was special because we had given it a name.

We called it, "The Let 'om"! At the former clubhouse, we utilized it for flipping on the mattresses in the backyard and raising pigeons that flipped also. At the new clubhouse, because we were all coming of age and sowing our royal oats so to speak, we flipped girls. If one of the homeboys brought a girl or girls there, she was most likely going to let him or let them have sex with her; hence, the name "The Let 'om."

The G-Ride had been untouched through the night. I slid on my brownie gloves and jumped in. As I cranked it up to get it started, I noticed it still had about a half tank of gas. Cool! Rolling the windows down, I made my way through the alley and onto the streets. I couldn't wait to roll past all the other kids who were walking to school! Slowly making my way across Normandie Avenue, students began to point and call my name as I cruised by, but I wasn't stopping. That was my show, and I was enjoying the attention. No time for explanations.

I am sure to have my pick of all the girls now! I am the man! So, I thought... Until a police car passed through one of the adjacent streets but didn't look my way. Too close for comfort! Snapped back into reality, I straightened up from my gangsta lean and rolled the windows up. I parked the car around the corner from the school and jumped out. That was close! After school, I ended up giving the G-Ride to one of the homeboys who wanted to handle some business.

I went home only to find out the bad news that Jeffery and Phillip's mother, Mrs. Bonk, was in the hospital. My mother told me Mrs. Bonk would have to get her legs amputated because of complications from diabetes. We were all shocked and saddened by the news. I have to admit, I didn't want to see Mrs. Bonk in a sad state. I had only seen her happy. She was the one making everyone else happy with her quick wit and humorous personality. I knew Jeffery and Philip were dealing with it internally when I saw them outside, but they never showed it outwardly. They hid their emotions well. I honestly don't know how they stayed so strong. I know now that it was only by the grace of God.

Chapter 22

Life Happens

Thank God! The weekend is finally here, and Uncle James' time is up on keeping his promise of letting me spend the night at his new apartment in Hawthorne. He had to move from his last place due to some Crips jumping on him on his way home from work one night. Uncle James could handle his own weight, but that time one of the Crips cracked a 40-ounce glass bottle over his head while he was fighting off the others. They didn't hurt him too badly, except for a small gash on the side of his head. He didn't even go to the hospital to get it checked out. Nevertheless, Uncle James was fed up with fighting "Cowards Running in Packs" (C.R.I.P.), so he called them.

"They already had me out numbered and still had to pick up weapons," Uncle James explained. "They can't fight, and they are scary! Stay away from scary dudes. They will try to kill you first because they're scared of what you might do to them."

As I stuffed some clothes into one of my backpacks for the weekend, Uncle James pulled a shiny chrome .25 caliber pistol out of his pocket. "Look what I got," he said.

"Cool!" I said as I took the gun out of his hand to get a closer look. "Where'd you get it from?"

"I bought it," he said. "Let them cowards come and try to jump me now! They only act tough when they're five or six deep."

"Yeah, this will back 'em up off you fa sho!" I handed the gun back to Uncle James.

"Are you coming with us, Joseph?" Uncle James asked.

"Naw, not this time," Joseph Jr. said, as he walked into the room. "I'm going to chill at the house with Pearl."

Pearl was Joseph Jr.'s new girlfriend, who he had started spending all of his free time with. Uncle James and I understood his case. He was in love like a kid in a room full of cupcakes and candy. He had a valid excuse not to chill with us. Maybe, he was still a little shook up from the last time he and I went to visit Uncle James. On the way back home, we were all crossing the street on Crenshaw Boulevard to catch the bus when Uncle James got into a staring contest with a guy sitting in his car at the light. All of a sudden, the guy hollered out, "What you looking at, fool?"

"I ain't looking at yo ugly self!" Uncle James replied.

Immediately, the driver pulled his car over into the deli parking lot next to the bus stop that we were going to. Plus, another car followed him. Two dudes jumped out of the first car and three out of the second, and they all tried to rush toward Uncle James ready to fight. To both my and Joseph Jr.'s amazement, Uncle James was handling all five of them at once, socking one in the face and jumping to the side before socking another!

Side to side, he danced, with the grace of a ram on a mountain side. His Jheri Curl swinging back and forth as he switched positions with all the jabs connecting, he seemed to shut them down one by one. They reluctantly got back into their cars, hollering out obscenities and dry remarks as if they had won the fight, such as "Next time, you'll watch your mouth," but they couldn't fade Uncle James. The bus pulled up, and we got on and went home.

That time, it would be just Uncle James and me. Uncle James' apartment was small, but it was big enough for him. I guess that's why they call it a single. It was one room with a closet that had mirrors for sliding doors. There was a full bathroom, but half a kitchen. The bachelor pad! But, it wouldn't be complete without the bachelor diet!

Fried chicken wings and Ramen noodles was all we needed for survival and, of course, cherry Kool-Aid.

"This is the life, man!" I shouted as I reclined back into my chair while raising one of my chicken wings high in the air.

"Yeah," Uncle James responded. "It's way better than my last place." He broke apart another chicken wing.

"I can't wait until I grow up and get out of school," I said. "I'm going to get me an apartment just like this one! No more sharing my bedroom, no more getting blamed for things my sisters did, and no more getting yelled at for no apparent reason."

"Hold up, nephew," Uncle James interrupted. "You sound like you're not enjoying your 'right now'."

"What do you mean, my 'right now'?"

"Your life right now," he continued. "You gotta enjoy it."

"I am enjoying it. I'm enjoying it right now," I said with a confused look on my face.

"No, I mean really enjoy it. Some people don't realize the good times in their lives until the good times are gone. You don't have any bills to pay right now. All you have to do is go to school, do your homework, and keep your room clean. Don't try and rush to get grown because one day you're gonna wish you were thirteen again," Uncle James explained.

"I already do those things every day," I said.

"Yeah, but you don't enjoy it," he said. "I'd give anything to be thirteen again and start all over, but I know it's going to get greater later. The worst is always first, but until then, I'll be out here dealing with these E-Rickets," Uncle James said as he pulled apart the gun and took the clip out.

"Ha! You gotta be quick on the draw," I laughed. "Handle them before they handle you!"

"Exactly," Uncle James said. "I'll be like, 'Freeze! Get against the wall!' Like I'm the police!" he said, running towards the mirrored closet doors, pointing the gun at his reflection.

"Ha haaa!" We both laughed.

"Then, you have to make your getaway before the police comes," I said.

"If one-time comes, I'll play crazy!" He put the gun to his own head. "Everybody, get back! I ain't playing!" Uncle James raised the gun in the air. BLAHHH! The gun went off! We both looked at each other in silent disbelief for about thirty seconds, mostly listening for any screaming responses coming from upstairs.

"I thought you took the bullets out, man?" I finally asked.

"I did…" he said. "Forgot one was in the chamber though."

We went outside to checked the angle that the bullet traveled. Everything seemed to be okay being that it traveled in the direction of the upstairs railing. We went back inside, and Uncle James immediately put the gun away.

"Thank God, nobody got hurt," I said. "You almost smoked yourself."

Uncle James kept silent. Maybe, he was thinking of all the hypothetical nightmares that could have happened. Maybe the short nineteen years of his life had flashed before his eyes. Whatever the case was, he didn't want to talk about it anymore. He had a look on his face as if he was wishing he had the power to disappear. We simply watched TV for the rest of the evening until we fell asleep.

On Sunday afternoon, I went back home, and as I walked into the apartment, Joseph Jr., Stephanie, and Ashley were sitting on the couch with their heads down.

"What's wrong with y'all?" I asked. No one gave me an answer. I was thinking that maybe one of them did something terrible, and Mama had whipped everybody. She usually did that if nobody came clean when she asked, "Who did it?"

As I walked past my mother's room to go to my room, I thought I saw Mama crying out of the corner of my eye and had to take a second look.

"What's going on, Mama? Why is everybody sad?" I was really concerned then. It was strange to see the whole family sad like that. Mama took some tissue to wipe the tears from her eyes as she looked up at me.

"Mrs. Bonk passed away, Ray. She's gone." She mustered out her words over the emotions in her throat. Her words shook me from the inside out. I couldn't believe what I was hearing. Mrs. Bonk was the only one who stood up for me when my mother thought it was a good idea to lock me in the house for punishment while everyone else enjoyed their summer vacation. I loved her for that. She would be truly missed. Although I knew her wisdom, strength, and unique sense of humor would live on through Jeffery and Philip, 37th Place just wouldn't be the same without her.

In a quick decision to make something out of his life, Jeffery decided he would go into the military. It was a chance to get out of the hood and away from the negativity. It was a good decision. Philip, who was only fifteen years old, could not enroll into the military just yet. So, he ended up moving in with Sharmaine and her family upstairs from our apartment. Sharmaine was already like family, so it only seemed natural. Philip fit right in.

It was kind of strange not seeing G-Nutt in the hood, but the streets didn't stop. The homies stayed grinding! The ups and downs of the street life, take the good with the bad, wins and losses. In between time, we still had fun though. A house party here or picnic over there. The year 1989 was coming to a close and ushering in 1990 full blast with the crime rate at an all-time high. Lil Loko ended up getting caught by the police and was sent to youth camp for juveniles, a vacation in disguise.

Gang violence was so rampant that the media stopped covering the stories and airing them on the news. Somehow, drive-by shootings became a sport. After the deed was done, gang members would rush back to the spot and catch what just happened on the news in hopes to see who got laid down. A very sinister sport it was. After the media stopped giving airtime to the hood, the phrase was coined, "The crook always returns to the scene of the crime." Well, at least most of the time they did, and quite a few "geniuses" were arrested due to their curiosity to go back and see what the results were. They were usually pointed out by a bystander and apprehended not too far from the scene of the crime.

I was lying down on my bed, looking up at the ceiling thinking of a scheme I could come up with to get some money quickly. My pockets were flat broke, and a girl wanted me to take her to the movies. Of course, the streets are going to pay for it. I just need the right plan to… LAAHH! LAAHH! LAAHH! LAAHH! LAAHH! Gunshots rang out and interrupted my thoughts. It sounded like a 9mm going off. It was probably one of the homies outside shooting in the air or chasing an unfamiliar car up off the block. I started to go outside and check the scene, but then I changed my mind, thinking to myself that the homies just wanted some attention, and they needed to stop wasting bullets.

The next morning, I made one of my famous egg sandwiches before anyone got in the kitchen. I left out the kitchen, without leaving any evidence. That was the trick, to make the kitchen look like you had never been in it. From falling asleep at night without washing the dishes so many times and getting an extra week to be on kitchen duty, I was actually getting pretty good at it. If there was a speck of food left on a dish, I could spot it! I had to! If I didn't, my mother would definitely notice it and that meant getting awakened in the middle of the night by a swinging belt, plus one more week added on of washing dishes. Nevertheless, I had unwillingly learned a skill that would benefit me for the rest of my life.

I decided to go outside before my mother found something else for me to do. Even though my Saturday morning chores were done, she seemed gifted in finding new tasks to be delegated. Luckily for me, I knew the solution for that. Out of sight, out of mind! Cowboy was in front of the apartments leaning against the fence.

"What's hatnin?" I exclaimed. "It feels good out here! The sun's shining, birds chirping, and I just ate a bomb egg sandwich that was on point! Where the bud at?"

"What's going on?" Cowboy shook my hand, as we both gave up the Brim sign. "Where mine at? I smelled it in there cooking..."

"Oh, you missed out!" I said, rubbing my stomach. "That was a one-man meal! You know what I'm talkin' 'bout?"

"Yeah, okay. You heard those shots last night?" He changed the subject.

"Yeah, I heard 'em. It sounded like a nine," I said.

"That was Killa Jess..."

"I knew it was one of the homies," I interrupted. "I was like, 'the homies need to stop wasting bullets!' Blood got a .38 though. When he get the nine?"

"That was Blood getting shot!" he said.

"Is that right?" My whole mood changed.

"Yeah, the homies just came back from beeing him at the hospital. He told 'em the Barlems came through the alley on him."

"Man!" I took a step back.

"It's a cold piece of work... They say he got shot five times. He told the homies that the bullets spun him around while he was standing up," Cowboy explained.

"He gonna be alright though, right?" I asked, hoping for a yes answer.

"Yeah, he going through it right now though," he said.

"Man! You know it's on now! The hood is about to be HOT!" I said.

"Exactly..." Cowboy responded.

Sure enough, Southwest Police Department doubled their patrols with the C.R.A.S.H. Units (Community Resources Against Street Hoodlums). They knew they could catch more gang members with guns right after friction starting between two enemy sets. Nevertheless, the homies were smarter than that. Everybody knew not to hang out too tough during war times. However, the police thought they were slick. They would bump everybody up during times of peace, so they could add you to the gang files. So when anyone got caught for something serious, they could add a gang injunction to their case, which made their sentence ten times worse as a labeled gang member and career criminal.

Lil Killa got out of the hospital in about a week and came back to the hood using a cane for support. He looked as if he had lost about thirty or forty pounds! The streets were waiting, and he didn't hesitate one bit. He jumped right back on the grind. His strength was a little weak, but he still kept it gangsta!

The police stayed hot in the hood for a long time. They thought for sure they would catch someone with a gun. A few months went by, and G-Nutt came home for military leave, or at least, I had heard he was home from my mother. I hadn't seen him yet. I couldn't wait to hear some of the stories and experiences he had had so far as a military man. It was May 22, 1990, when I came home from school, and Mama broke the news that Jeffery had gotten arrested. I couldn't believe it! Life was like that sometimes. Just too ironic. I found out later through the heartbeat of the streets that he and a couple other homeboys had gotten caught for armed robbery, but G-Nutt, being who he was, took the whole wrap and let the homies go free. He didn't want them all to have to suffer for the same mistake.

Not too many homies would have pulled such a selfless act as that one. Most would have stayed silent and let what fate they were given be just that. In the streets, we called it "sticking to your story." Whatever lie you told when you were caught, that's what you stuck with it until it somehow became the truth. Then, you had a small number of dudes that would roll over on you the first chance they felt it necessary. If it meant them or you going down, then the decision was unanimously you. These were, as they say in the old days, "rats," but in the hood, we called them "snitches." Someone like that, you stayed far away from because their future was not bright.

Chapter 23
Independence

"Good morning, students!" the dean of the school, Mr. Riggor, started the announcements as I sat in homeroom. "Summertime is coming up on us with the quickness in only one month! I am glad to announce that we have enough summer jobs this year for all who want to work and earn your own money! As long as you meet the age requirement of fourteen years of age, feel free to come to my office and pick up your application and request for a work permit for your parents to sign..."

"What?" I said out loud. "Did he say I could work? Oh, it's on now!"

Shanay sat across from me, shaking her head and smiling at me. I was super excited! I couldn't wait to work and have my own paycheck! Minimum wage was $4.25 an hour in 1990, and I wanted every bit of it! I couldn't wait to get my paper signed and sealed.

Later that evening, after Mama got off work, she signed the papers with no problem. She was just glad she wouldn't have to pay for my school clothes for the ninth grade. She kept saying "thank you" for some reason, but I didn't know if she was thanking me or God. Right in the middle of her appreciation rant, there was a knock at the front door. I could see through the screen door that it was Uncle James. He was standing there with a young lady by his side.

"What's up, Uncle James?" I said as she unlocked the door for him and we congregated in the living room.

"What's going on? What's going on?" Uncle James repeated. "I came to introduce y'all to my lady. This is Jazmine." Jazmine smiled and waved to the whole room.

"How are you doing, Jazmine? I'm Rachel," Mama introduced herself and shook her hand.

"I'm fine," Jazmine replied. She was a beautiful, petite young lady. I would guess of about eighteen or nineteen years old.

"It's nice to finally meet you," Mama continued. "James didn't tell us how pretty you are."

"Thank you," Jazmine blushed.

"I wanted you to see her for yourself," Uncle James chimed in. "What's pretty to me may not be pretty to you. Plus, I knew you would keep it real and raw."

"Well, I just tell the truth," Mama responded back. "Nonetheless, Jazmine, make sure you stick around. He needs someone in his life to keep him out of trouble."

"Amen to that!" Uncle James agreed.

"I'll try," Jazmine smiled.

We were all happy for Uncle James and his new girlfriend Jazmine. He had a few flings since he had been home from the California Youth Authority, but that girl he seemed really interested in. All seemed to be going well until the following week when Jazmine slapped Uncle James in the face outside in front of everybody. She slapped him so hard, his Jheri Curl shook! The homies didn't even trip out. I guess they were used to it. In a weird way, they kind of respected him for not hitting her back. Pretty cool, but Mama, who was there about forty feet away near her front door, had a different take on the whole situation.

Later, as soon as she got a chance, she pulled Uncle James to the side. "Look, let me tell you something, little brother," she started her intro. "Even though no one will ever mention it to you, people will start to look at you in a different way if you don't maintain your reputation in the streets. Don't ever let that girl slap you like that in front of all the homeboys. That was very disrespectful."

Why did she say that? It was like a light bulb switched on in Uncle James' head. He morphed into beast mode as he had just gotten confirmation from the commander-in-chief to drop a bomb he'd been holding too long. All passiveness left his body, and all that was left was pure aggression. Jazmine didn't know what hit her! (Pun intended.) Anything she did that even had a hint of being out of line or disrespectful, Uncle James was on her like white on rice!

One night, I was rolling with the homies Lil Skeet, Cowboy, and Red Flagg cruising down Crenshaw, which we called Brimshaw. Because we were close to Inglewood, I suggested we swing by Uncle James' spot and bick it for a while. Uncle James worked at night, but it was past time for him to get off, so I figured he would be home by then.

"Yeah, where Blood live at?" Lil Skeet asked. "I'm tired of seeing these low riders pass by anyway."

"Bool, turn on 111th Street," I said. I was familiar with the address being that it was Uncle James' grandmother's property. He had started renting the back house because it had become vacant recently. Uncle James' mother and grandmother still lived in the front house.

"He stay in the back," I said as we got out of the car. "Don't make too much noise in the front because Granny will pull out her gun on us."

"Ha!" Flagg laughed. He didn't know who he was dealing with. Granny had no problem with shooting a trespasser on her property. I think she wanted to test her pistol out anyway, just to see if it still worked.

"I'm serious," I said. "She's never seen y'all before, so be careful so she doesn't shoot." I proceeded to lift the latch on the front gate as quietly as possible, standing to the side as I opened the gate to let them in, so I could close it just as quietly as I had opened it. As he walked by the side of the house, Cowboy crunched a dry leaf under his foot. The sound made the hairs on the back of my neck stand up. That was too close! She must be sound asleep. Cool! We made it past the front house without incident. I slowly exhaled… I knew for a fact I only had about two seconds to yell out, "It's me!" as soon as I heard, "Who is that?" coming from the front house.

"Who is it?" the homie Spud from Center Park shouted out from inside the back house as I knocked on the door.

"It's Spike," I answered. Five seconds later, Jazmine opened up the door.

"Hey, nephew! What's going on?" She seemed excited to see us.

"What's hatnin?" I responded. "Where is my uncle?"

"Who Wee Wee II?" Spud interrupted from the kitchen table playing dominoes with the homie Taco from Centers. "Blood should be on his way home from work."

"Oh, okay. What's up wit you, Blood? What's brackin?" I said as I walked in and shook both of their hands. Then, I introduced them to the homies Lil Skeet, Red Flagg, and Cowboy.

"Where the bud at?" Lil Skeet asked.

"Yeah, we were trying to get blunted out," Flagg added.

"Oh, it's a spot around the way," Jazmine said. "If y'all rolling, I can ride with you over there."

"Cool," Lil Skeet said. Flagg went with them as they left to get the weed. Cowboy and I stayed behind at the spot with Spud and Taco. About five or ten minutes later, Uncle James came home and was happy to see us, shaking our hands and smiling. First thing he asked was, "Where's Jazmine?"

"Oh, she took Lil Skeet and Flagg to get some weed," I said.

"Is that right? She done burned her bridges," he said.

142

Cowboy and I laughed it off being that Uncle James was still smiling, but Spud and Taco held their peace and continued playing dominoes.

"Ha, ha!" Uncle James replied as his face turned to stone with no emotion as if he hadn't smiled all day. Just as we got outside, they came walking down the walkway with Jazmine leading the way. As soon as she got into arms' reach, Uncle James grabbed her and slammed her against the house. Then, he proceeded to use her as a heavy bag for about half a minute while she screamed from the body blows she was receiving. After he was satisfied, he slapped Lil Skeet and then slapped Flagg so hard he fell into the bushes. We all knew immediately that the party was over. That dude was trippin! We rode back to the hood in silence and never mentioned it again.

Summertime rolled around pretty quickly despite all the Scholastic Aptitude Tests (SATs) we had to take at school. I didn't fall asleep during any of them, so I think I did pretty well. I was too amped up about working over the summer to fall asleep anyway because Dean Riggor approved my work permit. There was a notice sent in the mail stating I should meet in front of the school a week after the last day of school to work for "Clean & Green"! Clean & Green was a company who hired youth to beautify the city. I had no idea the extent of the beautification until the first day of work. On the hire letter, it informed me to wear tan colored khakis and a T-shirt.

When I arrived and signed in, I was given a green hard hat and a green sweatshirt and T-shirt, which both had Clean & Green printed on them. I was excited! "It couldn't be too bad," I said to myself. I figured because there were about thirty youth with two vans parked in front of the school, each van would take half of us vacationing students and go throughout the surrounding neighborhoods picking up paper. Easy money! I was already thinking about what kind of school clothes I was going to buy for the coming school year. Mama made it very clear when she was thanking God that because I would be working my school clothes would be my responsibility that year. I didn't mind one bit.

As the two drivers/supervisors started to separate us by name, I found the first half of my prediction to be true. It wasn't until not after, maybe ten minutes into the ride, that we stopped in front of a house that sat next to an alley and got a rude awakening. I looked up and down the street and thought to myself, *This must be a piece of cake,* being that they were just a few pieces of paper in sight.

Then all of a sudden, a huge two-ton dump truck met us on the scene and backed into the alley. The driver/supervisor then informed us all that the alley was indeed our assignment for the day! The alley was a total mess! We proceeded to throw broken TVs, old couches, and other miscellaneous junk into the back of the dump truck. After all the junk was removed from the alley from one end to the next, we took a lunch break that was well deserved. Never before had I enjoyed a tuna sandwich and a bag of chips so much! I made an agreement with myself on the spot to pack two tuna sandwiches for the next day.

After lunch, we were instructed that the crew was then going to weed the alley and cut back any shrubs and overhangs from the trees. Cool! I immediately grabbed a pair of loppers from the back of the van. I figured I'd beat him to the punch before he assigned the worst job, which was chopping weeds with a hoe. No power tools allowed. I started trimming back the trees on the right side of the alley when another guy started on the left side. We had pullers behind each of us who tossed the cut branches into the two-ton truck. Behind them came the workers with hoes, chopping the weeds and crab grass down.

Then finally, behind the hoes came the rakes and shovels to bag it all up. After about two hours of procession line type landscaping, we finally made it to the end of the alley. I took a look at our finished work and was surprised at what before looked like a public dumping site had then brought a little more morale to the neighborhood.

All of a sudden, I was no longer there just for the paycheck. I got a certain gratification out of the finished product and the beautification of the area. As the job continued, alleys were not the single assignment of the day. Some days, we planted small trees on city streets. Other days, we painted over the graffiti on the neighborhood walls and even on the walls of some small businesses. That was the part that gave a little extra satisfaction being that most of the work that was done was in enemy territory. I would have painted over their hood writing for free. Just to look at it was like having a repulsive allergic reaction. I couldn't wait to whack it out.

As the fruits of my labor began to come in, there was also a new style of dance that was getting pretty big with the young culture. I always liked to dance, and the new dance attracted me with a strong urge to learn it. As I watched the Hip Hop music videos, the dancers on the screen were breaking down moves that I had never seen before. The last big dance scene in the Black community was with pop-locking and breakdancing, but the new dance seemed to combine the pop-locking and breaking with a more fluid type of rhythm. The moves were much more animated with creativity, and each dancer had his/her own style, like it was their handwriting. They called it "Housing"!

I began to practice on my own, adopting the moves that I saw on the TV screen and adding my own twist and flavor to them. I discovered I was pretty good at it and developed a passion for the whole movement. Along with the dance came a new style of dress, which included baggy jeans with multi-colored shirts, hoodies, and a variety of shoes. Because I had full power over my school shopping that year, I was very creative with my wardrobe construction. I even put an S-curl in my hair a day before school started back to top off the new look. I was serious about that thing!

The first day of school was always a live fashion show! Everybody was showing off their new clothes with a new attitude! Some students had gotten a little taller over the summer. I was 5'4," and the height police pulled me over permanently. Others had shot up like beanstalks! I was full of enthusiasm! Everybody was in good spirits, especially after Jessie Jackson had come to our school last year and told us to be leaders and to "Keep hope alive"! It seemed like everyone's grades stepped up a notch. I know mine did. I was also excited to be graduating from the ninth grade that school year. I couldn't wait to get to high school with Joseph Jr. and the homie Malik at Dorsey high. They always had stories of high school fun that made junior high seem like elementary school. Yet and still, I had all year to build up my reputation there at Foshay as a junior high senior.

"Hey, Raymond," Sheila interrupted my thoughts as I walked to the snack area to get myself a coffee cake.

"What's up, Sheila?" I responded. "How've you been?"

"I'm straight," she said. "You looking NICE though! How've YOU been?"

"Thanks," I said.

"Regina, look at Raymond. Don't he look cute?" Sheila called to Regina.

"Yes, he is looking cute. How are you doing, Raymond?" Regina blushed and smiled at me.

"I'm straight," I said, playing it cool as I kept walking to the snack lines. Sheila and Regina were cousins who also lived together. Sheila and I got along well because she was from Bounty Hunters, a Blood gang on the east side, but Regina wasn't into gangbanging. She was the girly type, just how I like them. Plus, she had the biggest booty at the school aside from Ms. Watkins, my science teacher. I think Ms. Watkins knew that us boys were just waiting for the perfect opportunity to brush up against her, so she stayed behind her desk whenever class was dismissed, just in case. Maybe, someone beat us to it in the past, and she grew wise. I was surely waiting for her to get caught slipping, so I could pull my behind the back trick and blame it on somebody else. Wishful thinking, I guess.

I stood in the middle of the yard, eating my coffee cake and checking out the scene. Everyone was grouped up into little small crowds, sharing their stories of summertime fun. The girls had their own groups, while the boys congregated to theirs. One of the groups of boys consisted of all the Harlem Crips of the school. They all knew me as being affiliated with the Blood gang, but they still showed me respect. I had a few of them in my classes where I talked to some individually, but I still kept my distance.

That was the crazy thing about gang banging. Each generation knew each other's first and last names because we went to the local schools together, but there were generations of deep hatred and lost loved ones that kept us rivals. It seemed that they had also taken a liking to the "house dancing" that was hitting the scene being that they were demonstrating and sharing dance moves amongst each other. Some were pretty good, but I had a few tricks up my sleeve myself that I was waiting to share at the first school dance.

"What's up, Raymond?" Byron came up to me smiling and shaking my hand.

"What's going on?" I shook his hand back. Byron was one of the outspoken ones who kind of admired my character. He had told Red Flagg last year that I was the hardest Blood at the school. I guess because I'd never checked out and went to another school.

"Why do you shake hands like that?" he asked with a perplexed look on his face.

"Shake hands like what?" I replied. I already knew what he was referring to. I was just trying to keep from verbally disrespecting his hood because we were at peace at the moment, but it seemed that may be about to change. The Harlem Crips all shook hands with both participants having their thumbs up, which gave an image of a large capital H formed by both hands. These kids were born and raised in the Harlem's, so that's all they knew.

"Aye, Tony!" Byron called out to the crowd of Crips. "Come and trip how Raymond shakes hands."

"Aye, what's up, Raymond?" Tony asked as he came over and put his hand out to shake my hand.

"What's going on?" I replied as I shook Tony's hand with my thumb down while Tony had his up. Tony just looked at me with the same perplexed look that Byron had as if I was some type of alien that they had just seen for the first time. He walked back over to the crowd as Byron proceeded to give me the rundown about a "tagging" crew they had formed over the summer call ATC.

"ATC?" I asked.

"Yeah, it stands for 'Addicted to Crime'," he explained.

"Is that right?" I replied as Sheila came walking up to me to hand me a small folded piece of paper.

"Regina said to call her," Shelia said with a devilish smile.

"Oh, okay. I'll see about doing that," I said as I took the piece of paper out of her hand and she walked off again.

"Man! You got it like that?" Byron exclaimed.

"A little bit," I replied, looking at him out the corner of my eye. "How many people in y'all click?" I asked, taking the attention off me.

"It's a gang of us!" Byron snapped back into former thoughts. "Everybody that you see in that crowd over there plus more, and we're still growing!" The school bell rang for lunch to end, and everybody started to head to their next class.

"Alright then 'B.' Y'all be bareful out in them streets," I said as I walked off to find my next class also. Byron just smiled ear to ear at me before walking toward the crowd of Crips. I don't know if that conversation was his attempt to recruit me or what, but I think my final comment gave him his answer. Anybody who joins that click would be just like joining the Crips, which was not happening on my watch. "Addicted to Crime"? It might as well stand for Avenue Thirties Crip. I'm cool...

All of my classes were pretty easy for me. Most of the time, I was able to finish most, if not all, of my homework before I left the school to go home. The system that I created gave me more time to practice my dance moves and go and visit some of those girls. I ended up calling Regina and even started to build a friendship, but I just didn't have enough time for her. They were too many pretty girls with brand new breasts at the school to be stuck with only one! Plus, it seemed like they were all smiling at me. How could I resist? Especially when they were willing to do the things I was planning to do with them.

It was all working in my favor. Until one day, a few of them got together and came looking for me- about three or four girls with attitudes. I don't know how they found me because I was usually hanging with the Belizean crew near the lunch table with my partner D-Ski from Belizean Blood Posse (BZP). That day, I was in the maintenance office with one of my childhood buddies, Darrell, eating tuna sandwiches that he had brought from home. Darrell was always in the maintenance office at lunch because his uncle was a maintenance worker.

"Slow down, bro!" Darrell said. "That sandwich ain't running away from you!"

"Man!" I replied with a side jaw full of tuna sandwich. "You already know... Your moms makes the bomb tuna!"

"Ha! Yep, I always tell her to throw an extra one in there just in case you come through," Darrel said as he walked to the door to check out the scene on the schoolyard.

"Is Raymond in there?" I heard a soft voice outside ask.

"Yeah, hold up," Darrell said.

"Aye, Raymond. You got a crew of girls out here looking for you, and they don't look happy. "

"Oh, okay," I said, getting up from the table, leaving a quarter of my sandwich. "Constant drama," I said as I walked past Darrell. He just looked at me in a state of wondering how I was going to get out of that one. As I walked out of the maintenance office, there were four girls: Chelsie, Laura, Alecia, and Trisha, waiting outside with their arms folded.

"Aye, what's going on?" I broke the ice.

"What's going on?" Chelsie replied. "I'll tell you what's going on. All these girls are saying they are your girlfriend, and I'm the one that supposed to be your girl. So, who's it going to be? You have to make a choice today."

"All of y'all are crazy!" I said in disbelief and walked back inside to finish my sandwich.

"That's it?" Darrell replied.

"Yep, that's it," I replied.

After lunch, I went to my locker to grab my books for my fifth period class. I had to pick up the pace because I had lost a few minutes joking around with Darrell and thanking him again for the tuna sandwich. I never liked being late for class. I was afraid I'd miss something. Hence, the reason I sat in the front of all my classes, so I knew what was being discussed as well as being a part of the discussion. Plus, Moms wasn't having it if tardiness became a pattern on my report card. My fifth period class was on the third floor, and there were two flights of stairs in between each floor. As I left the second floor, climbing the first flight to the third…

"Raymond," Chelsie called out to me from behind.

"What's up?" I asked as I turned to her in between the two flights of stairs. "Make it quick. I gotta get to class."

"I just want to talk to you for a minute," she said as she approached me a little closer and placed her hand on my chest and started to kiss my neck.

"Okay, hurry up," is what my mouth said, but my body was ready to stay there all day.

"You know I like you a lot," she said in between kisses. "Those other girls are not going to love you the way I love you."

"Oh, yeah?" I was at full attention. "And what skills in loving me do you possess that will surpass the rest?"

"I could show you better than I could tell you," Chelsea said, as she kissed me softly on the lips repeatedly. I liked it. Before I had realized it, I was kissing her back, books in one hand and the other hand everywhere else. Chelsea was a slim girl, but she was healthy in all the right places, even as a ninth grader. She reminded me of Jessica Rabbit. I just couldn't resist. We kissed and groped each other there in between floors for about five more minutes until I snapped back to reality, and it dawned me… I was late for class!

"I gotta go," I said as I started to pull away from her and move towards the upper staircase.

"No, just stay with me," she said, pulling me back into her arms.

"I'll see you later," I pulled away again as we both noticed Mr. Crosby coming down the upper staircase, and Chelsea quickly made her way downstairs to the second floor. I made my way up to the third floor, passing Mr. Crosby without speaking because of the obvious. I was halfway expecting him to scold me, but he said nothing. I guess he knew that wasn't my regular routine, so he kept quiet. Mr. Crosby was cool… I made my way to class, passing one of the third-floor fire escapes. If you know Foshay Junior High, you know that the fire escapes are secluded places. I couldn't help but think to myself that I should've taken Chelsea there and done some stuff to her.

Next time… maybe next time.

Chapter 24
May I Have This Dance?

"Good morning, students!" rang out a voice over the intercom in homeroom. "This is Tina, your student body president! I wanted to take this time to inform you all that the student body and I are already working overtime to make this 1990-1991 school year the best year of your educational career! We hope to…" she went on and on. I was thinking about the G-Ride I had parked around the corner. I wasn't sure if I had parked on the side of the street that was scheduled for street sweeping or not. If so, walking home would be part of the agenda if the parking enforcement noticed that it was a stolen vehicle while writing a parking ticket. "… I am happy to announce that we will be having our first lunch dance today for $.50, so come with your dancing shoes on to the basketball gym!" Tina concluded.

"What? Did she just say it's a dance at lunch?" I asked out loud to whomever would answer.

"Yep!" Heathcliff answered. "And, I got my $.50 on deck!" He was just as excited as I was.

"Oh, it's on now!" I said. I was pumped up! I couldn't wait! There were three more classes plus nutrition break to get through before lunch time would come. The anticipation was crucial! Although I knew I was ready, I still had some butterflies due to the fact that I had never "housed" in front of anybody yet. I had only practiced in my room, trying to perfect the skill and come up with unique moves and even elaborations on other moves I had seen on music videos. The dance would be the next level. Second period crept by like a slow freight train that wasn't sure if it was going in the right direction. Then, nutrition came, so I figured I'd put some food in my stomach, so I would be energized when the time came. What better way to energize than with a good old tuna sandwich from Darrell. So, I made my way to the maintenance office.

"What's up, bro?" I said as I went inside.

"What's hatnin', homeboy?" Darrell responded without even looking up from the Lowrider magazine he held his hand. "You going to the dance at lunch, huh?" he continued.

"Yeah, how about you?" I asked as I sat across from him at a table.

"Naw, I'm straight," Darrell said. "I'ma do my dance when they ring the bell at three o'clock to go home."

"Ha!" I laughed. "So, what's up with the tuna?"

"Oh, you trying to tackle it early, huh?" Darrell said, finally looking up from his magazine.

"You already know," I said, heading towards the refrigerator.

"You know where they at. You must have a 'hot date' at lunch?" Darrell smiled.

"Naw, I just want to have some energy when I hit that dance."

"What are you talking about, bro?" Darrell asked. "It's a dance, not a marathon!"

"For me, my brotha," I said, as I waved the sandwich in the air. "It's the Olympic games!"

Third period went by pretty quickly. It was my art class, and I liked art class. Fourth period was the only one that I didn't want to rush by. It was my history class with Mr. Gaither, one of the best teachers at the school. Mr. Gaither was the black version of Mr. Crosby, in that I never saw him following along with the textbook when he taught class. He knew the whole book and taught each history lesson by memory. Not only that, but he had a great sense of humor that kept you attentive, like telling the kids in the back of the class who were talking and not paying attention to be quiet because they weren't smart enough to be talking. What really made Mr. Gaither the best was his generosity, which certainly motivated the students to learn. He'd give five dollars for every correct answers to his questions. He even bought one girl a bike for passing a test. As Mr. Gaither began to conclude his lecture on the Great Depression, I began to get my books in order, so I could bounce out of there as soon as the bell rang.

"I know you guys are trying to run to that dance, but don't forget to read Chapter 7 tonight and answer the questions at the end," Mr. Gaither said as the bell began to ring and everyone scrambled to get out of the door. "And don't be stepping on these young ladies' feet in there! Leave some room for the Holy Ghost!"

I didn't know exactly what he meant by that, but I was out the door in a flash and headed to my locker to drop my books off, then out to the dance. Finally! Lunch couldn't get there fast enough! Then, it was time to play cool on the way to the gym. You never wanted to be the first in line like they were giving away free cheese inside. So, I slowed down my stride and let the line build up a little. I made my way to the line, and I could hear Ice Cube playing inside, "Jackin' for Beats." Inside, I was a rambling volcano about to erupt, but I played it cool as a fan. By the time I got to the front of the line to pay my $.50, I strolled in nonchalantly while the DJ played the "Humpty Dance" by Digital Underground. Individual crowds were gathering around different dancers, showing off their 'house' moves. A lot of the same moves I had watched on TV were going on. I wasn't hyped up enough yet to jump into a circle, so I continued to observe.

All of a sudden the DJ started to play the intro to "Heed the Word of the Brother" by X-Clan, and I knew it was time! I noticed Tony in a nearby circle quickly grabbing Heathcliff and starting to swing him around like a helicopter to open up the area. Tony put Heathcliff down and began some fancy footwork from side to side real smooth then ended his show by jumping over his own leg!

My turn! My energy was up then! I quickly slid forward into the middle of the circle with the illusion of running backwards. Immediately, I switched to slayer mode, slicing and dicing the air with upstairs and downstairs moves, as if all competition was being massacred! I took it downstairs with a few full body twist while parallel with the gym floor. My show was ended with a few spiral spins as I came back up to my feet, spinning out of the circle as Heathcliff took over. What a rush! My adrenaline level was sky high! After Heathcliff finished, I quickly took over the circle again! That time with my own fancy footwork that I came to call "liquid legs."

After the dance, I was ecstatic! The high that I received from the energy level was crazy! It was hard to believe that dancing could feel so good! From that moment on, I knew that 'butterflies' in my stomach was just like a fuse to a bomb. Only the bomb was a good thing, an adrenaline rush to be used for fuel. A weapon for life's 'fight or flight' moments. Whatever the case was, dancing had me hooked!

I started hitting all of the dances and event parties on the weekends. My hair has started to grow longer after I put the S-Curl chemical in it, so I decided to start twisting it into dreadlocks. My whole style had changed because of the housing lifestyle. I was a houser! Lil Killa saw me walking through the alley one day with my dreds and baggy jeans. I guess I looked too weird for him.

"I better never catch you 'Brim Walking' again," he said. I just looked at him and kept it pushing. I guess he had forgotten I was around there before he was. I knew he had love for me, but he was upset because I wasn't hanging out as much as I used to as I was engulfed in "housing." Expressing that was a different story. He adjusted the handle on the .38 revolver that was hanging out of his khaki pants pocket and went back inside the spot.

The next day at school, two seventh graders came up to me at nutrition and struck up a conversation about dancing. One of them suggested I start my own dance crew, and they wanted to be a part of it. It sounded like a good idea, so I agreed. We came up with the name "Based on Housing" or B.O.H. We began practicing our moves after school at my apartment. I'd bring my radio outside, and we'd share moves.

It really started to get real after Malik from around the corner on 37th Drive said he wanted to join the crew. Malik was in high school at Dorsey High with Joseph Jr. Because he was in the eleventh grade, he was allowed to go to more parties than I was.

"Aye, we need something that represents the crew," I said.

"Yeah, I know," Malik said. "There's a nightclub about to open up on Martin Luther King, Jr. Boulevard and Saint Andrews Place. It's going to be for teens only!"

"What?" I shouted. "Oh, it's on now!"

"Everybody is talking about it at Dorsey," replied Malik. He was surprised I had not heard anything about the new club.

"What's the name of it?" I asked.

"Club Nouveau," he said.

"Nice!" I said. "It's definitely a new thing!"

"We gotta be there!" Malik demanded. "All the best housers and crews will be there!"

"Exactly!" I replied. "That's just why we need something to represent us! How much time do we have?"

"Two weeks," Malik said.

That was big! The first eighteen and under nightclub of our time! Everybody was going to be there! We decided to go with gray sweatshirt hoodies with B.O.H. in bubble letters airbrushed on the back to represent our crew. I started to practice like never before! Stretching and proper breathing was a must. I wasn't playing! I had been to high school dances at both Manual Arts and Dorsey and found there was a higher level of skill there than I saw at the middle school dances. If the best on the west were going to be there, I wasn't about to come with no old garbage routines. It was time to show and prove.

While we were getting our things together on the dance scene, the world was still spinning. I'll never forget, it was a Wednesday night, November 7, 1990. I was out in front of my apartments, having some drinks with the homeboys, when a smoker rolled up on a bike frantically hollering out, "Aye, they just shot up Tim Stacks at Serbonne's!"

"Who shot Tim Stacks?" Multiple voices resounded in unison.

"I don't know! They was Crips though…" he responded.

Everybody mounted up! Jumping into whatever vehicle that was available and had room, we smashed out. As we approached the plaza of the grocery store, sure enough, the police had the entire parking lot taped off. We rolled past in silence… Everybody's eyes were fixed on Tim Stacks' white 1965 Chevy Impala with the doors opened, as police officers searched through it. As we circled around, we caught a glimpse of the white sheet that covered the body on the opposite side of the car. I thought to myself, *I will never hear his laugh again.* You knew when you heard "The Ghetto" by Too $hort from a distance that it was Stacks beating up the block in the '65 Chevy. He'd jump out of the car and shake all the homies' hands. That would never happen again… Smile now and cry later. There were no questions asked. Immediately, the streets went to war. Everybody knew the routine. No hanging out during wartime.

That Friday was the grand opening of Club Nouveau, and I was caught between two passions, two lifestyles, and two emotions. I wasn't really in the mood for housing, but I didn't want to let Malik down. That night was a big deal with the grand opening of the club; plus, we had already bought our sweatshirt hoodies with B.O.H. on the back. Of course, we could've waited until the next Friday, but it wouldn't be the same. So, I reluctantly showed up to Malik's house around the corner on 37th Drive and rang the doorbell.

"What's up, man? You ready?" Malik asked as he opened the door and shook my hand with an over the shoulder handshake.

"Yeah," I answered emotionlessly.

"I've been sharpening my skills," Malik said as he danced his way through the living room and into the dining room.

"They are not going to know what hit 'em! I'm about to chop 'em down!" He was full of energy like a kid who had snuck into the cookies and ate the whole pack.

I couldn't really blame Malik for not being as downcast as I was. He didn't really know Tim Stacks like I did. The night Stacks was killed, I had told Malik over the phone. He was sad and sorry to hear it, but the next day, he was alright. It be like that sometimes. I had a shoebox with a collection of obituaries; it was getting larger and larger. Although a lot of their true names weren't known until the day of the funeral, every now and then there was a bond formed in the streets when you had a real homeboy. You just couldn't continue your day with 'business as usual' when their life was snuffed out prematurely. At least, I couldn't.

"That hoodie looking pretty cool, dogg!" Malik said still wearing just a T-shirt with his baggy jeans.

"Yeah, where yours at?" I asked.

"Hold up! Hold up!" Malik ran into his room and quickly returned with the same identical grey hoodie with B.O.H. airbrushed on the back in colorful bubble letters. "Oh, it's on now! Based on Housing about to show and prove!" Malik strutted around the living room and kicked one of his mama's giant tomcats out of the way. I managed to muster up a grin. I only grinned because I hated those cats. They were sneaky, jumping around the house like two Cheshire cats. The homie Hotbox could not even go inside the house whenever he went over because he was allergic to the dander.

"Let me get a piece of that cake before we go?' I asked as I moved toward the lemon cake on the dining room table.

"Go ahead. Be my guest!" Malik snatched the lid off the cake holder. "You want some coffee with that? How about a V8? I need to get you hyped up before you fall asleep on the couch over there?"

"You got jokes, huh?" I responded to his sarcasm.

We left his house and went around the corner to my place because my mother said she would drop us off at the club.

"Whoa!" my mother shouted as we walked through the door with our hoodies on. "Who are you two, the dynamic duo?"

"Everybody got jokes tonight, huh?" I said.

"Let me drop y'all off because y'all look like you're ready to cut a rug in two," she said grabbing her purse.

"Yeah, it's almost nine," I said. "It started at 8PM, so it should be jumping by now."

Everything was copasetic. Joseph Jr. even decided to come along to check out the scene. We pulled up to a nice-sized crowd outside of the club. We were officially on the scene, but I still didn't feel like dancing.

"Y'all call me when it's over," my mother said.

"Alright," I said as we got out of the car.

"Thanks, Ms. Watkins," Malik said as he slammed the car door.

"Aye, when we go inside, don't jump in the circle until I'm ready," I told Malik.

"And when is that supposed to happen?" he asked.

"Oh, you'll know," I said. "Don't even trip."

"These girls are looking good!" Joseph Jr. said as we paid our entrance fees. "I might have to meet back up with y'all later. Watch out for 'pick pockets' on the dance floor."

"Ha!" I chuckled. "I am the 'pick pocket' on the dance floor."

The floor was packed! If you had an ariel view, it would look like something similar to a circus with multiple rings, but with dancers inside instead of circus acts. Malik and I made our way to the largest circle. Usually, the largest circle at a party was where you could find the best dancers. The bass of the speakers vibrated the room as the DJ spun "Can I Kick It?" by A Tribe Called Quest. Dreds and braids were swinging as the 'housers' grooved in the circle. Malik was amped up and vibing to the beat. I noticed he kept looking at me checking for signs of life. I'm not going to lie, it was rocking! Especially when Q-Tip asked on the record, "Can I Kick It?" and the whole club answered back, "Yes, You Can!" Yeah, that was nice, but I still wasn't there yet.

All of a sudden, the DJ stopped the record from spinning and started scratching the beat, IZZUB... IZZUB... IZZUB, IZZUB, IZZUB, IZZUB BOOM! The 45 King came on with "The 900 Number!" The whole club went crazy! It was no holding back then! I was ready to rock! Malik noticed also and started to smile, but neither one of us could get in the circle because of the hype.

"Swing me around and open up the circle!" I hollered out to Malik. He quickly grabbed me under the arms and started swinging me around. At first with my knees forward, then with my legs fully extended, kicking whoever didn't get the picture. When the circle was once again a circle, he put me down, and I spun away from him and twisted down then went into a 190° spin on one arm with my feet facing the ceiling. I then dropped down to my forearm and into a back spin, hopping up to my feet with side to side sweeping footwork. I gave a few more 'upstairs' moves before twisting out of the circle since I started with a spin.

Then, it was Malik's turn! He quickly slid into the circle before anyone else could take it over. He began to flow with elbows and slashing motions like he was cutting the crowd. It was tight! That's when I understood what he was saying at his house about "chopping 'em down." Everybody knew we were a team because we had on the same hoodie with the B.O.H. on the back. It stood out well on the back of Malik. He continued killing the competition with his 'upstairs' massacre before ending with some shovel moves that insinuated digging their graves.

Next, the circle was up for grabs, so one kid jumped in with dreds in his hair, wearing African attire with sandals. He had a unique style with his moves. They seemed to be liquefied as he contorted and twisted into different positions. The ability to apply his skill to dance was kind of dope. Many others also came with moves I had not seen before, which was pretty cool. The night went on as we continued to trade moves until midnight when the DJ shut the party down.

That Monday when I went back to school, the talk of the campus was Club Nouveau! Even those that didn't show up or weren't able to were talking about it, mostly asking questions. It looked as though Club Nouveau would be the Friday night spot. Who knew? Maybe it would last and maybe it wouldn't. But for then, we would create some awesome memories. Dancing was not only fun, but it was my stress reliever, especially when all else seemed to fail and there were no answers. I'd turn on the music and go into my zone. Kind of like when you read a book and you feel like you're in the time and place of the story. When I turned on the music, I entered the song and the beat took my moves wherever they wanted to go. I loved it!

Chapter 25
A Gentleman and a Scholar

Sitting in my algebra class, I decided to write a letter back to G-Nutt in the penitentiary because I was done with my assignment early. G-Nutt's name was ringing in the streets of how he had hands in the pen. I wasn't surprised because he was beating dudes up with ease on the streets. The pen was just a change of location. I was glad he was taking care of himself nonetheless.

"Raymond, you have a summons to the counselor's office," Mrs. Davis interrupted my letter and handed me a hall pass.

"Do you know what it's for?" I asked.

"They didn't say, but take your books with you just in case the bell rings before you get back," she said.

"Oh, okay," I looked at her sideways, trying to think of what I had done wrong lately.

"I wouldn't worry if I were you," Mrs. Davis said, reading my mind. "If you were in trouble, the summons would have probably been to the dean of the principal's office."

"Alright," I responded, feeling a bit of relief but still skeptical.

On the way to the counselor's office, I put my books in my locker along with a bag of weed that I had in my pocket for later. I didn't know what to expect. Better safe than sorry.

"Hello, Mr. Watkins," Mrs. Ringles greeted me as I walked into her office. Her use of my last name kind of made me paranoid. Kind a like when your parents call out your full name when you've done something wrong.

"Hey, Mrs. Ringles," I responded. "How are you doing? Is everything alright?"

"I'm doing well," she said. "Thanks for asking. Go ahead and have a seat."

I sat down, waiting for the bomb to drop. Mrs. Ringles was a smiling lady. She was always smiling, but that day I thought her smile was still at her house on the kitchen counter next to the coffee pot. She looked at me with evaluating eyes, as if she wasn't sure if she could trust me. *I think I better run up out of here while I have the chance! Wait a minute. I'm innocent until proven guilty. I didn't do nothing, and I'm sticking to my story...*

"Okay, Raymond," Mrs. Ringles started in. "I'm going to cut to the chase. There is a Japanese bank called Yasuda Trust Banking Company, and they are giving away $5000 scholarships to one student from each Los Angeles Unified School District junior high school. They have stipulated that ten students could be chosen from each school to compete for the scholarship at that particular school. I have chosen you, Raymond, to compete amongst the ten students here at Foshay Junior High. Do you think you're up for this challenge?"

"Sure," I said as I relaxed and loosened my 'defense mode' grip on the arm of the chair. "So, what exactly is the competition?" I continued. "Are we running fifty yard dashes or arm wrestling or something?"

"No, silly." She finally smiled. "You must write a 500-word essay on the importance of going to college and how this scholarship would benefit you."

"Oh, okay. That shouldn't be too hard," I said.

"Raymond," she snatched her smile off again. "This is very important. I am recommending you, so I don't want you to let me down."

"I understand," I said. "How much time do I have to write the essay?"

"You have until the end of this week, Friday. That's four days from now," Mrs. Ringles pointed to her calendar on the wall.

"Alright," I said as I stood up to leave the office. "Oh, Mrs. Ringles?" I stopped at the door.

"Yes?" She looked me in the eyes.

"Thanks for recommending me," I said.

"You're welcome, Raymond." Mrs. Ringles smiled again as I left the office.

What a great opportunity! Of course, anything beats being in trouble, but Mrs. Ringles was putting on the pressure earlier. I didn't want to disappoint her, so I went home and jumped right on it that night. I figured 500 words was only about a page and a half or two pages.

As I began to write on the topic that was given, "The importance of going to college and how the scholarship would benefit me," I began to go into detail of how much college would play a part in my maturing into adulthood. Also how a scholarship, although it wasn't a full one, would be a great motivator to even go to college. The words began to flow onto the paper and before I knew it, I was done. I had two and a half sheets of paper. That should suffice for the 500 word count.

I walked into Mrs. Ringles' office the next day with my essay nicely rewritten and placed into a folder. "Good morning, Mrs. Ringles. Here you go," I said as I handed her the folder.

"Good morning, Raymond. What's this?" she asked as if we didn't even have the scholarship conversation yesterday.

"That's my essay," I said, feeling agitated. "Do you remember asking me to write it yesterday?"

"Yes, I remember, Raymond, but I also said you have until Friday to complete it," she said. "You want to make sure you give it your best."

"Yes, I know," I responded. "I realized how important it was and how much faith you put into me, so I wanted to get it out of the way. Believe me, I gave it my best. Right away."

"Oookayyy," she sang. "I still need to receive the other nine essays from the other students by Friday, and then, we'll make a decision next week."

"Alright, you have a nice day, Mrs. Ringles," I said, walking out of her office.

"You do the same, Raymond," she said. As I walked out, I noticed she opened my folder and started to read my essay.

When lunch came, I headed out to the yard to go and hang with the homie D-Ski and the Belizean Blood Posse. Before I could reach the kicking it spot, I got sidetracked by the homegirl Kiera. Kiera used to live upstairs from us on 94th Street, but she and her sister Maisha just recently moved to 37th Place.

"What's up, Ray?" Kiera stepped right in front of me, stopping me in my tracks.

"What's going on?" I said, wrapping my arms around her. "If you wanted to hug, all you had to do was ask."

"No, crazy!" she said, pushing away from me. "But, my friend likes you."

"Who?" I was interested.

"Her name is Sharol," Kiera explained. "She just checked into school a week ago. She and her family just moved to L.A. from Mississippi, but since she's been here at Foshay, she's been watching you."

"Is that right?" I looked around and said, looking for surveillance cameras. "Where is she? Is she cute?"

"See for yourself, silly," Kiera giggled as she pointed toward the coffee cake line. "She standing right there with the flowered blouse and blue jeans on."

"Whoa!" My eyes got as big as golf balls, and my mouth stayed in the same position of the 'whoa' I had just spoken for about thirty seconds. The girl Sharol started to look over at Kiera and me.

"She wants to know if you have a girlfriend," Kierra said. I continued to look at Sharol as we locked eyes. She was super thick and bowlegged like she had just rode a horse all the way from Mississippi. She was cute and sexy, and I wanted to get to know her right away!

"Thanks a lot, but I think I'll tell her myself," I smiled at Kiera and started to make my way over to Sharol. Sharol noticed I was headed towards her, and she started to adjust herself: fixing her hair and straightening her clothes. She had on one of those blouses with the elastic around the top that was pulled down, so her shoulders were exposed. Very sexy. To top it off, she was wearing lip gloss on her lips. My weakness! I had to tell myself not to grab her although it was hard not to. If all goes well, she'll give me unlimited access later.

"How are you, Sharol? I'm Raymond," I said as I walked up and shook her hand.

"I know exactly who you are. I'm fine. Thank you," she said with a smile and her southern drawl.

"I like that accent," I said. "Kiera told me you are from Mississippi. Which part?"

"Yes, I'm from Hattiesburg," Sharol said. "I've only been in California for a week now."

"I don't know how I missed seeing you around school for a whole week! You are beautiful!" I looked her up and down.

"Thank you," she smiled.

"So how do the women in Hattiesburg, Mississippi treat the men in their lives?" I asked.

"With southern hospitality," she said with a coy smile. "That's until you do us wrong."

"Well, let me have your number because I want the hospitality part, if you don't mind," I said, gently grabbing her hand. I couldn't help it. I had to touch her.

"Wait a minute, slick," she said, pulling her hand out of mine. "Where is your girlfriend? I see the way these girls look at you, and I know you have at least one. Where she at?" Sharol asked, putting her hands on her voluptuous hips and looking me straight in the eye.

"Well, what happened was, we recently broke up," I responded.

"Is that the truth?" She looked at me sideways, trying to catch any signs of lying.

"That's the truth, and I'm sticking to my story," I said pulling an ink pen out of my back pocket. Sharol took the pen out of my hand and started to write her number on the inside of my hand.

"Alright, I don't want to be caught up in no mess," she said, looking up from the writing. "I'm a generous girl, but one thing I don't want is to share my boyfriend."

"Likewise," I responded. "Be real with me, and I'll be real with you." I was being honest. I was 100% single. I didn't have a girlfriend. That was the truth, but the part that I failed to mention was that about four or five of them almost jumped me when it all hit the fan. That time, I would be more careful. Plus, Sharol seemed like a good girl. Maybe, she was worth the monogamy thing. I would try it for a while and see how it went. After all, she was like a trophy that was placed in my hand.

Club Nouveau was a little different that week being that I invited Sharol and Kiera to go and check out the scene. I had to balance my time between Sharol and the dance circle, but Sharol was cool. She understood my addiction to the beat. I noticed Joseph Jr. getting more interested in Kiera, and she didn't seem to mind. As usual, Malik was rocking the house with the dope moves. I took a break from the dance floor and went to find a restroom.

As I closed the door behind me and the noise of the music faded, I began to hear another type of noise. Only that noise was in my head. The voices I used to hear that I thought were gone, all of a sudden were back tenfold. It was as if ten or twenty people were all trying to talk at once. I kept telling them to shut up, but to no avail. Instead, they got louder. So, I got louder. I started to shout, "SHUT UP! SHUT UP!"

I went into a stall and locked the door behind me. I knew I needed to pray, but I didn't know how to pray like the preacher did at church when I was little, using scriptures that were fitting for the occasion. So, I just hollered out, "GOD, HELP ME! I NEED YOUR HELP!" Nothing happened... The voices persisted. I decided to just close my eyes and try to make sense of what was being said in the arguments in my head. It was as if a room full of angry men were having multiple conversations in a courtroom and the judge could not call order.

I began to make out some of the phrases that were being said like, "YOU ARE NOT WORTH IT!" "KILL YOURSELF!" and "DIE!" I knew if I could find the right scripture, it would help. But, I couldn't remember any. Something had to give. I was not leaving that restroom stall until they were quiet, or else someone would end up putting me into what the old folks called "the crazy house."

I just stayed in there quietly with my eyes closed, listening to the argument of condemnation that was going on in my head. After some time passed, (I don't know how long. It seemed like forever.) something came to my remembrance. It was a song we used to sing as kids in Sunday school. It wasn't a scripture, but it was the next best thing. I figured what did I have to lose. I couldn't remember the verses of the song, only the chorus came to mind. So, I began to sing it slowly and very low, almost in a whisper, "Yes, Jesus loves me. Yes, Jesus loves me. Yes, Jesus loves me. For the Bible tells me so." To my surprise, the volume of the voices went down to a mumble! So, I put a little confidence in my singing and some bass in my voice.

"YES, JESUS LOVES ME. YES, JESUS LOVES ME. YES, JESUS LOVES ME. FOR THE BIBLE TELLS ME SO."

The voices stopped... I inhaled deeply, then exhaled, as I lifted up my hands and gave God the glory while continually repeating, "Thank you, Jesus!" *How come nobody ever told me about this part of life?* I was thankful and angry at the same time! I came out of the stall to wash my hands and face before returning to the dance floor.

That same night, I ended up going out to Baldwin Park after the club with Red Flagg and Cowboy. They were about to head out there with the big homie Smokey in the '66 Chevy Impala.

"What's up, Spike? Let's roll!" Cowboy said as I got out of my mother's car. After what I just went through at the club, I needed to get away and clear my head.

"Y'all about to roll out now?" I asked.

"Yeah, what it do? You rolling?" Smokey asked.

"Alright, hold up," I said. "Let me grab some clothes out the house real quick."

They had been trying to get me to go out there and spend the weekend ever since their granny recently moved the whole family out there. It was a refreshing change of pace. The environment was quiet, and I didn't feel like I was practically being hunted like I did in L.A. I needed the break. After that, I knew where I could go to get a short vacation from the hood although it was only twenty minutes away. Leaving the hood was one thing, the only problem was that the hood was in us.

On Saturday morning, Flagg and I went and ate breakfast at the grocery store that was around the corner. Nope, they weren't giving away free meals, and we didn't have any money to buy any meals either. We simply ate what we wanted while simulating a shopping spree up and down the aisles. The munchies were starting to kick in because we smoked one of the two blunts Flagg had rolled up that morning. I was grubbing on Honey Buns, Doritos, and beef jerky while Flagg was working on some donuts with O.J. The ZOOM ZOOMS and WHAM WHAMS were going up! We almost got away with it until Flagg decided to make a turkey sandwich while I slowly pushed the basket. Suddenly, the manager came up on us.

"What's going on with you two?" he asked "You plan on paying for all that food you opened?"

Immediately, we tried to turn and make a break for the door, but there was a giant of a security guard standing right behind us.

"Oh, no!" The manager smiled as we turned back towards him. "No place to run, and no place to hide! Only place you two are running to is jail!" After we accepted the fact that we were caught, we willfully followed the manager into the office in the back of the store. Of course, we were followed by the giant security guard.

"So, what is you guys' excuse for stealing today?" The manager asked as he took a seat behind his desk. "Give me a good reason not to send you to Juvie."

"We are actually here to help, so that you don't have to throw away the old stuff," I said.

"Exactly," Flagg chimed in.

"Ha!" the manager laughed. "You two are funny! I used to be you guys' age, so I'm going to give you a break this time. Give me your phone number, so your parents can come and pick you up."

Flagg gave him the number to call Granny, and the manager put her on speakerphone. After he gave her the news, Granny said, "I'm not coming around there to that store. Just send them home, and I'll take care of them."

"No problem, ma'am," the manager said before hanging up the phone. "You heard what she said, right?" he asked us. "She said she's going to take care of you when you get home. Now, this time I'm giving you guys a break, but if I catch you in here again pulling what you pulled today, you are definitely going to jail."

"Alright," we both said. "Good looking out."

"No problem," he said. "You guys be careful out there."

Flagg and I walked out of the grocery store with our heads held high.

"That was close," Flagg said as we crossed the parking lot.

"On Bloods," I agreed. "Let's go smoke that blunt and let Granny cool down."

"You already know," Flagg replied. "Let's go chill in the back with the Esés."

"Cool," I said.

We made our way to the back of the apartment complex where the Esés were hanging out and walked up on what looked like a crime scene. I suspected the worse, but we hadn't heard any gunshots, and there was no blood. Nevertheless, two Hispanic gangbangers were laid out on the ground on their backs. Another one was passed out sitting on his butt with his legs out slumped over against the building. Then, there were two that were conscious; one that was midway up a flight of stairs holding an aerosol can with a tube connected to it, and the other stood by the guys that were knocked out on the ground.

"What's up, Redd Flagg?" said the one standing.

"What's going on, Bandit?" Flagg replied. "You socking out the homies now?"

"Naw, homes," Bandit gave a half smile. "They're back here taking flight off that computer cleaner." He pointed to the can in the other guy's hand. "I'm just watching their backs."

"Is that right?" Flagg responded. "Aye, this is my homeboy Spike."

"Aye, what's up, Spike?" Bandit shook my hand with a five pound, Esé style. "You want some of that stuff, man?"

"Naw, dogg," I responded. "You know the brothers don't get down like that. We leave the exotic drugs up to y'all."

"Exactly!" Flagg laughed. "We're about to take flight on the blunt though. You can hit it if you want to."

"Yeah, I'll hit it," Bandit said. "I don't mess around with that other stuff either, but the homies need someone to watch their backs while they're buzzing."

While Flagg sparked up the blunt, the other guy sitting on the stairs started to inhale from the tube that was connected to the aerosol can he held in his hand.

"All the time," I said while watching the guy on the stairs. He started to freeze up as his eyes got as big as golf balls, and he exhaled slowly while making a straining sound. All of a sudden, his eyes closed shut, and he rolled forward down the stairs and was passed out like the other three.

"You see what they've signed up for?" Bandit asked.

"Yeah, I'm real cool on that," I said as I took the blunt from Flagg and pulled on it. "That's not the career move I want to make."

"Wise man," Bandit responded as he took the blunt from my hand. "By the time we finish this blunt, they will pass out two or three more times each."

"That's crazy," I said.

Sure enough, they began to wake up in chronological order, repeating the process with the aerosol can after prying it from the former victim's hands. I thought to myself that this couldn't be fun, but for them it was a trip to another dimension. It was bad enough I drank alcohol and smoked weed, which is what they called the gateway drugs. Supposedly, once introduced to a mind-altering substance, it's really easy to graduate to something stronger depending on a person's tolerance build up. At least that's what they taught us in the sixth grade

D.A.R.E. Program. For me, that was one graduation I did not plan to attend.

Back in school, I sat in homeroom, twiddling my thumbs as the attendance for the day was taken. The voice of Mrs. Ringles rang out over the intercom, as she gave her portion of the daily announcements. She talked about the importance of being on time to class and not having any absent days. She mentioned an earthquake drill that was supposed to take place on Friday and how everyone could bring a beach towel or something to sit on because we were going to be outside for a while. Then, she said, "Also today, I have the results of the essay contest for the Yasuda Trust Banking Co. Scholarship." Suddenly, I was more attentive than ever as she continued. "The winner of the $5,000 scholarship is our own ninth grader RAYMOND WATKINS! Congratulations, Raymond! Come to my office at nutrition time for more details."

"Whoa! I won!" I said in shock.

"Congratulations, Raymond!" the whole class echoed and began to clap.

"Thanks a lot! I appreciate it!" I said.

I was excited! When Mrs. Ringles asked me to write that essay, I just wanted to please her. I really didn't expect to win. I guess she saw something in me that I didn't see. Living in the ghetto didn't show me too many positive promises of a bright future, but then, my hope started to rise! It was a definite chance that I could go to college! Somehow, my essay proved I had potential. It was then time to, as my mother would say, "Get on the ball!"

At nutrition time, I made my way to Mrs. Ringles' office, smiling as I walked in.

"Good morning, scholar!" Mrs. Ringles smiled and even came from behind her desk to give me a hug.

"Good morning, Mrs. Ringles." I hugged her back. "So, how did I manage to win? I'm still waiting for the catch."

"There is no catch, Raymond." She looked me in my eyes. "You are the winner of the $5000 scholarship! The judges really liked your essay and your writing skills. They will be giving you $500 each semester you are enrolled in college."

"Thanks, Mrs. Ringles," I said. "I appreciate all you have done for me."

"Don't thank me." Mrs. Ringles sat back in her chair behind her desk. "You earned it. Not only was your essay a number one pick by the judges, but your attendance, workmanship, and academics speak for themselves. You're on your way to college, young man. You must stay in the books and keep up the good work. Great things are in store for your future."

I left Mrs. Ringles' office feeling like I could conquer the world! No one had ever encouraged me the way she did. It was like a new light switched on in my head. A new way of thinking. Thoughts of success and not failure, building a future of accomplishment and not destruction. Although I had to constantly shut out those other voices in my head, they couldn't stop me from shining!

After school, I exited the building and headed up 37th Place. I noticed up ahead among all the students was Sharol walking with Kiera. She was a brick house at the age of fourteen! You couldn't miss her walking down even a crowded street. She was even putting grown women to shame in those jeans she was wearing. I hurried up and caught up to them.

"I thought you lived back towards Western?" I asked putting my arm around her neck.

"I do," Sharol smiled. "I'm about to hang out with Kiera for a little while."

"Congratulations on winning the scholarship," Kiera jumped in.

"Oh, yeah! Congratulations!" Sharol echoed.

"Thanks," I said.

"What college are you going to?" Sharol asked.

"I don't know yet. It's still fresh," I responded as we all turned into Kiera's yard and made our way inside. Kiera's older sister, Maisha, wasn't home. Immediately, I began to play out in my head, trying to devise a plan to get Sharol alone, away from Kiera. To my surprise, Sharol walked into the restroom as we talked but didn't close the door. She stood in the mirror fixing her hair while talking to me. I thought to myself, *I can't pass up this opportunity*. It was like finding money lying on the ground. So, I followed her inside the restroom.

Kiera had gone to the kitchen and was no longer a part of our conversation, so I closed the restroom door behind me. The situation made it inevitable that things were going to get hot and heavy, and they did. Sharol lost her virginity that day... on the cold floor of Kiera's bathroom. I don't know if Sharol told her mother where she would be after school that day, but I highly doubt that she knew her daughter was with a fourteen-and-a-half-year-old boy like me: a parent's worst nightmare.

Sharol was cool though. I didn't dog her out like I did the others. I liked being around her and the conversations we had. So, I made her my "main girl." She came before all the extras. I even introduced her to my mother. Well, I kind of had to because we were caught in the house after school one day doing what we weren't supposed to. My mother told Sharol, "I don't mind you coming over to see Ray, but it has to be while I'm home, and you have to sit in the living room." So, we tried our best not to get caught again.

Everything was falling right into place according to my desires. My confidence was at an all-time high! Nothing was impossible! My grades were up, I was popular at school, I had my own dance crew, and a southern girlfriend, who was thicker than my mother's cornbread! What more could I ask for? Nothing that I could think of…

Until one day when I got a call from Lizzie who used to live across the street from me, but she had moved across the street from Foshay Junior High. Lizzie did not attend Foshay; she went to Audubon Junior High. She had called to invite me to a house party she was having on a Saturday. I was all in, especially because Audubon was known to have a few more pretty girls than Foshay, and I knew a few would be there. Nevertheless, my main interest was on the dance scene. Audubon was also known to have a good group of dancers there, and I loved to compare moves. I quickly accepted the invitation. It was a no-brainer. I didn't even inform B.O.H. I just went on my own.

As I stepped into the party, which looked like it had just begun, Lizzie greeted me with a hug and introduced me to the six or seven people who had shown up before me. I heard her say their names as I shook each of their hands, but for some reason, I quickly forgot every one of them. I hate it when that happens. Because I looked like I was fresh off A Tribe Called Quest video with baggy jeans, water moccasin shoes, a colorful rayon shirt with dreadlocks in my hair, I guess they figured I would come in and immediately start dancing. Nope. I sat down on the couch and watched the scene while twisting my dreds every now and then.

The party goers continued to congregate in the middle of the living room. Sporadically, one or two of them would bust a dance move, but nothing too fancy. The crowd began to increase as more and more teenagers showed up at the door. They even started a dance circle as Vanilla Ice rang out through the speakers with "Ice Ice Baby," but I still wasn't feeling it. I continued to twist my dreds and watch…

One of the girls Lizzie had introduced me to came and sat on the couch with me. I really didn't pay her any mind; I just continued to watch the crowd. A few more people came through the door, making the crowd a little thicker.

"How come you're not dancing?" the girl next to me asked.

"I'm not hyped up yet," I answered with a smile. Just as I spoke those words, the 45 King "The 900 Number" blasted through the speakers! I immediately jumped up and headed to the circle, and the girl on the couch followed. One kid was already grooving in the middle of the circle with upstairs moves. He had a cool style, breaking halfway motions and cutting the air. I was definitely hyped then! I couldn't wait to enter the circle!

As soon as the kid started to look tired as if he was running out of moves, I bolted in before anybody else could. I expanded the circle with crossover footwork all around before rocking with the bows from side to side, then breaking it down giving two fake launches. On the second launch coming back in with a corkscrew twist, falling down into an Indian style seated position then kicking out side to side with sweeping kicks while still close to the floor. I paused on my right knee with my left leg kicked out to the left and horizontal to the floor. Then, I pulled into a ball and quickly spun out and up to my feet into a steady up rock with my short dreds bouncing as I grooved out of the circle.

The 45 King kept on banging as the girl who sat next to me on the couch entered the circle. *Uh oh, it seems like she got a few skills!* She bounced into the beat with popping movement. Each time the beat dropped, she gave another pop. She even gave simulations of pulling back on a bow and arrow, which was dope. Her hair was in a ponytail of individual braids, whipping back and forth, giving her moves extra emphasis. She was tight! Everybody around the circle pumped her up even more with bouncing hands screaming, "Yeah! Yeah! Yeah!" I had to give it to her. She rocked it!

More dancers showed up who attended Foshay that I knew. We all shook hands as they entered the party. Then, it was officially live! The circle stayed active for the duration of the party! Everybody rocked it multiple times over!

As it began to get late, a woman came through the door to pick up her child. I had no idea who she was picking up until the girl who had sat next to me on the couch went to grab her coat, and a bunch of girls hollered out, "Bye, Rose!" *Rose! That was her name! Yeah, now I remember. She was tight...* I also left shortly after, thanking Lizzie for inviting me and grabbing a few snacks from the table as I headed home. It was a good party.

The following Monday, after school, I received a phone call from Lizzie.

"Hello," I said after my sister handed me the phone.

"Hey, Ray. This is Lizzie," she said.

"Hey, what's up, Lizzie? That was a cool party you had on Saturday! Thanks for inviting me," I said.

"No, thank you for coming! You helped make it into what it was," Lizzie said. "But that's not why I'm calling."

"Okay. What's up?" I asked. "Did someone start fighting after I left?"

"No, not at all," she said. "Do you remember the girl named Rose?"

"Yeah," I closed my bedroom door, so I could hear her more clearly. "She's the only one whose name I do remember of those you introduced me to."

"Good because she likes you," Lizzie giggled. "She wants to know if she could have your number or if you could give her a call."

"Interesting," I said. "Yeah, give me her number. I'll give her a call..."

Chapter 26

Rose Johnson

That girl Rose was really cute. She stood out from the rest, in a wholesome way. When I saw her at the party that night, I had a feeling she didn't live around there in the hood. I knew she would be worth it, so I waited until the next day after Lizzie gave me her number to give her a call, just so I wouldn't seem desperate. Even though she was the one who asked for my number, a little anticipation is always healthy.

"Hello?" A small sweet voice answered my call.

"Hello, may I speak to Rose?" I responded.

"This is she," she said. I had never heard anyone respond in that manner. It sounded so sexy to me! I was used to girls saying, "This is her," or repeating their own name. Already, we were off to a good start. She seemed interesting.

"How are you doing? This is Raymond from Lizzy's party."

"Yeah, I recognized your voice. By the way, you have a nice voice."

"Thank you. So do you," I responded. "So, what's up with this about Lizzie saying that you like me? How come you didn't mention it at the party?"

"I guess I was too shy to come out and say it, but I did give you hints," Rose said.

We began to converse about each other individually, revealing things we liked and disliked, such as favorite foods, colors, and pet peeves. We even got a little deep, discussing our grades in school, things we'd like to aspire to do in the future, and even believing in

God. She mentioned her parents were strong believers and attended West Angeles Church of God in Christ on Crenshaw Boulevard. I gladly accepted the invite she gave me after I told her I wasn't currently attending any church. We talked about our talents and skills, as Rose explained her mutual love for dancing and how she was taking modern dance at Audubon Junior High. She also had a beautiful singing voice, which she demonstrated over the phone and instantly stole my heart.

The phone calls became a daily thing after school in the evening time and first thing in the morning on Saturdays and Sundays due to the fact that Rose liked how much deeper my voice was first thing in the morning when I answered the phone. We began to build a relationship over the phone, and on shortened days and minimum days after school, I was at Audubon, visiting Rose until her mother came to pick her up. I was stuck between a rock and a hard place because I still had Sharol also, but my feelings for Rose were growing stronger and stronger. I was thinking, *I have found a new "main girl."*

Things were really starting to change. Not only in my relationships, but with the homies in the hood. There was an exchange of freedom going on. Lil Loko was released from juvenile camp, and the homies got him faded. The next day, he jumped straight on his hustle with no breaks! Lil Loko knew how to get money, so everybody wanted to get money with him. It was his season to get paid. Just as we gained one to the streets, we lost two to the cage. Insane Dre and Lil Killa Jess got gaffled by the police and went to Youth Authority. The homies were gangstas, so it came with the territory.

That was the difference between the majority of the youth in the suburban areas and the youth in the inner-city ghettos. The youth in the suburbs went on vacations to Florida, Europe, Australia, etc. with their families, while the youth in the ghetto went on vacation to Camp Miller, Camp Kilpatrick, and Youth Authority - away from their families. Of course, there were some exceptions, but due to financial differences and broken homes, that was the reality for the majority.

"Here, Ray," my mother said, coming into my room with the telephone on a Saturday morning. "It's for you."

"Alright, thanks," I said still half asleep. "Hello?"

Rose's voice came through the phone as I put the receiver to my ear. "Good morning, Mookie!" Her smile came through the phone.

"Good morning, Pookie," I smiled back.

"Are you still sleeping?" she asked

"I was just wrapping up a dream about you," I said.

"You're lying, but you sound sexy, so I'll let you slide…"

"No, I was," I interrupted her. "We were both on top of a giant banana split, and we had to eat it all up together before we could climb out of the bowl and get back on land."

"Sounds like teamwork," Rose said.

"That's what I was thinking," I agreed.

"We're the 'Dynamic Duo'!" Rose declared.

"Ray and Rose!" I confirmed. We both laughed.

"Well, I'm inviting you to come to Six Flags Magic Mountain with me next Saturday," Rose said.

"Is that right?" I asked. "You know they have an after sundown dance party scene now, right?"

"Yes, my parents offered to take us as a Christmas gift to us, and they are paying your way as well," she said.

"How could I say no to that?" I asked. "What time will you pick me up is what I need to know."

"Around 9AM," Rose said.

"Oh, okay. Well, let me go and brush my teeth and stuff, and I'll call you back later," I said.

"Okay, yuck mouth," Rose giggled.

"Bye, bugga nose," I said.

Cool! I hadn't been to Six Flags in about a year. Maybe they've built a new roller coaster. Who am I kidding? I couldn't wait for the dance party after sundown! I had been practicing some new moves and couldn't wait to show them to the world. It was also cool that Rose's parents offered to pay my entrance fee into the amusement park. Of course, they could afford it. Her father was a police officer, and her mother was a schoolteacher. They were living comfortably in a four-bedroom house in Lynwood. Rose was the only sibling still living at home. She had an older sister who had her own apartment and an older brother in the military. Yeah, the baby of the bunch and Daddy's little girl. I already knew I had to be careful with her. Officer Johnson most likely had already ran my name through the police computers.

The next Saturday rolled around, and the Johnson family was outside my apartment in their minivan at nine o'clock a.m. sharp! I love it when people keep their word. I came out and waved at Estelle, Rose's sister who followed behind the minivan in her own car full of friends. As I jumped in the back of the minivan, I made sure to thank Mr. and Mrs. Johnson personally for the trip as I gave Rose a hug.

"Awe, you're welcome, Raymond," Mrs. Johnson said.

"It's no problem," Mr. Johnson said.

"How are y'all doing this morning?" I asked.

"Fine, fine," everybody said.

"You sound like you came from back home," Mrs. Johnson smiled from the front passenger seat.

"Where is back home?" I asked.

"Little Rock, Arkansas," she said.

"Oh, no!" I smiled back. "It's just a little broken English. I was born and raised right here in L.A."

"Yes, Rose told me," Mrs. Johnson giggled. "It's just that every time I hear someone say the word 'y'all,' I think of back home."

"Oh, okay. Sounds like it's time for a trip back home," I said. "Do you still have a lot of family there?"

"We both have a lot of family in Little Rock, and yes, we plan to go back this coming spring for spring break," she said.

We continued to talk about this and that as Mr. Johnson weaved through the traffic on Interstate 5. I had come to the conclusion, about twenty minutes into the ride, that Rose had some pretty good parents. Now, I had been to church with them once and had gotten rides home from Audubon by Mrs. Johnson while thinking, *Okay, they're just on their best behavior*, but that was different.

The ride to Six Flags was forty-five minutes, and the whole trip there, they didn't argue or disagree not once! Mrs. Johnson didn't give Mr. Johnson one instruction on how he should be driving or which turn he should make. To top it off, I never heard one curse word come from either of them. No curse words came from my mother's mouth either, but Cleophus by now would have cursed out half the motorists on the freeway. The Johnsons were a good example of a Christian family with actual evidence of living a Christian lifestyle. I had never seen anything like it. I was impressed.

We pulled into the amusement park just as the small talk started to die down. The place was packed! People were everywhere, coming from far and wide! The most important thing was remembering where we parked. Once we got inside and paid our entrance fees, Mr. Johnson gave us his separation speech.

"Okay, you two," he started with Rose and me. "We are not going to have a battle between the young and the not-so-young today just to see who can keep up with whom. So, we are going to let you guys go your way, and the Mrs. and I will go ours. Here's $20 for each of you for snacks, and we will be back here in this spot at the closing of the park. We'll go and get some dinner after we leave tonight."

"Okay. Thanks, Dad," Rose said, grabbing a $20 bill from his hand.

"Thanks a lot, Mr. Johnson," I said also grabbing a $20 bill from his hand.

"You're welcome," Mr. Johnson said. "We'll see you two later."

And, we were off! The fun times began! The first ride we headed to, of course, was the Revolution because it was one of the closest to the entrance. After about a thirty-minute wait in line, we were speeding through twists and turns, ups and downs, and then a big loop! The whole time, Rose was screaming and holding onto me as tightly as she could! I started to think to myself, *Whoever invented roller coasters did all couples a favor.* I couldn't wait to get on the next one! Coaster after coaster we went. Although we spent the majority of the day standing in thirty minutes to hour-long lines, we still had fun.

After the sun had gone down, Rose and I started to hear hip-hop music coming from a distance.

"You know what that is right, baby?" I asked Rose.

"Yeah," she smiled. "The sundown dance has started."

It was what we had both been waiting for, the main reason we had both come. Rose started to put her individual braids into a tighter ponytail as I tightened my shoelaces. We started to make our way over to the dance area as they played Digital Underground's "The Humpty Dance." As we entered in and made our way to the center of the area, we noticed some of the dancers had already formed a dance circle and were housing up a storm. There were housers from all races with major skills on the floor!

I was feeling the scene. It was definitely jumping. I noticed Rose was starting to bob her head to the beat, so she was getting hyped as well. The DJ started mixing and scratching then mixed in LL Cool J's "Mama Said Knock You Out!" That was my cue! I went into the circle with some upstairs pop-locking while the DJ extended the intro over and over as LL kept saying "Come on, man!" I ticked and popped down to the ground and made my way back up while the DJ mixed.

After a minute or so, he let the song ride out, and LL hollered out, "Don't call it a comeback! I been here for years!" I immediately went into some of the new moves I had been practicing at home. One move I called 'the handlebars,' where I held the imaginary handlebars which determined which direction my body would face while I had some crazy footwork going on. I made my way out of the circle back next to Rose to give someone else a turn to control the floor.

One guy leaped in from the opposite side of the circle, giving some crazy side to side footwork. There were about four or five other guys cheering him on, so I assumed they were together as a crew. The guy started to dance in the direction of Rose and I, giving metaphorical moves as if he wanted to battle. Immediately, Rose launched into the circle with twists and kicks, forcing him back to his crew! She took over the circle with her flexible moves with breaking speed and popping her arms and legs. She even went into the splits, combining her skills from modern dance class. She rocked it!

Rose made her way back to my side as another one of their crewmembers took to the floor. He also had skills with flexibility, but he only did the basic usual moves. He did a few flip-flops, a pretzel walk on his hands with his legs behind his head, a turtle walk on his hands and feet with his chest to the sky; then, he came out of it with a twist and a standstill backflip. It was then back on me! The battle continued!

I shuffled my feet into the circle with side slides and crisscross foot action that made it seem like I came in on a conveyor belt gliding. I started to break it down and hit some groundwork as the DJ mixed in Ice Cube's "Jackin' for Beats." I hit my leg swipes and windmills before I spun back to my feet, bouncing with some of Malik's slashes and chops. After dicing them all up, I spun out of the circle and posted a B-Boy stance. Immediately, two of their crewmembers shot out into the circle! They started to house rock side to side then hit random moves while getting pretty close in front of me. That's when Rose hollered out, "Don't get mad at my man because he's dope!"

They faded back, and they all seemed to have a defeated look on their face, knowing they had lost the battle. The crowd started to cheer and broke up the circle. Some even came up to Rose and me saying, "That was dope! Good battle, bro!" Everyone returned to dancing individually as Rose and I danced together for the rest of the night. We had fun! It was everything we had hoped it would be. The anticipation was all worth it.

On the way home, we all stopped to grab burgers and fries, including Estelle and her small entourage. We even saw some of the dancers along with the crew we had battled. The burgers were universal, one size fits all. The battle was over, and everybody subconsciously agreed it was time to eat. Getting full of double cheeseburgers was the goal. Rose and I ended up recapping all of the dance moves in the backseat as Mr. Johnson headed to my place to drop me off.

About an hour later, I woke up to Mrs. Johnson saying, "Raymond, we are here."

"Oh, okay," I said. "Thanks for everything! I had a blast!" Rose woke up also and lifted her head off my shoulder. I immediately took the opportunity to steal a kiss. "Good night, Rose. Stay sweet."

"Good night, baby," Rose whispered into to my ear.

"You're welcome, Raymond," Mr. Johnson said. "Glad you two enjoyed yourselves."

"Good night, Raymond," Mrs. Johnson said with a sarcastic tone and a smile. Apparently, she got a glimpse of me kissing her daughter.

"Thanks again," I said smiling as I got out of the minivan. It was a good day! One definitely worth remembering. At least that's what I was thinking as I went inside and got ready for bed.

Chapter 27
Hood News

1990 was quickly approaching to the end. It was a full year from beginning to end with activity and excitement. There was never a dull moment in the hood, and New Year's Eve was no exception. I was out in the front of my apartments, sipping cognac and pineapple juice with the homeboys. The usual dice game was going on while everybody either increased or gambled away the money they'd hustled for that day. As midnight started to approach, a few of the homies couldn't wait and started shooting their guns in the air. The surplus stores and pawnshops were exceedingly grateful in L.A. because a lot of people bought boxes of bullets just for New Year's Eve.

Midnight struck, and everybody let off over the city! It was officially 1991! One of the big homies pulled up with a fully automatic Uzi and sprayed bullets in the air. Classic! The sounds of gunfire went on well into the night all over L.A. as if it was a war going on! It was the perfect cover for murder. That's why everyone stayed extra careful on New Year's Eve, just in case someone was looking to settle a grudge. The same precautions were taken for the Fourth of July because gunshots were covered by fireworks for the getaway. Also, Halloween was not exempt. Because everyone was wearing masks, the Grim Reaper was almost guaranteed to get away. All he had to do was switch masks. It was as simple as that.

I was up early the next morning, on New Year's Day. Not because I was still celebrating from last night, but because I had to use the bathroom. That Hennessey and pineapple juice was still making its way out of my system. The phone started to ring as I came out of the bathroom. Everybody in the apartment was still asleep, so I went into the living room and answered the phone.

"Hello?" I asked.

"Ray." It was Uncle James' voice.

"What's up, Uncle James?" I asked. "What happened to you last night? I was hoping you and Jazmine came through to ring in the New Year with us."

"I killed her," he said.

"What?" I chuckled. "Man, quit playing. Where you at?"

"I killed her," Uncle James started to cry. That's when I knew he was definitely serious. "Let me talk to your mother. I only get one phone call."

"Man!" I was in somewhat of a shock. "Alright, hold on. Hey, Mama!" I knocked on her bedroom door.

"What?" she asked.

"Come and get the phone. It's Uncle James," I said. She came out of the room and took the phone, closing the door behind her to not disturb Cleophus.

"Hello," she said. "What's the matter with you?" she asked uncle James. "Why did you do that, James?" She started to cry. "What happened?"

Uncle James told my mother he was cleaning the gun, and it went off. He thought he'd unloaded all of the bullets, but there was one more in the chamber. Turns out Jazmine was also pregnant with what would have been Uncle James' first child. After the trial and investigation, Uncle James was sentenced to sixteen years for manslaughter. It was a sad time. My favorite uncle was back behind 'the walls' again, but that time it would not be Youth Authority. That time, it was the penitentiary.

Let Me Tell You How I Got Saved

Although my grades were at a 3.0 GPA level, I kept doing stupid stuff to mess up my life. I was fifteen and in the ninth grade and already I was becoming an alcoholic. One day, I decided to take some Super Socko and gin to school. I wanted to feel that mellow feeling in the daytime for a change. There was clearly a problem growing, and I didn't even know it. I sipped on my mixture at nutrition time straight out of the Super Socko bottle. I didn't even get to finish it before someone smelled it on me and went and told the security guards. They came straight to me and took my bottle before placing me in handcuffs. They called my mother to come and pick me up, who was highly upset because she had to leave her job at USC in order to deal with my 'foolishness.'

When we got home, she broke out that leather belt with the steel rings down the center, which I had never actually saw her wear with an outfit. It was officially 'the whooping belt.' I received the majority of the whoopings in the house, so I guess the real title would be "my whopping belt." One time I hid it, but it obviously wasn't a good hiding spot being that she had it that day. I tried to hold in the pain and take it like a man as she gave me my issue, but she had a different goal and that was not to give up until I let it out. My goodness! I should've thrown that belt in the trash.

Once I got off punishment for the umpteenth time, I noticed a lot of the homeboys had grown taller. Red Flagg and Les Dogg were then about six feet tall! Others grew just a little bit like Lil T-Bone and Insane Dre, but Lil NoGood remained short like me. What a relief! At least I wasn't the last of the shorties. How long was I locked in the house anyway? Some who were already done with their growth spurts were growing their pockets instead, like D.G. and K-Luv. Getting money was the new hobby, and there was enough for everybody. Lil Loko had made it his religion, by any means necessary! Everybody wanted to get money with Lil Loko because he knew how to go and get it, and he wasn't scared. Be it robbing, stealing, or dope dealing, he had his hand in it somewhere and somehow. He went and bought himself a set of chrome Dayton wire rims with tires right after he bought his first car, which was a 1986 Buick Regal. I had stacked the rims in my room for him until he had gotten the car out of the paint shop. Jet black on chrome Daytons, he was sitting nice!

The sun was making its way down on a Friday evening, and I was already feeling kind of sleepy. Usually, I'd be somewhere hanging out on a Fruit Friday, but that day I think I smoked a little too much weed. I was ready to lie down, at least for a little while. As I went inside, I walked to the kitchen to get a glass of water, and on the floor was what looked like a plate of food that someone had dropped and left there. I immediately doubled back out of the kitchen with a military about-face and went to the bathroom and proceeded to drink my glass of water from the sink. Somebody was definitely in trouble, and it was not about to be me! As I came out of the bathroom, I saw a glimpse of my mother passing through the hallway going towards the kitchen.

"Who left this food on the floor like this?" she yelled from the kitchen.

"I don't know. I just came in here," I said as I walked to the living room.

"Stephanie and Ashley!" she yelled to my sisters who were in their room.

"Yes!" they yelled back.

"Who left this food on the floor?" she asked.

"Ray did that!" they yelled back. *The audacity!*

"No, I didn't," I responded quickly. "I just came in here!"

"Yes, you did!" my mother said, as she walked past me towards her room. "Let me get my belt!"

I shot straight out the front door and down the street. I was fed up! *That's it! No more whoopings for me!* I was thinking to myself that I should've done that a long time ago! *She can't keep beating me for general purposes! I'm getting too old for this!* As I walked past the Foster's house, the homies were in the front yard hanging out.

"Aye, where you going, Blood?" Lil Loko asked.

I didn't even answer him as I looked behind me and saw my mother running to catch me! I broke out running again! Especially because the homies were out. She might've asked them to catch me for her, and they probably would've done it. I got ghost! I turned left down Raymond Avenue towards Exposition Boulevard with a steady stride while breathing at a deep even pace. I thought, *For sure, she probably turned around by now. She wasn't running every day like I was at school during physical education. She's probably tired by now.*

As I got to Exposition and was about to cross the railroad tracks, I turned to look behind me, and sure enough, she was still coming! I broke out running faster! *This lady is crazy!* I forgot that she was only thirty-five years old. I was just twenty years younger than she. Maybe she was running every day at the college on her lunch break. I didn't know, but I was done doubting her skills. I put the burners on up Exposition, all the way to Normandie Avenue and made a left. I kept going another block and made a left on 38th Street and started walking. *She should be tired by now, I guess. At least, I bought myself some time before she bends that corner on 38th and Normandie.* As I reached the middle of the block, I saw two of the homeboys, Smokey and Red Flagg about to get into a car.

"Spike! Where you going, Blood?" they asked.

Just as I did before, I turned to look behind me and saw my mother coming and took off without an answer. There was no time for conversing. I was literally running for my life! Had I let her catch me after the obstacle course I'd put her through, she would've probably murdered me right there on the 'eight block.' After I bent the corner to the right on Budlong towards Martin Luther King Jr. Boulevard, I didn't see her again. Maybe, Smokey and Flagg took her home. I don't know. Whatever the case, I slowed down to a power walk until I made a left on King, looking back periodically. I made a left down Vermont Avenue and headed back towards 37th Place, but instead, I cut down 37th Drive and headed to Malik's house.

"What's up, homie?" Malik asked, as he let me in the front door.

"What's up, dogg?" I responded. "You don't mind if I crash here tonight?"

"You ain't gotta ask that, bro," Malik said, welcoming me in with no questions asked. I was glad he did because I was sure enough tired from all the running and walking. Knowing Malik's mother, she probably called my mother and told her where I was. They were cool like that. Plus, most of the homies' parents had each other's telephone numbers. I crashed on the floor in Malik's room like a coma patient.

I woke up early the next morning and walked around the corner. I appreciated the love and hospitality from Malik and his family, but there's nothing like sleeping in your own bed. I had decided I was going to face whatever punishment, other than whoopings, that was coming my way. I even tightened my belt another notch, just in case she wanted to run another marathon. As I approached the front of the apartments, I stopped at the edge of the property on the sidewalk as I noticed Cleophus and my mother leaving out of the apartment with Cleophus leading the way. I didn't know what to expect. I was bold, but I wasn't stupid. I kept my distance away from my mother as Cleophus approached me on the sidewalk.

"Hey, Ray," Cleophus said. I just looked at him, trying to discern whose side he was on. "I had a talk with your mother last night. Everything is alright. You can go ahead and go in the house."

"Alright," I said. "Thanks."

It was still too good to be true, so I walked past my mother with extreme caution. To my surprise, she didn't explode or even give me a 'mad dog' look as I walked by and went inside. She simply followed Cleophus and got into the car. I don't know what Cleophus said to her last night, but whatever he said, it should have been written down and sold for top dollar because she never attempted to whoop me again after that day.

Chapter 28
Too Close for Comfort

Up until now, every girl I had was a conquest, a goal to be accomplished. I don't know what it was about Rose, but I wanted more from her. Her presence was one of the things I couldn't get enough of. She was so smart and talented with a songbird voice that could send chills through your very soul. Maybe, that's why she was chosen to play the role of Josephine Baker at the Wiltern Theater. She was awesome!

It was no longer about taking her virginity just for trophy rights. Although I was physically attracted to her in a major way, it had already been three months, and I hadn't pressured her about sex not once. I realized that was the first girl that I truly began to have feelings for. Whenever it did eventually happen, if it ever happened, I wanted it to be more than a sexual experience. I wanted to make love to her.

One morning, I was in the kitchen cooking a breakfast sandwich for breakfast before I went to school. There was a technique I had for wrapping the napkin halfway around the sandwich after I stacked the scrambled eggs and sausage onto the bread, so I didn't lose any scrambled eggs along the way as I walked to school. Every bite was important. While I was getting my sandwich wrapping down to a science, I heard the phone ring in the living room.

"Hello," I said as I answered the phone.

"Hello, Ray?" Rose asked. It sounded like she was stopped up.

"Good morning," I said. "Is everything alright? You sound stopped up."

"No, I feel terrible," Rose whispered. "I caught a cold from somewhere, and it seems to be getting worse."

"Awe, baby," I said. "You should stay home and get you some rest."

"That's why I called you," Rose whispered. "I'm staying home from school today, and you can come and see me if you'd like."

"Of course," I said quickly. "What's your address?" Then, I was starting to whisper as well. Rose gave me her address in Lynnwood, and I told her I would be on my way before I hung up the phone. Looks like me and my breakfast sandwich were changing directions that day! Of course, I had to walk around the whole block to make it seem like I was on my way to school. You'd be surprised at who was looking out their windows at 7:30AM. The whole neighborhood had eyes, and they had my mother's telephone number.

After taking two buses, one southbound down Vermont Avenue and another eastbound down Imperial Highway, I was there in about an hour. Rose answered the doorbell and opened the front door, looking just how she was sounding over the phone, stopped up. She was still in her pajamas with a bathrobe tied closed. Her eyes were puffy and nose reddish from blowing it.

"Good morning, stranger," Rose said as she wrapped her arms around my neck and hugged me tightly.

"Good morning, Sniffles," I said as I hugged her back even tighter.

"Did you have a hard time finding me?" Rose asked.

"No, I just followed the directions you gave me," I said. "They were detailed enough to lead the way."

"Okay, good," she said. "Let me show you around the house."

"Alright." I followed her around, and she gave me the tour. As we got to her parents' room, she began to show me her father's guns. He had a 9mm under the mattress, facing the door, with a .38 revolver under the mattress on the opposite side. Then on the same side, there was a shotgun under the bed. Officer Johnson was not playing! He was ready to show any intruder they had picked the wrong house!

"Is your dad preparing for a war we don't know about?" I asked jokingly.

"No," Rose laughed. "He just likes to be safe."

"I think he has accomplished his goal," I said examining the 9mm in my hand. Mr. Johnson was lucky I loved his daughter because that one would have come up missing had I cared less about her.

"Come on. Let me show you my room," Rose said, as she put the gun back in its place.

"Lead the way, my lady," I responded. She led me to a room that was full of purple, which was her favorite color. Even the walls were painted purple. "For some reason, I want a purple Laffy Taffy right now," I said as I surveyed the room.

"Ha! That's funny," Rose giggled. She grabbed my hand and took me back into the den in front of a 55" floor model television. "Make yourself at home, baby," she said, as she handed me the remote control. "I'm going to make you some breakfast."

"Cool," I said. I didn't tell her about the egg sandwich I had earlier. Plus, it was the perfect opportunity to taste her cooking. Turns out, she knew what she was doing around the kitchen. She brought me a plate of pancakes, scrambled eggs, and a fried hot link that was cut in half.

"I like cooking for you," Rose said. "It makes me feel like a wife."

"Well, let's see if it tastes as good as it looks, and then maybe, we can discuss our future," I said as Rose smiled. Rose began to dance around to the music video that was on the TV.

"The food is really good, baby," I said, as I dipped more pancakes into the syrup. "Let me see you do the splits."

"I know it's good," Rose smiled, as she slid down into the Chinese splits. For a moment, I had to stop chewing my food as I watched how graceful she was. She was amazing!

"You got skills, baby!" I told her.

"Thank you," she smiled.

We continued to enjoy each other's company like it was our house, and we didn't have a care in the world. Rose was easy to get along with. Almost too good to be true! I even got her to sing a song for me, which got me so aroused I grabbed her in the middle of a high note and kissed her like her mouth was the source of all good things. We both got a little carried away, until I tried to pull down her pajama bottoms, and Rose said, "No, I'm not ready… Next time, okay?"

"Okay," I responded. I realized she was trying to fulfill a mental list of do's and don'ts that almost all girls had, and I respected her wishes. So, I backed off before my boys turned blue. As it began to get closer to 3:00PM, I started to get ready to leave before the officer and the teacher got home. Our day of living vicariously in her parents' house had come to an end. Yet and still, we stood at the front door hugging and kissing as tears rolled down Rose's face for about fifteen minutes.

"Why are you crying?" I asked the obvious.

"Because I don't want you to go," Rose sniffled.

"If I don't leave soon, you're going to have to feed me dinner under your bed," I laughed.

"I wouldn't mind that one bit," Rose said, contemplating the thought. "Thanks for being my medicine today. I feel so much better."

"No problem, baby," I said, as I gave her one more kiss and opened the door to leave. "That's my job, making you feel good."

"I like that," Rose smiled. "Call me when you get home. I love you."

"Alright," I said as I walked out the door. "I love you, too."

On my way home, I examined my day, thinking how I wasn't really disappointed as I would usually be if I didn't put new points on the scoreboard with a potential prospect. I must have really loved that girl.

No doubt, two weeks later, it definitely went down, and it was all that I expected it to be. After we had opened Pandora's box, Rose began to find all kinds of reasons why she needed to stay home from school. In turn, I was getting very creative in forging absent letters from my mother in order to return to school the next day. I was addicted to Rose. Some might say I was sprung. That's okay because she was sprung also. We both shared a mutual fantasy of us spending the night together, which we almost pulled off when Rose's parents went on a weekend getaway. What we didn't contemplate was Rose's sister, Estelle, coming to check on her. I guess her parents didn't give her that memo. Estelle came pulling up in the driveway while Rose and I were in the den watching TV like it was our house, big chillin' with our feet up.

"Run! Hurry up!" Rose jumped up, as she heard her sister's car engine in the driveway outside. "Go to my room and get under my bed!"

"Alright," I said as I grabbed my shirt off the couch and dashed to the bedroom. Estelle came into the house with two other voices that I heard from under the bed. They were laughing, talking, and greeting Rose. *What a reality check,* is what I was thinking as I lay there underneath Rose's bed, which was too close to the ground. The box spring rested right on my back. If I needed to shift positions, I had to raise the bed a little and adjust myself. That was crazy! I hoped I didn't leave anything else on the couch.

All of a sudden, I heard, "Come here, Rose. I need to talk to you for a minute." Estelle and Rose came into the bedroom and closed the door. I watched their feet as Estelle went on and on about how she ran into her two friends at the mall and now they wouldn't leave her alone.

They hadn't seen each other in a while, so she wanted to spend some time with them, but she already had plans to go and hang out with her boyfriend. My goodness! I had to lay there and listen to that stuff!

"So what should I do, Rose?" Estelle asked. "You're my sister. Help me out."

"Tell them to follow you in their car, and then, leave them in traffic," Rose said.

I can't do that," Estelle said. "That's cruel! Plus, I'm not a getaway driver. They'll catch me every turn I make." Actually, I thought it was a good idea. It was a little cruel, but also clever.

"Well then just take them with you," Rose said. I was starting to get uncomfortable. I needed to shift positions real quick, and it didn't look like the Johnson sisters were coming up with a solution anytime soon. So, I started to slowly raise the bed off the rails with my shoulders in order to reposition myself.

"What is that?" Estelle immediately hollered out. "Who you got under there?" I was busted! I came out from underneath the bed to see the shocked look on Estelle's face. "Raymond? What are you guys doing in here?" Estelle was trying to make sense of it all. "You cannot stay here, Raymond."

"Alright. I'm leaving," I said, as I put on my shirt and shoes.

"Rose, what were you thinking?" Estelle asked another one of her rhetorical questions, as I let myself out of the front door. Man! Maybe that was a sign that we needed to calm down. Estelle was cool about it though. She didn't mention the situation to their parents. Now, that was some sister love at its finest.

As I got off the bus at Vermont Avenue and Exposition Boulevard, I saw fireworks in the air in the neighborhood. It looked like they were coming from 37th Drive. Right away, I knew it had to be Pepé. Pepé always went down to Tijuana around that time of year to bring back all the fireworks he could get his hands on to make a nice profit before the

Fourth of July came around. Of course, I had to go and check out his inventory.

"Pepé! What's brackin?" I said as I entered Pepé's front yard. He was about to light a cannon in his driveway that shot straight up in the air.

"What up, Spike?" Pepé said just as he lit the cannon and stood back. BOOM! POW! The rocket shot up in the sky and burst into multiple colors as I gave Pepé dap.

"That was tight, dogg," I said. "You got a gang of those?"

"You know it!" Pepé smiled. "You ain't seen nothing yet! I am selling these, but the best ones I'm saving for me and the kids for the Fourth of July. Look, this is a quarter stick of dynamite."

"Is that right?" I asked taking the firework out of his hand.

"Yeah, you can have that," Pepé sad. "That's way louder than an M-80."

"Bool! Good looking out," I said.

"Don't even trip, homes," Pepé said. "Tell the homies I got 'em."

"Yeah," I said as I walked off, thinking of a good place to bust that thing.

Monday morning, I went to school excited! I had a plan for my quarter stick of dynamite. Just lighting it in the street was too easy. After thinking long and hard about it, I'd come up with the most diabolical decision. The quarter stick of dynamite had a destination and the address was at my school. Yet and still, just lighting it on the playground or in the hallway was not enough. It had to be special. I decided at nutrition time I was going to blow up the Crips!

I had it all thought out. The stem on the dynamite was the same as an M-80, and I knew it would give me about thirty seconds once I lit it to get out of dodge. I couldn't wait until nutrition time! Everyone was going to see blue khakis on fire and blew All-Stars falling out of the sky!

As soon as nutrition time came, I put all of my books in my locker and headed out to the food court. I got in line to purchase myself a coffee cake, so I didn't look too suspicious. Plus, I needed to kill a few minutes, so the Crips would have time to sit down in their usual hang out area, which was under the canopy of the food court at two of the twenty-foot long wooden fiberglass benches. I got my coffee cake and approached the benches eating pieces of it.

They were all congregated at the further end of the benches closest to the edge of the canopy. Most of them were there, the Warlocks, the Kilowatts, and a few other reputables from Harlem Crips. They took up the first ten feet of the two benches, laughing and talking to one another. I knew them all by their first and last names, and they knew who I was also and where I was from, which is why they kind of got quiet when I went and sat in the middle of the bench. They were all probably wondering what I was up to because I had never sat over there.

"What's up, Ray?" C-Rag broke the monotony.

"What's up?" I responded like everything was normal and continued eating my coffee cake. They all looked at me for a moment and resumed talking and laughing amongst themselves. Once I felt they had forgotten about me, I pulled the quarter stick of dynamite out of my pocket along with a lighter. I bent down and started dusting off my shoe, only to set the dynamite underneath the bench and light it.

Once it was lit, I got up and walked towards the playground as the fuse stem burned slowly. The further I got, the faster I began to walk. Then, as I glanced to my right - BOOOOMM!!!! The quarter stick exploded with about a four or five foot tall ball of fire! I continued to walk towards the basketball courts. As soon as I got to the courts, the two school security guards came walking up to me.

"Put your hands on the back of your head and don't move," the huskier of the two said with his hand on his gun.

"What did I do?" I asked.

"Come on, Raymond," he said while his partner put the handcuffs on me. "We know it was you. Don't try and play us like we are dumb."

I didn't say anything else as they walked me past everybody into the main building to the police car in front of the school. I found out later that C-Rag had snitched on me. When I got to the police station, the security guards began their scare tactics along with another LAPD officer at the Southwest station.

"So, where did you get the explosive from?" the LAPD officer asked.

"I don't know what you're talking about," I said.

"Come on. Give it up," the husky school police officer said. "We have a witness that told on you. Plus, a few students are complaining about their hearing."

"It wasn't me," I said.

"If you think you're gonna get away with this, you're sadly mistaken, young man!" his partner yelled.

"Explain this cigarette lighter that you have in your pocket," the LAPD officer said.

"I smoke weed," I said. "A gang of people smoke weed at the school. They probably got lighters in their pockets, too!" I said, pointing to the school police.

"You think you are smart, huh?" the officer asked.

"No, you think I'm smart," I said.

They went on and on and back and forth for about ten more minutes until they finally gave up and handcuffed me to a bench. Because I was a juvenile, they had to call my mother to come and pick me up because apparently no one had filed any charges on me. They were highly upset. The school didn't even suspend me. I went right back to school the next day. I'm guessing they didn't want me to ruin my grades for the scholarship. The logical thing to do would be to straighten up, but I didn't believe that fat meat was greasy.

Finally, graduation came around, and I was voted "best dressed" and "best dancer" in the school yearbook! That was pretty cool! Rose even came to my graduation, looking extremely beautiful in a money green and white skirt suit. Afterwards, my mother took us to Harold and Belle's Creole Restaurant, and Rose's mother joined us. I couldn't believe I was headed to high school! Tenth grade- here I come! I had already applied to the magnet program to attend Dorsey High School with Joseph Jr. and Malik. If you had exceptional grades, the magnet program allowed students to be bussed to schools that were outside of their local radius that had better college prep classes. Plus, Dorsey was a Blood school. That was the main reason I wanted to go. Rose had one more year to complete the ninth grade before she graduated, but she was already planning to attend Crenshaw High.

The school summer program ended up calling me for summer job at UCLA. It was a blessing! All I had to do was file paperwork in folders in alphabetical order and place them in file cabinets. The only problem was all of the student workers had to get picked up and dropped off by a school bus in front of the L.A. Coliseum. I wasn't trippin' though. The homie Les Dogg had given me his snubbed nose bulldog .38 revolver to hold onto for him. She was a pretty chrome. I took her to work with me every day in a camera case. Fortunately, no one asked if they could check out my camera or if I could take their picture, but best believe if any of those Crips ran up trying to show out, they were going to get more than a flash.

One Thursday evening, Rose called me up with some good news as I was flipping through the TV channels after work, trying to find something good to watch.

"Hey baby," Rose greeted me on the phone as I answered it.

"How are you doing, baby?" I responded.

"Fine," she said. "How do you feel about spending the night with me?"

"You are ready know," I said, putting the remote control down. "That's our ultimate fantasy!"

"Yes, it is!" Rose said. "To wake up in each other's arms and me fixing you breakfast."

"All the time," I said. "That'll be the day…"

"Well, the day is tomorrow, my love," Rose said.

"Yeah, right," I said. "How we going to make that happen?"

"My parents are going to be out of town for the weekend, but their flight doesn't leave until early Saturday morning," Rose explained. "I can hide you under my bed Friday night until they leave Saturday morning."

"You got it all planned out, huh?" I asked.

"Yeah, I want you the whole weekend," Rose said.

"So, how am I supposed to get into this fortress with your parents in the house on Friday?" I asked.

"They are going last-minute shopping for their trip tomorrow evening after my dad gets home from work," Rose said. "I figured you could head over here after you get off work."

"Cool! I'm game," I said. "Let's do it!"

The next day, I couldn't wait to get off work. I hurried home to stuff a change of clothes into my backpack along with my toothbrush and deodorant. I was not playing! Of course, I had to grab the heat for protection. Les Dogg had come and picked up his .38, but Lil Loko had dropped off his favorite heat to me the other day- the chrome .380. I tossed it in the front pocket of my baggy jeans while I dialed Rose's number on the phone to let her know I was on my way.

She said, "Okay. Hurry up. My parents just left to go to do their shopping. Remember, when you get here, if you see the minivan in the driveway, it's a no go. Turn back around!"

"All right, bye." I hung up the phone and darted out of the front door. There was no time to waste. For sure, the bus ride there would take about an hour at the least. Hopefully, the Johnsons had a lot to shop for. A bus ride to Lynnwood and back to South Central L.A. just for general purposes was not what I was hoping for. I hated dry runs, so I tried not to think about it along the way.

About an hour and a half later, I arrived on Rose's street. I proceeded with swift steps, hoping that the minivan was not in the driveway. As I approached the house, I noticed an empty driveway. That's when my eyes got bigger and my steps got quicker! That was a crucial moment. It will be all bad if Rose's parents pulled up with me on their doorstep looking lost. I had to hurry up and get inside! Rose must've had the same idea because before I could knock on the door, she was opening it.

"Come in! Hurry up!" she said in a quick whisper. I hurried in as Rose closed and locked the door behind me then peeked through the blinds.

"I made it!" I said with relief.

"Yes, you did, baby," Rose said, wrapping her arms around my neck and giving me kisses.

"That was close," I said. "Have they called to check on you?"

"No, but they're probably on their way home," she said. 'Let's go in my room. When they pull into the driveway, you're going to have to get under my bed quickly and stay there until they go to bed."

"Until they go to bed?" I asked.

"Yeah, then you can come out and play a little while," Rose giggled.

"Well, let me make sure I don't need to use the restroom," I said, walking to the bathroom that was next to Rose's bedroom. Now is the time to make it happen. Unfortunately, I tried to use it, but nothing came out. So, I washed my hands and met Rose in her bedroom.

"Is everything copacetic?" Rose asked.

"Apparently yes," I said taking the .380 out of my pocket and placing it on the dresser.

"Nice gun," Rose said, picking up the gun off the top of her dresser. She examined it for a moment and then walked to her closet. "I'm going to put it up for you."

"Alright, cool," I said. "I have another gun for you also." I looked at Rose with wanting eyes as she peaked over her shoulder and blushed at me. All of a sudden, we both heard the sound of a vehicle outside, pulling up in the driveway.

"Hurry up! Get under the bed!" Rose said, as she quickly grabbed my backpack off the floor and stuck it in the bottom of her closet then left out of the room. I laid there under the twin bed thinking to myself, *Here we go again.* That time, I would be a little more cautious about my movements. I couldn't afford to give myself away that time.

Rose's parents came into the house conversing or should I say, Mrs. Johnson was talking about her outfits that she'd just purchased, and Mr. Johnson simply listened.

"What did you get, Mama?" Rose interrupted her.

"Come in my room and help me pack, and I'll show you," Mrs. Johnson said.

"Okay," Rose replied.

The sound of shopping bags rustling was starting to get louder and closer as they went into the bedroom next to Rose's. I could hear Mr. Johnson starting to flip through the channels on the floor model TV in the den. I listened along for about an hour to the old John Wayne movie that Mr. Johnson had found while channel surfing. He had turned the volume up considerably to drown out the girl talk that was coming from his bedroom. Finally, Rose came back into her bedroom and closed the door. She lay down on the floor on the side of the bed where I was.

"Hi, boy toy," Rose said smiling.

"Shut up," I responded, and we both laughed.

"Shhh," Rose said. "You're going to get us killed!"

"I think that was your plan," I whispered.

"I'm sorry, baby. You look so miserable under there." She kissed me sideways.

"Yeah, next time, let's wait until they're officially out of town," I said.

"I agree," she whispered.

"Now, give me some more of those kisses," I whispered back.

We kissed, and we touched, and somehow we managed to make love as Rose undressed and laid her situation next to the bed. I couldn't believe that it was happening! We were both CRAZY! I tried to run it through my mind again just to try and make sense of it all, but it still was not registering to be sane. I was actually stowed away in the house of a police officer with three known guns in the next room, while only a thin wooden door separated us as I committed ungodly acts to his youngest daughter. Yeah, I had to be NUTS!

"You know I'm hungry, right?" I asked. "What's going on in the fridge?"

"Yes, I'm going to feed you," Rose said as she got herself together. "I'm gonna go check right now. When I left out my mother's room, she said she was about to start dinner. So, she should be done or almost…"

"Alright, cool," I interrupted. "Just don't bring me a piece of chicken in your pocket."

"I'm not." Rose lay back on the floor next to the bed. "Stop being mean. I do have to eat out there first, and then make your plate like I'm getting seconds."

"Alright," I said.

"Don't worry," Rose said, turning on the TV on top of her dresser. "I'm gonna hook you up."

Rose left out of the room for what seemed like twice as long as the first time. I say that because I'd managed to doze off while listening to the TV, so it could have been shorter. I awoke to Rose coming back into the room and closing the door behind herself with a plate of food in her hands. It was about time! I thought I was going to have to go in there and ask, "What's taking so long?"

"I'm so sorry, baby," Rose started in. "I tried to come back as soon as I could, but my daddy was talking to me. Once he gets going, it's hard to get away." Rose settled down on the floor next to the bed with the plate in her hands.

"No problem," I said. "What did Mrs. Johnson cook tonight?"

"White rice, collard greens, corn bread, with meatloaf," Rose whispered. "Now say your grace and bless the food before you eat."

"Jesus wept. Amen," I said.

"Amen," Rose agreed, as she started feeding me from the plate of food while I lay under the bed.

"The food is really good," I said.

"Thank you," Rose said. "Too bad I can't relay the compliments to my mother."

"Oh, I'll just have to accept you as her representative," I said.

"Right," she replied. We both smiled at each other as Rose continued feeding me the food. After she took the empty plate back into the kitchen, Rose came back with great news. "You can come out from under the bed now. My parents have gone to their room, but you must be very quiet," she whispered.

"You haven't said nothing but a word," I said, as I eased out from underneath the bed. I proceeded to stretch as about five of my bones popped. Rose gave me a hug looking so apologetic as she expressed how much she loved me. She turned out the light and left the TV on as we talked face to face on the bed. She mentioned I would have to get back underneath the bed before daybreak, which I was not looking forward to. As it began to get late in the night, I asked, "Are you going to turn off the TV?"

"No," Rose replied. "I sleep with the TV on."

"Alright," I said.

After making love to her once again, I needed to use the bathroom. Rose suggested I use the bathroom that was close to the kitchen and not the one next to her room. She further explained that if her parents heard me taking a leak, they would know right away there was a male in the house. She was right. The only problem was I had to walk past her parents' bedroom to get to the other bathroom.

"Alright, when I leave out of here, you can't make any noise because they will think you've already left the room," I said.

"Okay," Rose whispered. "Hurry back."

I left out the bedroom, closing the door behind me. All the lights in the house were off, but I was familiar with the house, so I proceeded to walk on through the hallway. Quickly, I noticed Rose's parents' bedroom door was wide open, and Mrs. Johnson was lying in bed close to the door, and she was facing me. I kept it moving down the hallway passing through the den until I reached the second bathroom, which was close to the living room. After locking the door behind me and turning on the light, I let out a deep breath of relief. That was close!

After I did what I had to do, I turned the light back off, but I waited for about a minute for my eyes to adjust back to night vision. I knew I needed to get back inside Rose's room as quickly as possible without a sound. Being that Mrs. Johnson was right by the door, I risked the chance of her opening her eyes and speaking to whom she thought was Rose. If she asked me to bring her a glass of water, I would be dead! Even worse, what if Mr. or Mrs. Johnson met me in the hallway to take their turn in the restroom? Hesitation time was over. I immediately left the restroom and made a bee-line straight back to Rose's room and closed the door behind me.

"What took so long?" Rose whispered. "I felt like I was holding my breath the entire time."

"You and me both," I whispered.

We talked a little while longer until we both fell asleep in the twin bed. I was sound asleep when I heard a loud deep voice in the room.

"AWE, NAW!" Mr. Johnson exploded. "THERE'S 'BOUT TO BE SOME QUESTIONS ANSWERED UP IN HERE!"

I rose up to gather my senses and noticed Mr. Johnson had already left the room. Rose and I were both in the bed naked, but while I was asleep, Rose had covered me with her sheet and blanket. The only problem was my dreds were not covered on the pillow next to Rose. Mr. Johnson had been coming in to turn off the TV in Rose's room, which was never mentioned to me that that was his routine every night! Rose and I scrambled to find our clothes.

"Raymond?" Mrs. Johnson came into the room, turning on the light. "Rose? What's going on?"

"I apologize, Mrs. Johnson," I said as I put on my clothes. "We should have never done this."

"You better grab those clothes and get out! He's in the kitchen with his gun, talking on the phone to his friend," Mrs. Johnson said as she went out of the room to check on Mr. Johnson.

"Give me my gun," I said to Rose.

"You not about to shoot my daddy!" she replied.

"I'm not about to let him shoot me either," I said. "Look, I'm just trying to get out of here. Give me my gun, so I can leave."

Rose finally went to her closet, brought out the .380, and gave it to me. I kissed her goodbye and walked straight through the house and out the front door. *Man! That had to be the dumbest fiasco yet!* I thought to myself as I made my way up off Rose's block before Mr. Johnson got any bright ideas. *What was I thinking?* It was a disaster waiting to happen from the start. I tried not to worry about it too much. What's done was done. I just hoped Rose wasn't being killed right then. I had to figure out how I was going to get home at 2AM with the bus going down Imperial Highway probably not starting until 5AM.

On a mission to make it home, I made my way to the corner of Imperial Highway and Martin Luther King Boulevard. There was no time to waste. It was late night in the city of Lynwood, and I had the heat in my pocket. I had never experienced Lynwood Police Department and didn't want to start that night. There was no puzzle in the decision. A taxicab was the answer to my dilemma. The only problem was that I wasn't trying to pay an arm and a leg to get back to South Central L.A.

Because I only had $40.00 in my pocket, I decided if the fare meter went too high, I was going to jump out the car and run once the driver got to the hood. I knew every shortcut and backyard over there. There was no way I was getting caught by Mr. Taxi Driver. So, I used the payphone that was there near the bus stop, which was right in front of a small plaza. There was a sticker with the number for a taxicab company, right on the side of the payphone for my convenience. I told the company my location and ordered the taxi before sitting down on the bench at the bus stop to wait. The operator had mentioned it would be about fifteen minutes before the driver showed up to my location. I just needed to get off the empty streets.

A few minutes later, a dude came walking down Imperial toward me. He carried in his hand a clear plastic bag and was dressed as if he'd just got off work on the night shift. Then again, he could have also just been released from county jail. My antennas went up immediately. I stayed posted on the bus stop bench with my hand in my pocket on the heat, slightly facing the direction he was coming from. As he approached the bus stop, he continued walking past about ten feet to the pay phone. I stood up to get a better look at my surroundings. He stood there fidgeting with the telephone receiver, but he was not pushing any buttons, as if he was contemplating his next decision.

"Aye, homie. You got some change?" he finally asked, hanging up the phone receiver and facing me.

"Naw, dogg," I replied as I took the gun off safety. He just stood there looking at me and looking around. I could tell he wasn't going to take no for an answer.

"You don't have NO change, homie?" he asked again. I stepped into the street, as if I was looking for the bus and cocked the .380 back…

Click! Clack!

Placing the heat back into my pocket but keeping my finger on the trigger, I stepped back onto the sidewalk looking him straight in his eyes.

"I ain't got no change, dogg," I stood there with about ten feet between us awaiting his next move.

He must have decided that finding out if I had change or not wasn't worth it as he continued walking up Imperial Highway. I watched him as he got further and further away before putting the heat back on safety. Then, I watched him periodically until he was out of sight. Still no taxicab! It was well over fifteen minutes since I called. *Maybe, I should call back and check on the status…* Just as I was in mid thought, a police car passed by riding slowly! I was spooked!

As soon as the police car turned the corner, I went to the trashcan that was in front of one of the stores inside of the small plaza, and I put the gun in a brown paper bag and put it in the trash. About five minutes later, after I had sat back down at the bus stop, the taxicab pulled up. As I waved him down, I shouted out, "One moment!" Then, I ran to go and get the gun out of the trashcan. As soon as I turned back around, to my surprise, the driver sped away!

I didn't blame him. If I had been the driver, I would have done the same thing. I just ran to get a gun out of the trashcan, trying to get into his taxi. Plus, I had little to no intentions of paying for the ride anyway. It was time for Plan B: Agitate the concrete. I ended up walking from Imperial Highway to Florence Avenue where I finally caught the westbound bus to Vermont and then the Vermont bus to the hood. I didn't get home until almost 6AM.

Later that morning, I was awakened by my little sister Stephanie holding the telephone. "What do you want, girl?" I asked, still half asleep.

"Here, it's Darrell on the phone," Stephanie said, handing me the phone.

I put the receiver to my ear still lying down on my pillow. "Lil Loko, what's brackin'?" I asked.

"Aye, I'm about to come and get that," he said.

"Alright, come through," I said. "I'll be out there in a minute."

I got out of bed, put on some jeans and a sweatshirt, and then got the gun from underneath my bed. I took a moment to wipe my fingerprints off. There was no telling what he was about to go do. Plus, I figured he was probably calling from the payphone around the corner by the dairy, so I had a couple of minutes.

After I was done wiping it down, I wrapped the .380 in the red flag I had been using and then tucked it in my waist. I went outside to find a light drizzle coming down. As I went to the front of the apartments, Lil Loko was already at the curb sitting in the Regal on Daytons. I had to admit, that fresh black paint looked good in the rain. The closer I got to the car, I saw he had Lil T-Bone in the passenger seat, so I went around to the driver's side and got in the back seat.

"What's brackin'?" I took the gun out of my waist.

"What's brackin' wit you?" Lil Loko asked.

"Man!" I began to tell him what happened in Lynwood with a little hesitation. I thought for sure he was about to give me a speech on being bareful and ask why I took his gun all the way to Lynwood, but after I told him what happened, he just laughed with that high-pitched laugh of his. I started unwrapping the gun and handed it to him, but I kept my flag.

"So, you straight?" he asked.

"Yeah, I'm straight," I said. "Just tired. I'm about to go lay back down."

"Alright," he let me out of the car. "Be bareful out here, Blood."

"Yeah, y'all too," I said. "Be bareful."

I went back inside to get a little more sleep, while thinking to myself about how even though there was no problem getting a heat from any one of the homies, I needed my own.

Chapter 29
High School Days Begin

Things just kind of died down with Rose since the night with her parents. Even though we kept in touch from time to time, there was no time spent together like we used to. Maybe if I had gone back over to her house to have a sit down talk and apologize to her parents, things may have gotten better, but I wasn't thinking about preserving my first love. Rather than deal with the issue, I just started focusing more on Sharol.

Meanwhile, I started tagging my housing name on the walls. I was about to start high school in the tenth grade once fall came, so I had to make sure my name was up. My tag was ERCL, pronounced Ur-sl, but the home Big G-Dogg saw it written on the wall and started calling me ERKL, and the name spread like wildfire! One more nickname added to the list. I didn't mind too much because I know words have power, and names were no exception. Those who had names like Crazy-K and Demon Rat usually took on the characteristics of their name. Because I was associated with having intelligence, I was cool with that. Most nerds became bosses of the world anyway.

The first day of school came around, and because we were in the magnet program, Joseph Jr., Malik, and I had the option of riding the school bus free. The only problem was we had to get up extra early to be at the bus stop by 6AM. I already knew that that was going to be for emergency purposes only.

"Don't even trip, homeboy," Malik said. He and Joseph Jr. were seniors that school year. "I'm going to introduce you to some of the best housers in L.A. and probably the world. The best of the best, hands down."

"Yeah, maybe I'll learn some new moves," I said.

"Fa sho!" Malik replied. "Plus, I gotta introduce you to the NATURALS, so you can get some real writing done."

The NATURALS were the N.K.S. taggers, which stood for "Natural Kings" or "Never Kaught Slippin." Most of the members were also from Black Pee Stones up in the Jungles and few other hoods. Young Bloods were writing on the walls.

"Yeah, I'm about to put up some dope styles!" I said.

The bus driver continued to make stops along the way, picking up more students.

"You know I'll be introducing you to all the ladies," Joseph Jr. said. The young ladies always flocked to him like a magnet. I could count on him to introduce me to most of the twelfth grade girls and even some eleventh graders also. He had already told about three girls on the school bus that I was his brother. Just as it was in the seventh grade, but the tenth grade was ten times better. I gained instant popularity as they passed their portions to me.

As soon as we hit the schoolyard, there was a group of dudes standing around because we had almost an hour until the first class started. They all had backpacks with N.K.S. written on them.

"Aye, there they go right there," Malik said as we walked up to the crowd.

"What's up, Nester!" one of the guys hollered out to Malik.

"What's hatnin'," Malik responded. "Aye, this is my homeboy ERCL. He wants to write with us." Malik motioned towards me with his hand.

"What's up?" I responded as I started giving dap to all the writers as Malik called off their names. The first two were the founders of N.K.S., KLUE and KAPER, who I found out later were brothers and both sons of the infamous T. Rogers, who brought the Black Pee Stone Gang to L.A. from Chicago. Next was Upper, who reminded me of Lil Loko. He had that same wild spirit like he was the only child of his parents.

"What's hatnin' wit you, ERCL?" Upper said with a firm handshake. "You trying to get up? Cause we got what you need," he said, opening a backpack full of spray paint and permanent markers.

"Oh, fa sho!" I said. "You already know!"

"We don't get along with N.B.T. (Nothing But Trouble) tho, so watch your back," Kaser said, which was Nester's cousin. "Or M.L.K. (Mobbin Like Krazy) neither."

"Our brothers are K.W.S. (Kings With Style)," said ANEK, who had a little sister, DEM, who wrote.

"Oh, okay," I said, taking it all in.

More and more members started to show up as they gave me the run down on other important information, like which clothing stores were good to steal from. We called it 'racking.' If anyone was caught or if security was beefed up, you were to report back immediately that the spot was burnt. The artist in me was attracted to tagging. I liked to draw a little bit and tagging was like putting your artwork on the wall for everyone to see, except tagging was illegal without the owner of the property's permission. As you can see, there was a whole lifestyle and culture that came with it, with a history dating back to the 1960's. It was artwork gone rogue! I was in…

It was almost time for school to start, so I had to get to my homeroom number in the hallway of the main office. I began to see a lot of familiar faces of students who graduated with me from Foshay, including Sharol. She was filling in those jeans with her Mississippi curves that even had teachers turning their heads. She came up and gave me a hug.

"Good morning, Spike," Sharol said, giving me a kiss on the lips.

"What's up with you?" I responded. "You looking good."

"Thank you. So do you," she said.

"We need to celebrate soon," I said. "We'll make a toast to high school."

"Okay, let me know," Sharol smiled. "But, I know you want more than a toast."

"You already know," I said, looking her up and down. "I was just trying to be nice. I'll see you later tho."

"Alright," she said, as we walked off in separate directions.

High school was already looking up! Even my classes were not as hard as I thought they would be. It seemed like I already knew most of the students at the school thanks to Joseph Jr. and Malik. Even my old buddy Ben was there and Lil D-Mack from the hood, but the circle wasn't complete until Friday came around. Yep, you guessed it! The first lunchtime dance! It was off the chain! As soon as lunch came, everybody lined up to fall into the basketball gym. I got inside and went immediately to the circle. Malik was already there with all the housers as the DJ spun Main Source, "Looking at the Front Door."

"What up, my boy?" Malik shouted, giving me two sideways fives.

"What up, dogg?" I said. "It's on up in here!"

"This is it, man!" Malik shouted. "You're about to see some of the best get down! Check it out! That's Gizmo in there now!"

Gizmo was in there, wrecking the circle with his dreds swinging doing some crazy upstairs moves! He was tall, so the circle naturally got wider as he broke into some downstairs swipes. The DJ switched up the track with Public Enemy "Can't Truss It," and an albino kid with dreds jumped in the circle.

"Aye, that's Hobo! He dope!" Malik shouted.

Hobo broke in with some tribal-style locking. His baggy clothes added a rubber band effect to his moves. Then, I couldn't resist! I jumped in the circle with shovel moves and locking up bows as I went into a twist before walking it out with some bowlegged box struts. Just as the DJ switched it up with Tupac "If My Homies Call," in came Secret, sliding in on his dreds with his feet in the air! I already knew Secret was dope. I remembered him from Club Nouveau, but now he had his girlfriend Manomi with him, who was just as dope as he was.

They tag teamed back and forth with moves I had never seen before. I had already made a mental note to practice that head slide he did. Secret had a liquid flow with his moves. It was impressive just to watch him. I definitely made another note of his sideward swipes as Manomi hit a front flip over his head and landed on the floor in the splits. Everybody was hyped! The energy was sky high, and everybody was fighting to be next with a new move to bust! We couldn't get enough! Unfortunately, lunchtime was only thirty minutes, and the DJ had to shut it down.

The following Friday, there was a scheduled meeting after school on Manchester Avenue and Arlington for the N.K.S. and K.W.S. crews. All of the NATURALS mounted up on the RTD bus with some form of fake bus fare, about thirty deep. I had a bus pass with a handmade monthly sticker that I manufactured myself. Several others had the same. Some had transfers that they'd snatched from other bus drivers. Others had stolen bus passes that they passed back to the guy behind them to use multiple times. We packed the bus in before the diver closed the front door and left some to catch the next bus.

Immediately, everybody pulled out a marker or a scribe to tag the bus up. I was in the back of the bus turning over the advertisements and tagging ERCL N.K.S., as the bus driver continued to make more stops. Apparently, two other taggers had gotten on the front of the bus, started tagging their crews, noticed they didn't get along with each other, and immediately started fighting on the front of the bus. The bus driver jumped up to break up the fight and another tagger jumped into the driver's seat and proceeded to drive the bus! It was hilarious! He pulled the bus over once we got to Manchester Avenue on Crenshaw Boulevard, but the doors did not open quickly enough as the bus driver yelled out, "Nobody's getting off this bus! You're all going to jail!"

That's when we almost simultaneously pulled all emergency stop and release levers and jumped out the windows and the back door! We ran across Crenshaw laughing and walked the rest of the way to Arlington Avenue and Manchester. The little park on the corner was full of taggers with baggy jeans and backpacks on. There had to be about two or three hundred strong from all the local high schools and junior high schools. We talked about new clothing stores and art supplies that were easy to rack from, new beefs with other crews, squashed beefs, and other random topics, like which cars were easy to steal, etc. Those who had weed smoked it just before the police came and dispersed the crowd. Meeting adjourned.

One day, I was sitting in English class when I received a summons to the counselor's office. That was all of a sudden and too random for me, especially because I was doing the most… It was a long, slow walk to the office, as I tried to sort out what I could have been caught for. Maybe, someone had told the counselor who had been writing ERCL on the walls. I didn't know. *Maybe, I should hop the fence and go home.* Unfortunately, facing the music seemed like the best logical choice. If I avoid the outcome, it would only get worse. Plus, I was at the office already. I went in to see Ms. Manuel.

"How are you doing, Raymond?" Ms. Manuel smiled at me, but that could mean anything. I stayed on guard.

"I'm fine, and you?" I stood at the door of her small office within the main office. "How are you doing, Ms. Countee?" I hollered into the small office next to hers.

"Hi, Raymond," Ms. Countee smiled. Joseph Jr. had introduced me to them on the first day of school, so I was hoping they would remember and show me a little leniency for whatever reason I was there.

"Come on in, Raymond," Ms. Manuel said. "Have a seat." I went in and sat in the chair that was opposite her desk and she began. "Well, young man. You are quite impressive."

"How come you say that?" I asked.

"I just got off the phone with a representative from Yasuda Trust Banking Company, the bank that's giving you your scholarship, and now I'm reading through your transcripts, and I like what I see," Ms. Manuel said.

"Oh, okay. Thank you," I replied. I was able to relax a little because she was on a positive note.

"You're welcome," she said. "The representative contacted me to inform you that the bank is going to have a competition between all the scholars from the different schools who won their scholarships for an opportunity to take a trip to Tokyo, Japan as ambassadors from America."

"Wow!" I responded. "When is this competition?"

"In two weeks," Ms. Manuel said. "Now, there are three categories of the competition that will be judged. First, you must write a speech that you will recite about an item that is significant to you, and you must bring the item with you."

"Okay," I said. "What else?"

"Then, you will be tested on your ability to work in groups, and the last category will be making quick decisions," she said. "So, you have two weeks to write that speech and memorize it."

"Okay, thanks!" I said with a new attitude. "So, how long does the speech have to be?"

"Oh, I'm sorry," she said. "Only one page. You can do this, Raymond. I'm going to be there with you cheering you on. The bank is sending a memo to your house for your parents to attend."

"That'll be good," I stood up smiling.

"Oh, one more thing before you go," she leaned back in her chair.

"Yes, ma'am?" I asked.

"Stay out of trouble, Raymond," she said. "I've seen the group of kids you're hanging with, and it's not a good bunch."

"Alright," I said. "Thanks for your support in everything." I walked out of the office.

"I'm serious, Raymond!" Ms. Manuel yelled after me.

"Okay," I hollered back, as I left out.

I began to think about what would be a good object or item of significance for me. Whatever it was, it had to be something good. I couldn't write about why I liked weed! Let alone bring some with me. They'd probably kick me out of the place with the quickness. So, the best thing I could come up with was the flute. I was still in band class, so it wouldn't be a problem with borrowing one from the band room. It was time to write!

Two weeks later, my mother and I arrived at the hotel where the competition was being held, and Ms. Manuel met us there in downtown L.A. There were about thirty students and their parents in a banquet room with a podium placed in front of all the chairs. Everyone was ready with the significant item in hand. There was no pattern, just random items, such as a teddy bear, a clock, a hat, flowers, etc., and I sat there with my flute.

"You're going to do great!" Ms. Manuel leaned over and reassured me.

"Thanks," I said, looking up from studying my speech for the umpteenth time.

"Good morning," one of the bank representatives announced.

"Good morning," everyone responded back.

"Welcome to Yasuda Trust Banking Company's Young Ambassadors to Japan Competition," he continued. "My name is Haru, and I will be officiating the program today. There will be three categories in the competition: the first is articulation of a speech, using a significant item, the second will be testing the student's ability to work in a group in a very unique way, and the third category will be testing the student's ability to make quick decisions. There will only be eight winners today, who will have the opportunity to travel as young ambassadors from America to Japan for ten days, all expenses paid. So, without further ado, let the competition begin."

Haru began to call names one by one to come and present their speech at the podium. One young man got up with a face towel in his hand. He started to explain how he never leaves home without it, and he feels naked without it. He mentioned that sometimes he washes it, but he stands right by the washer and dryer until it is done. Everyone looked at each other in disbelief, but he was dead serious.

A girl got up and spoke about the pearl necklace she was wearing. It fit perfectly around her bare neck without any hanging space. She explained how the necklace used to belong to her grandmother, who gave her the family heirloom just before she passed away. The necklace had skipped her own mother, who died while birthing her. The young lady told her story as tears rolled down her face and many other faces in the audience also. I adjusted my tie thinking, *This is going to be tough.*

"Raymond Watkins," Haru called. It was then or never. I got up with my flute and headed to the podium.

"Good morning, everybody!" I smiled.

"Good morning!" the audience resounded back.

"My name is Raymond Watkins, and this is my flute. I began playing the flute in the seventh grade. At first, I didn't like it, but then I began to get pretty good at it. This flute is significant to me because it's my peacemaker. It keeps me at peace, kind of like a stress reliever. The soothing tones played, no matter what time of day, bring a tranquil calm over me. It doesn't matter where you are, the flute brings its own ambiance. Note by note, the flute can change your day or set the tone in the morning. I usually just start to play a peaceful melody, and it relaxes me right away. I've noticed that the less stressed I am, the easier I can deal with life's situations in a more rational and logical way. Most of the youth today are angry and bitter for some reason or another. Unfortunately, there are not a lot of positive outlets in the ghetto, so that energy is turned towards negative pathways. We know that's when the crime rates start to climb. Ultimately, we make our own decisions at the end of the day. Of course, there are gangs. Of course, there are drugs. There are even suicidal thoughts, but before I turn to any of those things, I play my flute. Thank you."

I turned and walked to my seat, holding the flute high in the air as the people applauded. Although I was already gangbanging, tagging, housing, drinking alcohol, and smoking weed, they bought it! My mother, on the other hand, gave me half a smile because it sounded good, but she knew good and well, I was lying through my teeth.

When it was time for the second category, "Working in Groups," Haru led us all to a larger room that was next to the one we were in. There were several other bank representatives on a stage in the front of the room, pouring out buckets full of Legos.

"Okay, everybody," Haru began. "This is the second category. We'll be judging your ability to work in groups. You'll be divided into three groups, and you'll be given five minutes to build the tallest building you can using these Lego pieces. So, all students line up in front to receive your group number."

As soon as we were separated into groups, I shared my master plan with my group. We isolated ourselves as I began to share. "Alright, guys," I whispered. "We have to build a strong wide base first, like a pyramid. Then, we could gradually go straight up with our building."

"Sounds like a plan," one boy said.

"I was thinking the same thing," a few others responded.

"Alright, cool," I said. "Let's do this!"

Haru marked the time on his stopwatch, and we all got straight to it. We began to build as planned, and it was working like a brand new engine! The other two crews were impatiently building their Legos straight up as fast and as narrow as possible. They were getting really high, but their buildings had no foundation and would slowly collapse. My crew, on the other hand, was working with a solid base, like the Eiffel Tower and gradually getting taller. Haru announced that we had one minute left. That's when we built straight up. It was a beautiful plan! One of the other crew's building actually fell over the moment Haru called time, and the other building wasn't tall enough due to the fact that the group tried to adapt my group's plan at the last minute. It was evident who the winners were! Champ status was granted!

"Okay," Haru started. "For the third and final category, the students will be separated from the parents for a short while. After which, we will all enjoy refreshments in the luncheon hall next door. Students, could you please exit to my right?"

All of the students were led to another room with a giant 'business meeting' table inside that was about thirty feet long and six feet wide on each end, but it was ovaled out to about ten feet in the middle and made of cherry wood. It was beautiful and was surrounded by fifteen leather executive chairs. Fourteen of the students and I sat down around the table, and those that remained standing were taken to another room that I assumed was a twin of the one we were in.

"Hello, everyone!" One of the bank representatives stayed with us and closed the office door.

"Hello," we responded.

"My name is Chieko, and I'll be giving you the final test of making quick decisions." She walked slowly around the table as she talked, passing out a sheet of paper and an ink pen to each of us. She was beautiful. "I'm going to give you a scenario that you will have five minutes to answer on the sheet of paper placed in front of you. When you are done writing your answer down, please turn your papers face down until the five minutes are up."

After we all had writing stationary, Chieko set the remaining pens and paper that she had to the side and continued walking around the table. "Okay, so here is the scenario," Chieko began, as we all listened closely. "Planet Earth is going to explode in twenty hours. You have a spaceship with knowledge of another habitable planet's location. Unfortunately, you can only fit fifty people on your spaceship. Who would you take with you? Your five minutes starts now. You may begin to answer the question."

I jumped on it! It was a very good question. I knew there had to be some thought put into it. Chieko was picking our brains and whatever she pulled out would determine if we went on a trip to Japan or not. An educated answer was a must. I wrote down the best logical outcome of the situation I could think of and turned my paper face down and waited.

"Okay. Time's up," Chieko announced. "Make sure your name is on the top of your paper. We will go over your answers and then collect them. If your name is at the top of your paper, I will collect your ink pen now."

She collected the pens and began to call on us to read our answers going clockwise around the table. The first few students said they would take their whole family, starting with their immediate family first. One young man said he would take himself and fifty beautiful women, so he himself could populate the planet. Another said he would take twenty-five family members, five friends, and twenty women.

"Okay, Raymond Watkins, who would you take with you?" Chieko asked.

"Alright. I know I need to populate this new planet, but I also need to sustain life, so we could survive for more than two generations," I said. "First on my list, I have ten scientists of different sorts in order to test the water, minerals, and other things in the ecosystem. Preferably, five women and five men along with their textbooks and notes. Then, I would have ten doctors, also five women and five men, along with their textbooks and medications to work with the scientists to make new medications with the new planet's resources because we're going to be having a lot of babies real soon." Everyone giggled.

"Then, I would choose ten farmers, five women and five men, who would also work with the scientists to test the soil and cultivate the ground to grow food. They would bring seeds from Earth, but they would also test the native fruits and vegetation to find out what's edible. Then, I'd search for ten skilled workers, five women and five men, skilled in the areas of carpentry, masonry, ironwork, casting, etc. in order to build our new homes and other buildings and also to make new tools, fixtures, and gadgets. Last on the list would be five immediate family members and five teachers of the opposite sex of my family except for two women for me because my parents wouldn't need another mate."

"Okay, two women for Raymond," Chieko teased. "Why not?" Everybody laughed and continued around the table reading their answers.

I was confident in my answer. A few others had similar answers along the same lines. It was a good contest overall. The only category that I was worried about was the speech. The flute talk was still up in the air. No worries. We all had fun with the event. Over refreshments, we were told we would be notified in one week if we were winners.

The following week, I had almost forgot about the contest until Ms. Manuel got on the intercom during homeroom.

"Good morning, students," she began. "Today, I'd like you to join me in congratulating our own Raymond Watkins as one of the eight winners of the Yasuda Trust Banking Company's contest to become a young ambassador from America to Japan! He and seven other students along with several chaperones will spend ten days in Tokyo, Japan, all expenses paid, in the springtime next year 1992. Again, congratulations to Raymond Watkins on a job well done! I'm so excited for you! Please come to my office later today for more information on your trip!"

Awesome! Everybody applauded! Some even shook my hand, including the homeroom teacher. It was a great accomplishment, even greater than winning the scholarship, in my opinion. It felt good!

The rest of the year seemed to drag by as I prepared to be internationally known. I was taking driver's education as an elective and would be taking driver's training the next semester in order to get my driver's permit. So, I started focusing on my license to take my mind off Japan. I would be sixteen in January and able to take the DMV test. My homeboy Oscar said his mother would allow us to use her car for the test. That would be great! At least, I would have a license while driving those stolen cars.

"My gangsta! My gangsta!" Cowboy said as he and Red Flagg jumped out of the homie Smokey's '66 Chevy Impala.

"What's up, dogg," I responded.

"Aye, you seen Lil Loko?" Cowboy asked.

"Naw, why? What's up with Blood?" I asked.

"Blood talking about taking a helicopter ride to Catalina Island," Cowboy said.

"Is that right?" I asked. "That's bool! You know Blood gonna make the streets pay for it."

"Exactly!" Red Flagg responded. "Aye, Spike, you coming back with us to Baldwin Park for the weekend?"

"Yeah. Smokey gonna roll out?" I asked.

"Yeah," Flagg said.

"I'ma try to get Lil Loko to roll, too," Cowboy said. "Blood need a break from these streets. Plus, Granny hasn't seen him in a while."

I already knew that was going to be a hard task to do. It was February 1992, and Lil Loko was getting his paper non-stop! A few moments later, a few more homies started to pull up. They jumped out of their cars and started chopping it up.

I went into the apartment to use the restroom real quick, but as I was going back out, there were about ten pings on the screen door, and I quickly closed the door back. I looked out again, and it was Lil Loko out there with a CO_2 hand automatic BB gun, shooting at people. Blood played too much. After he finally put the gun away, we shared a few bottles of Hennessy while chopping up game and having a few laughs. As it started getting late, everybody started to smash out little by little. Then Cowboy, Flagg, and I rolled out with Smokey headed to Baldwin Park for the weekend.

"Where's Loko?" Flagg asked. "He's gonna meet us out there?"

"Naw," Cowboy said. "He said he wanted to come, but he has something to do in the morning."

"Is that right?" Flagg asked.

"Bang that beat, Smoke!" I said, as Smokey turned up the music and we put a few joints in rotation on our way to Baldwin Park.

The next morning, we were in Flagg and Cowboy's auntie's apartment looking for some breakfast when Cowboy's little sister came from next door.

"Granny said for y'all to come here," she said. We all dropped what we were doing and went next door. Granny was in the living room watching the news. "They killed Darrell, y'all... Darrell is gone."

"Nooo!" We all immediately broke down. We took a look at the "Breaking News" on the TV, and there was a person on a stretcher with a sheet covering him with the right foot hanging out from underneath the sheet. That was confirmation. It was the same brand new Jordan's Lil Loko was wearing the day before. Lil Loko was gone... We couldn't believe it. Cowboy took it real hard, socked the wall, broke his hand, and had to go to the hospital.

We knew from the news that Lil Loko was involved in a robbery, but we had to make it to the hood to get the whole story. When we did make it to the hood, we found out that Lil Loko and two other homies were supposed to be robbing the Fedco on La Cienega and Rodeo Road, but Loko saw that the armored truck was there slipping and decided to rob them. Lil Loko managed to get two bags of money, each containing $500,000, away from the truck. He had two homies waiting in the car, one driving and another in the back seat. Lil Loko then put one of the bags into the window of the front seat in order to free his hand to open the door, but when he did that, the driver took off and left him.

Lil Loko then began running with the second bag in his hand onto the back streets while being chased by the armored truck security. The armored truck security said himself that had the driver let him in the car, they all would've gotten away because they didn't get the license plate numbers or anything. As he chased Lil Loko, the security stated he emptied out his gun, firing after the suspect. Lil Loko was in the process of hopping over a fence of a residence, and the last bullet hit him in the temple.

The driver of the getaway car came back to the hood to try to give an excuse or explain why things turned out the way they did. But, one of the homies knocked him out. After he woke up, he left and never came back for fear of something worse happening to him. The whole hood was in an uproar! It was like a wheel that had lost its hub. A whole lot of unity was lost that day, and the hood wasn't the same since.

Before I grew my dreds, I had done a little studying on them, so I knew a little something about what I was doing. In an article that I read, it stated that in some cases, people cut their dreds in honor or respect for a lost loved one. So, I decided to cut my dreds for Lil Loko. The dreds came off, but not only did my hair change, my whole mentality started to change. The things I did for fun were no longer fun anymore. There was no more tagging. No more housing on the dance floor. Just West Side Fruit Town Brim Gang! The demons that were oppressing me were then ten times stronger, and they tied me up good.

The funeral was packed! There was a movie coming out called "Darrell's World." It was right on time. We had many of the movie's hats with the title on them. Many people put their hat inside the grave along with a large amount of money, different kinds of weed, Hav a tampa cigars, red flags, and more. We all took the shovels from the grave diggers and buried his remains ourselves. It was a very sad day in the Fruits.

Thinking back to our childhood when we made up our own games like, "No Touch Cement" and "The Belt Game," even then he was still just a kid with his life snuffed out way too early at the age of eighteen years old. Life was just beginning. We definitely had enough fun for a whole lifetime. It was just hard to let go when change was forced upon you like that. To tell the truth, I didn't know how to deal with it, so I opened my vent onto the streets and decided I was going to be dedicated to the Brim thang until the wheels fell off!

Ride or die, I became a full-fledged gang member doing the things that members do. The big homie Sike told me to do my dirt by myself. That way, no one could tell on me. I took his advice most of the time, but of course, there were exceptions. I decided to show my dedication and loyalty and went and got my first tattoo at Shopper's World on La Brea and Rodeo Road. I went and got the Gunslinger himself, Yosemite Sam, on my arm. I told the artist to have Sam's fingers throwing up the Brim gang with Brimz written above him. It wasn't told to me, but I found out later that tattoos can be addicting. Shortly after, I went to Harpy's and got my second tattoo, "B.I.P. (Brimin' In Peace) Lil Loko."

Chapter 30

Japan

Yasuda Trust Banking Company wasn't playing when they said, "All expenses paid." They even took all the winners downtown L.A. to take pictures and to get our passports processed. It was on! It was the beginning of April 1992, and we were ready to go to Japan! There were eight winners of the contest: four males (including myself): Deon Reid, Jamaican; Thomas Park, Korean American; Mitchell Hernandez, Hispanic American; along with four females: Rita Haywood, African American; Laura Franks, African American; Nancy Kim, Korean American; and Sarah Nunez, Hispanic American. We were also accompanied by eight adult chaperones to show us around and complete the agenda of the day.

The flight to Tokyo, Japan from LAX lasted thirteen hours, flying across the Pacific Ocean. It was my first time aboard an airplane, and I had no idea of what to expect. As the plane gained altitude, we began to experience some turbulence, which caused the airplane to violently shake up and down and gave the effect of the plane's wings seeming to flap like a bird. No one was panicking as I looked around, so I guessed it was normal. I didn't want to be the first one to shout, "HEY, WHAT'S GOING ON?" Then, everybody would've known it was my first time flying, so I kept it cool.

Once we were through with the turbulence, the flight was pretty smooth, and we were advised we could take off our seatbelts and move about freely. After watching about four movies, having a meal, and taking a nice long nap, we were there. The pilot then advised us to put our seatbelts on to prepare for landing. I braced myself, but it was much smoother than the takeoff had been.

Once off the airplane and into the airport, I have to say, the way the Asians breath smells in the United States, the entire atmosphere smelled that way in Tokyo! Fortunately, as we ate the local foods, we also began to smell the same way, so we adapted. Everyone had their own rooms as we checked into the Hilton in Tokyo. Everything was top of the line. We were treated like royalty! The first night, all of the students were congregated into one hotel room, as we became more acquainted with each other and broke the ice with friendly games of "Truth or Dare" and "Spin the Bottle." It was the weirdest game of the sort that I had ever played, being that the Korean girl only kissed the Korean boy because of "tradition." Yet and still, there was a whole lot of kissing going on.

After the games were over, everyone went to their own rooms, except for me. I was too riled up like a cat without a toy. I ended up in Rita's room, trying to release some of the energy, but all she would allow me to do was just more kissing. I wasn't satisfied, so I left and went to Laura's room, which was more of the same. I couldn't take it any longer, so I scooted back to my room and went to bed in pain. Well, turns out Rita went to school at Audubon Jr. High and was in the ninth grade with Rose. Rita didn't like what I did with Laura, so she later told Rose what I had done, but she never mentioned her part in the situation of course.

The next morning, we all met downstairs for the awesome continental breakfast that was prepared by the hotel for us. Each day, we were taken to meet two or three dignitaries of the government and the Yasuda Trust Headquarters Bank. It was tradition to exchange gifts, so we had been instructed to bring small souvenirs from America to exchange. In return, each dignitary would give each of us 20,000 yen, which is equivalent to $200.00 USD. It was definitely time to go shopping! The money gifts came in handy while attempting to bring home souvenirs for family members. Japan is really expensive!

On another day, we took a trip on the Bullet Train to Sanrio Puroland in the city of Tama New Town, Tokyo. There was an amusement park about an hour away from the hotel, but the Bullet Train, traveling 360 miles per hour, got us there in about fifteen minutes. It was super-fast! Sanrio Puroland is home to the cat Hello Kitty and the frog Kero Kero Keroppi. It was cool. We took many pictures, but the most impressive attraction of the theme park was the food court! The food court was like a living cartoon with a multitude of various dishes and desserts, coming out of the ceiling on a conveyor belt type of roller coaster, dipping and curving all around the room. Whatever dish or dessert you liked, you just grabbed it off the roller coaster. Very creative.

We had more fun on the next day as we visited the local high school. The students gave us a tour of their campus, and we then took school busses to travel to their basketball gym, which was a different location from the school. The Japanese, being so much of a country of germaphobes, even played basketball without shoes on! In the USA, I'll have to admit that I wouldn't be considered a very good basketball player, but in Tokyo, Japan, the students said, "Oh, he's like Michael Jordan!"

"Ha!" I laughed.

I was ballin'. *Maybe I should move to Japan and be a basketball star!* You have to respect the Japanese for their cleanliness. I did not find even one piece of paper on the streets of Tokyo! Not even a cigarette butt, when probably 90% of the adults smoked. They took very good care of their country. Plus, littering fines were strictly enforced. The only area that was considered "the ghetto" was a small section of the city where former students who had dropped out of school lived due to the fact that their families had disowned them for doing so. Education was top priority in the Japanese family.

That night, after we came from a nice restaurant where we ate deep fried seahorses, we returned to the hotel to find Kiyoko, one of the students from the high school, waiting for us.

"Kiyoko!" we all shouted.

"What are you doing here?" Deon asked her.

"Yeah, have you been waiting a long time?" Laura asked.

"No, I just got here," Kiyoko said. "I came to have fun with you guys!"

We took Kiyoko to Rita's room. She was carrying a big bag on her shoulder.

"What's in that bag?" I asked.

"Have you guys ever had Saki?" Kiyoko asked.

"No," we all responded.

"Well, you're going to have some today!" she said, taking a portable burner out of her bag with a small pot, individual shot glasses, and a large bottle of Saki. She proceeded to heat up the Saki while we watched, as if she was a brand new infomercial on television. "This is some of the best Saki. You guys have to try it while you are here in Japan." Once the Saki was warm, Kiyoko poured each of us a shot. I took a sip of mine and was cool on it. It tasted like rubbing alcohol.

"What else you got in that bag, Kiyoko?" I asked.

"My clothes," she said. "I'm going to sneak you guys out tonight and take you dancing!"

"How are you gonna do that?" Mitchell asked.

"I have my dad's Mercedes Benz downstairs," Kiyoko said.

"Cool!" I said. "As long as I get to drive!"

"If you know how to drive, I'll let you drive," Kiyoko said.

"Yes, I do," I said. "Get dressed, and I'll show you."

Kiyoko went into the bathroom and changed out of her private school uniform and into a superstar model! She was beautiful!

"Hey, what did you do with Kiyoko?" I asked.

"Ha! Ha!" Everybody laughed.

"If that's your way of telling me that I'm pretty, then thanks," Kiyoko smiled.

"Yeah, you know I have to switch it up," I said. "I'm pretty sure everyone tells you that you're pretty."

"No, they don't," she said as we walked out to the elevators. "Only my dad."

We made it to the parking lot, and sure enough, she had a black Benz waiting with the steering wheel on the right side of the car. *This is going to be fun, driving on the left side of the highway,* I thought. Kiyoko gave me the keys like she had been knowing me for years, and we all jumped in. Kiyoko and I were fine up front, but everybody else was in the backseat sitting on each other's laps.

"Is everybody in?" I asked.

"Yes, let's go," they said.

I drove out of the parking lot, following Kiyoko's directions. It seemed weird at first, driving on the right side of the car on the left side of the street, but I got used to it real quick. I wasn't trying to crash in Japan. Plus, I had given my word that I could drive. Left or right, I had to make it happen. Kiyoko had me turn into a carport where the nightclub was supposed to be. We had made it without incident.

"What about our IDs?" Laura asked.

"Oh, they don't ask for IDs here," Kiyoko said. "You have to be twenty years old, but nobody follows the rules."

"Cool," we said.

"There's a different genre of music on each floor," Kiyoko said, as we walked into the sky rise building. "Which floor do you guys want to go to first?"

"Hip Hop," all the dudes spoke up.

"Okay. Hip Hop it is," Kiyoko said.

We stayed on the Hip Hop floor for a while until the girls wanted to go to the R&B floor. That's when getting off the elevator, we ran straight into our chaperones, who were getting on the elevator!

"Heyyy! What are you guys doing here?" We all said the same thing to each other. They were cool though. They didn't send us back to the hotel or anything like that. We all enjoyed the night and had a good time dancing.

There was much fun in Japan! I don't want to say that it was a once in a lifetime opportunity because I may go back in this lifetime. It was definitely a blessing to be able to go.

The flight back to Los Angeles, California was only eleven hours, as we flew against the world turning. We all said our goodbyes and exchanged information to keep in touch as we prepared to enter back into our own individual realities. We didn't realize it yet, but the experience we shared had changed our lives a little bit. Being on the other side of the Earth made me broaden my horizons. There was not a goal that was too big to reach. The impossible had just become possible!

Chapter 31
Banged Out

About two weeks after returning from Japan, Rodney King, an African American who fell victim to police brutality back in March of 1991, awaited the verdict of the LAPD officers involved. The brutal beating was caught on video tape, so the rest of Los Angeles waited along with Rodney expecting justice to be served. On April 29, 1992, the verdict was in- not guilty.

The entire city went into an uproar beginning at the intersection of Florence Avenue and Normandie Boulevard, with the near fatal beating of a white truck driver named Reginald Denny. Seeing the scene unfold on the news was as if a green light went on for everyone else to let the rioting begin! The L.A. Riots lasted over five days, with over 2,000 people injured and leaving over fifty dead. The city was up in smoke with over 1,000 fires.

Yes, I was also involved in the riots, but to what extent is not important. There were too many people telling on each other then and still are today. One young man came to school bragging about the things he and his family had accumulated, and the very same day, he was placed into custody on school grounds by police officers.

The point of mentioning the riots is to show that life still happens no matter your status, race, skin color, or educational background. After everything was burned down and we couldn't even go to the corner store because it wasn't there anymore, almost everybody had to use the bartering system. We had to find out who in the neighborhood had what we needed. Some may have had to exchange some toothpaste for a roll of toilet paper. Maybe not literally, but you get the idea. Under that thick cloud of smoke, everyone was in the same position.

Despite all the drama, Joseph Jr. and Malik were at the pep rally hollering out "'92!" as they prepared to graduate in June. They were passing the torch to me, and I had to carry it with the strength of my own for two more years. It shouldn't have been too hard given they had done a good job preparing me. The only thing was I had no one to pass the torch to. My kid sisters, Stephanie and Ashley, were five and six years younger than I was.

Summertime was approaching fast, and I was all the way wrapped up in the streets. Instead of getting a summer job like I usually did, I was already selling crack cocaine, staying out sometimes all night, especially at the beginning of the month when the smokers got paid. If there was a drought with cocaine coming to hit the streets, the prices doubled and tripled for the size of the rock. They say fast money doesn't last, and they were right. As soon as I would make money, something would come up that would take away the profit. Selling crack was just not my path to success, but it took me a few years to finally realize it. As long as I had my re-up, I could keep money in my pocket while I was out in the streets, but I made more money usually in the dice game gambling.

I was always into something, hanging with my road doggs, the Belizean Baby NoGood or Lil KB, doing what gang members do. Lil T-Bone was the first of the Tiny Gangstas to get a car after the riots and then Lil D-Mack. Transportation and a gun changed your status of living in L.A. in a major way. I didn't have my own car yet, but because I had my driver's license, smokers would let me rent their cars for crack. That was my usual, aside from the occasional G-Ride. It was safer to be mobile in the streets, especially after the homies roll through with the heads up that the Crips just got laid down. Wartime was no joke in the hood! "Watch your back and not your sack," is what the OGs told me.

In the end of '92, I caught my first dope case and went to juvenile hall. As I was processed in and sent to my unit, I ran into the homeboy Deen from the Belizean Blood Posse. He was in the same unit that I was placed in, Unit AB on the B side. He and the other inmates were finishing their lunches in the day room as I was brought inside. I sat over against the wall by the window, and Dean came over after he was done cleaning up.

"What's up, Spike?" Dean shook my hand.

"What's up, Blood?" I responded. "What's brackin' with you? You alright?"

"Yeah, I been in here about a month," Deen said. "What about you? You straight?"

"Yeah, I'm straight," I said. "What's up with these dudes in here? Where they from?" There was about five blacks and three Hispanics sitting at the tables.

"I don't know, but that dude right there is from Barlem," Deen said, pointing at one of the Black dudes that was about my height.

"Is that right?" I asked. "I'm gonna take off on him tomorrow during line movement."

"Okay. I get out tomorrow," Deen said.

"Alright," I said.

It was mandatory that I get him. I had heard stories about Lil Loko running across the field just to take off on a Harlem Crip. After the staff shut the program down for the evening, they put me in a two-man cell with one of the Hispanics, and I jumped straight on my push-ups.

The next morning, the staff lined us up for school. I noticed Deen was already gone. The staff told me I had to take an assessment test before they could place me in a class. I took the test while the rest of the unit separated into other classrooms. After the test was over, we all had to fall back in line for movement. Then, what do you know? They lined the dude up from Harlem right behind me. It was on! Right before the line moved, I turned around and gave him a three-piece combo! Bing! Bing! Bing! We locked up for a moment until the staff pulled us apart.

"What that Fruit Town Brim like?" I mad dogged him.

As I turned around to see the rest of the unit, all of the blacks were throwing up Harlem, hollering it out, and disrespecting my hood! I knew it was really on then! I was the only Blood in a unit with five of my worse enemies. The staff let me off with a warning that the next time, I would go to the box, which was solitary confinement.

The next day, another dude from Harlem tried to get a pencil to stab me in the classroom before the teacher called the staff in to break it up. There was a whole lot of activity going on. A few of the dudes ended up getting transferred or maybe they went home. I didn't know, but one day another dude from Harlem came down from Youth Authority in order to go to court. He had to be in his early twenties on swoll.

He would ask to go to the restroom, and on his way there and back, he'd be hollering out Harlem Crip, so that I could hear it in my cell. I jumped on my pushups! I knew I would have to fight the big dude, so I made myself stronger. I remembered what the homies said as they shared their war stories in the hood. They said to take off fighting as soon as someone disrespects you. It didn't matter what size they were. Win, lose, or draw, make sure you get down! I also knew from Uncle James that I had to fight hard. It was a life and death situation in there, and nobody showed any mercy.

Fortunately, the next day, I went to court, and the judge released me with three years summary probation. I went home to my comfortable bed at peace that I didn't have to fight that silverback gorilla. My mother had to check me back into Dorsey, but I received my same classes, so I was straight. I was fresh out from my first trip to "gladiator school" with two weeks in the Halls, and I did pretty good. Had to admit, I was kind of proud of myself with about ten more pounds of muscle and a few more fighting skills. I didn't know that I was shining so much until I went to the hood after school and the homie K-Luv pulled up on me.

"What's up, Blood?" he said. "You been to the Hall; now you got your chest poking out, huh?"

"Ha ha!" We both laughed.

It was 1993, when I got the news we were moving out of the hood. It was bittersweet because I didn't want to move out of the hood, but we were moving twenty blocks away into a house. Once we had moved, I was still in the hood every chance I got. Malik started coming over to the new house with his first car, a Cutlass Oldsmobile. Then, he came with another car, a small Toyota. Then another car, and I asked, "Man! Where are you getting all of these cars?"

"We Bubbling, homie!" Malik said. "I be with Scotty on the east side selling weed in the Swans. We got a tight crew!"

"That sounds shady, dogg," I said. "You be careful over there."

"Oh, we straight," Malik said. "Don't even trip. The spot is rolling!"

I left the issue alone, but I knew it wasn't cool. The Swans was a Blood gang on the east side of L.A., and Scotty was someone we had gone to elementary and junior high school with. Scotty was cool, but the only problem was he was a Harlem Crip, and all of his crew were Harlems. I knew the Swans were not going for that in their hood. Plus, Malik had never been a gang member, so he didn't fully weigh the politics and consequences of it all. He just saw all the money.

The hood was calling! It was time for me to hit the streets myself and get my grind going. It was the first of the month, and I was planning on staying out all weekend to get my money. I hit the block with the ten toes down with my rocks already individually wrapped in plastic. That time, if the police rolled up, I could toss them in my mouth and swallow them. Couldn't afford to get caught slipping. Before the block started popping, I jumped in the car with Lil D-Mack to go and get the blunts and beers from the store.

As I walked past the video rental store, I noticed a short bowlegged girl inside, checking out the movie cases. She was a little skinny thang with a nice shape. My variety of girls didn't include a skinny one. It was time to try something new. I approached her, and she told me her name was Kara. She gave me her number, and I later found out I had gone to elementary school with her brothers. So, we hit it off, and I got her to the house a few times to play. She was cool, but I loved the streets more.

One night, I had come home from a long day in the hood and was about to eat something and then lay it down when the phone rang.

"Hello?" I answered.

"Ray?" It was Malik's mother. "THEY KILLED MALIK!" She broke down.

"NOOOOO!" I broke down with her.

A few days later, Scotty ended up turning himself in to the police, admitting he made a deal with the Swans to set up his own crew. They were four deep in a tow truck, transporting a lowrider to the shop. When the shooter caught them at a red light and began to unload, Scotty slipped out of the truck and gave his boys up as prey. Scotty ended up getting life in prison. Malik was one of a very few that I could call my friend. That was another life gone too soon, not able to even see twenty years old. I was growing tired of collecting the obituaries of my friends.

Late night in the hood on the grind with dirt bikes were Belizean Baby NoGood from the set, Nutty Boy from the Jungles' Black Pee Stones, Trigger Ru from the East Side Blood Stone 30s Piru Gang, and me on a hood patrol mission. It was a good night. We had a pocket full of money after shutting down the Walton Block. We pushed through to the 20s on the dirt bikes because Nutty Boy wanted to get a wet stick of PCP; then, we pushed back to the hood. We posted up on 36th Street upstairs in an empty apartment with a view out the back bedroom window that overlooked Jefferson Boulevard.

"Fire it up, Blood!" Trigger Ru said.

"If this is the same batch, it should be bomb," Nutty Boy said while pulling out the stick. I lit up a weed joint while he did his thing. Those were my gangstas. A lot of homies hit the wet every now and then, especially after Lil Loko died, but I had never hit it before.

"Erk, you should hit the sherm stick for Lil Loko!" Baby NoGood said.

"I don't see what's the big deal," I said. "How come y'all like this stuff so much?" I took the stick from his hand and gave him the joint. I hit it two times and passed it like it was a joint and waited for the affect. It didn't really feel any different, but I liked the taste of the chemical smoke. "I don't feel nothing, Blood," I said to Nutty Boy. "It must not be a good batch like you thought."

"Look, Blood!" Baby NoGood said, pointing out the window to a black cloud of smoke that looked to be coming from Walton on the north side of Jefferson Boulevard.

"Something on fire, on the B!" Trigger Ru said.

"Come on. Let's go over there," I said.

We all jumped on the dirt bikes and raced over to the scene. Sure enough, the homie Denny Ray was over there, watching the fire department put out his car.

"What's up, Ray!" I asked as we rolled up on the bikes. "You alright?"

"Yeah, Blood," Denny Ray said. "Some smoker came and said you did it, but I know better than that."

"Is that right?" I responded in disbelief. It was good that he knew my character and that I wouldn't do him like that. Setting the big homie's car on fire and then rolling up on him at the scene would have been pretty crazy or better yet, stupid. That could have cost me my life. Plus, Denny Ray already had an idea of who had done the deed.

Later, when I was in the hood, I found myself hitting the sherm stick whenever the homies had it around. Then, before I knew it, I was buying my own. The drug started to pull all kinds of anger out of me and put it on my sleeve. It would heighten all senses and eliminate all stress. Despite the occasional zombie-like state depending on the batch, I liked it. I even smoked it at school a few times. I didn't know it, but PCP (phencyclidine) was slowly changing my life.

A smoker dude came to the hood with a stick shift Datsun and wanted to rent it to me for some crack. I had never driven a stick shift, but I'd heard about it, and it didn't seem like it would be hard, so I took him up on his offer. To prevent him from changing his mind, in case I didn't shift gears correctly, I waited until he walked off the block before I jumped in the car.

Once he bent the corner, I jumped in the car and thought of all of the instructions people had told me concerning driving a stick shift. First, I remembered I had to start the car with the clutch in, and there was no park gear, only the emergency brake held the car still. *Okay, so far, so good.* Once the car was in gear, I remembered someone saying to ease off the clutch while slowly pressing the gas at the same time.

Cool, I started rolling to the corner of 37th Place and Catalina and turned north on Catalina. Someone else had told me to wait and listen to the engine to tell if it's time to shift the gears. The engine revved, and I shifted to second gear and then to third, and I was rolling! I knew how to drive a stick shift in a matter of minutes. The next day, I drove the car to school and parked it behind the auto mechanics building on campus. That was my spot whenever I brought a G-Ride to school.

Lunchtime came around, and I ran into the homie CK-Bomb from the Pueblos.

"What's up, Spike?" He shook my hand. "How you, B?"

"I'm brimtaining," I said. "West brackin'?"

"You know the sun rose in the east this morning, right?" he responded.

"Yeah, but last night, it turned red on the west!" I jabbed back, and we both laughed.

"Look what I got." CK-Bomb opened the backpack that he was carrying and showed me a nice black .32 automatic handgun.

"That's nice," I said. "That's real nice."

"On point, huh?" He closed the backpack again.

"Yeah, aye let me hold it for you. I'll bring it back Monday," I said.

"Alright, where you gonna put it?" he asked.

"Come with me, and put it in my locker," I said. "I got a backpack in there."

We put the gun in the locker and went to our next class. I already had plans going through my head of what I was going to do with the gun. First, I was going to make a trip up to Crenshaw High School to visit Rose after school. I knew she would be waiting for her mother to pick her up like she used to do at Audubon. I had only seen her once since the incident at her house with her parents, but in my mind, she was still my girl. Reality hadn't hit that maybe she had another boyfriend already.

As soon as school let out, I jumped in the Datsun with the .32 on my lap and headed on over to see Rose. Crenshaw High was known to be an all Crips school, the Rollin 60s to be exact. But, I wasn't going to be up there slipping either, nor was I doing any playing. I rolled down Crenshaw Boulevard and was almost to the school when a police car pulled up next to me at a red light! There was a female cop in the passenger seat and a male driver. Immediately, I was wondering, *Can she see this gun on my lap?* I tried not to look suspicious. When the light turned green, I turned down the backstreet, and the cops followed me and turned on their lights. Man! I put the gun under the seat and pulled over.

"Driver, step out of the vehicle," the female officer said with her hand on her gun. She must've seen the gun. I stepped out of the vehicle with my hands on my head. I was immediately placed in handcuffs and seated on the curb, while she searched the car.

"Do you have license and registration for this car?" the male office asked.

"Yes," I said. "My license is in my back pocket, and the registration is in the glove box in the car."

Sure enough, his partner came back with the .32 in her hand, and I was on my way to the police station. Because the car was registered and I had a driver's license, they didn't impound the car. The gun must've come back clean because I was able to call my mother to come and pick me up because I was a juvenile.

"You need to stay out of trouble," my mother said, as we walked out the station and to her car.

"Yeah, I know," I said. "I need you to take me to the car I was driving. They left it on the street." I directed her back to the car and drove it home as my mother followed me. She pulled up alongside of me as I parked.

"Man! You were driving that stick shift like it was an automatic!" she said. "Who taught you how to drive a stick?"

"I taught myself yesterday," I said. She was surprised because she had tried to learn how to drive a stick shift but didn't quite get the hang of it. For me, it was second nature.

January 8, 1994, the block was rolling since the first and hadn't stopped yet! I was trying to get it, at least all that I could because I was planning on taking a break on the next day to celebrate my birthday. That night, I had posted up on the Walton block with Baby NoGood and a few other homies. I was sitting on the stairs halfway up when somebody yelled, "ONE TIME!" Then, everybody broke out running in different directions to escape the police. Because I was halfway up the stairs, I ran to the top. I had run out of plastic earlier in the day, so I had my dope wrapped in a paper bag. I quickly threw the drugs on the roof of the apartment building and started knocking on doors to see if someone would let me in, but no chance.

"Put your hands up and walk down the stairs!" one of the police officers shouted, as they flashed their bright lights on me. I walked down and was told to put my hands on the hood of the police car. More cars started to pull up, and they searched the area. One of the officers ended up climbing on the roof of the apartment building, and I took a deep breath, hoping he didn't find what I had thrown up there. I stood there as the officer ran my name through their computers. The other officer came down off the roof and walked towards the rest of the officers with my drugs held high in his hand and smiling. They went over my information in the computer and circled around me singing "Happy Birthday." They were happy that I was about to spend my birthday in jail. I was hot!

I was taken to the Southwest Police Station and placed in a cell. The officers weren't satisfied with their taunting. They waited until midnight, as I turned eighteen years old, to book me as an adult. So, instead of juvenile hall, I was going to the county jail in the morning. I didn't care anymore. I started thinking of which homies I would see in the Blood Module. I knew Sugar Bear and Red Cap were in there still fighting their case, but I didn't know who else.

The next morning, they called me out to line up with a bunch of other dudes to put on a chain of handcuffs, linking us together by two's to head to the courthouse. They loaded us up on a prison bus that everyone kept calling 'the grey goose." As we got to the courthouse, we were unloaded off the bus and into the building, and the cuffs were taken off. Then, we were led through a hallway and stopped.

"Alright, listen up!" one of the correctional officers shouted. "We're going to be separating the Crips from the Bloods to go into separate holding tanks! I'm going to need all of you to step closely to the wall and put your nose against the wall!" No problem. We all stepped to the wall and followed the directions, except for one dude who just stood in the middle of the hallway.

"Sir, did I make myself clear?" the officer shouted again, "Step to the wall and put your nose against the wall!"

"I ain't putting my nose against NOTHING!" the guy shouted. "You want to separate me? Separate me from where I stand. I'm a MAN! You talk to your kids like that!"

"I'm going to need some assistance in H2 ASAP!" The officer made a call on his radio. In less than half a minute, there were four other officers surrounding the man. They all rushed him at once, slamming him against the wall and giving him punching bag style body blows.

"GET AGAINST THE WALL!" they shouted.

After the smoke cleared, the man stood against the wall, trying to catch his breath with his face bleeding.

"Okay," the officer continued. "Let me have all the Bloods take two steps backward. I was the only one that stepped back. They placed me in a holding tank with two other Bloods, and I noticed one was Firebug from 62 Brim.

"Spike, what's up, Blood?" Firebug shouted as we shook hands. "You going to the Module?"

"Yeah," I said. "You done gained a little weight up in here, huh?"

"Blood! I just beat my murder case! I'm going home." He was grinning from ear to ear.

"Is that right?" I responded. "Oh. Okay. Congratulations!"

"Yeah, man!" he said. "I'm out of here."

A few minutes later, after I carved the hood in the wall with my fingernail, my name was called for court.

"Alright, Blood! Be up!" I shook Firebug's hand again, as I walked out the door.

"Alright, Blood!" Firebug said.

Inside the courtroom, the judge grabbed my file and read over my case. He looked closely at the procedures the officers had taken. All I could do was wait patiently knowing I was already on three years summary probation for another dope case. I just wanted to know how much time I was getting. Then, the judge started to speak to the arresting officers who sat in front of him.

"You waited until 12:00 midnight to book this young man as an adult?" the judge began. "This young man was supposed to go back to juvenile hall. Case dismissed."

My eyes got as big as golf balls! I couldn't believe what I had just heard! My birthday saved the day! I got up out of there as quickly as I could!

I had been growing out my hair, so I wanted to see if it was long enough to be braided. There was a girl I was dealing with at school who was called Lady, who acted as though she really liked me. Maybe, she just liked Bloods because her brothers were Bloods. I didn't know. If she really cared, she would braid my hair. So, I brought her to the hood to figure it out. Turns out, my hair could be braided, but I still didn't know if she cared. She was still on trial.

I was focused on getting some money together in order to buy a Monte Carlo, sitting on laces, that the homie Black from Swans was trying to sell. I was about to bust fresh for the summer! Plus, G-Nutt was coming home from the penitentiary in a couple of months after doing four years. *We about to turn Los Angeles upside down!*

Sure enough, two months rolled around real quick. It was already spring time.

"Y'all better make room for Jeffery in that room," my mother said. "He should be coming home tomorrow."

"He's gonna be alright," Joseph Jr. said.

The next day, G-Nutt came home on swoll with the long G-Braids. I was waiting to hear all the new raps he'd written while he was locked up. G-Nutt was always rapping since we were kids, so I knew he had gotten better at it. He came home and started handling his business immediately. A couple days later, he went and bought a clean '86 Buick Regal and put the major beat in it. I was also ready to pick up my car. I had it towed to a shop to put a V8 engine in it that I bought from the homie Lobo. It was ready for pick up, money green on laces! It was on! We were tearing up the streets! Out doing what members do. Much love to the homies from Van Ness Gangstas that came through for us when we needed it! Big CK Moe, D-Loko-B, and Mr. B., even the homegirl, Tinkerbell. Good looking out!

The night of the twelfth grade prom, I didn't attend due to the fact that I blew my head gaskets on the freeway a couple of weeks earlier while racing with Lil KB, trying to take some girls to the beach. I was gonna save some money to fix the car. While my classmates were dancing the night away, I was in the middle of a gang war and got shot in the leg. G-Nutt didn't make it any better by scaring my mother half to death over the phone, talking about, "Hello? Have you heard from Ray?" G-Nutt said.

"No, what happened?" Moms asked.

"You didn't hear what happened?" G-Nutt said.

"NO! WHAT HAPPENED, BOY?" Moms was frantic.

"HE GOT SHOT!" This dude…

"OH, MY GOODNESS!" She was distraught.

She came and picked me up from the hospital the same night. Thank God, the bullet went straight through. It had only been a flesh wound. The next day, I had to go to the other homeboy's funeral on crutches. Somebody had killed Nutty Boy from the Jungles... Word on the street was some Crip had pulled up next to his car and started bangin' on him. Nutty Boy banged back, and the Crip shot him. That happened on May 29, 1994. It wasn't too long after that G-Nutt got pulled over by the police and got caught with a gun, which sent him back to the pen. The summer was just getting started, and we had already lived fast enough for the whole year with no breaks. So much activity but no need to speak of it all.

Chapter 32
Jackson State University- College Days

It was getting about time for me to calm down and get ready to leave for college. I had been accepted to attend a college down south for the Black college experience. With everything that was going on in L.A., I almost forgot I was going. I could have easily run the streets clean through the fall. Self-motivation was a must because the streets were constantly calling my name.

Before I left, I had to go and visit Lady and have her mother pray for me. Mrs. Jackson had a good relationship with God, and I knew she could pray a good prayer for me as I left for college.

"Hello, Deacon Ray," Mrs. Jackson greeted me as she opened the front door. She would always call me a deacon from the first time I met her. She said I would be a deacon in the church. Her daughter Lady and I just shined it on, figuring Moms just had wishful thinking because we all knew I was lost in the streets. I eventually began to get comfortable with her calling me Deacon all the time. It became normal.

"How are you doing, Mrs. Jackson?" I responded as I went inside.

"I'm blessed," she said. "Lady, told me you were about to leave for college."

"Yes," I said.

"Well, you know we got to pray, right?" she asked.

"Yes, ma'am. I was hoping we did," I said.

We three held hands as she began to say a powerful prayer over my life, pleading the blood of Jesus. The first time she prayed that way, I did not understand what pleading the blood of Jesus meant. No one had ever prayed for me that way. The first person that came to mind that went to church every Sunday was Rose, but even after she explained it to me, I was probably more confused than before I called her. She was talking about being protected by Jesus' salvation power that came by the work of the cross.

"Okay. But if He died for me and rose again, why do I need to be covered by His blood over and over again?" I asked.

"Because even though you accepted Christ as a child into your heart, you are now out of God's will because you are living in sin," Rose said. "You need to repent and ask for forgiveness, turning away from the bad things in your life. Then, the blood of Jesus keeps you and protects you from demonic attack by God's grace until you willfully sin again. Then, you'll need to repent again."

"Um, okay. I'll talk to you later," I said. She was breaking it down, but it wasn't clicking in my head. I needed understanding.

It came time to go and receive part of my scholarship from Yasuda Trust Banking Co. They were going to be giving me $500 per semester, so I used part of it for my plane ticket to Mississippi. My buddy Ben said he was going down there as well to spend time with his mother and siblings until Christmas, so we could hang out sometimes. Everything was going according to plan. As I stepped out of the airport in Jackson, the humidity hit me like a blanket. I had never been in that kind of weather before. It took some getting used to. The campus was nice. Ironically, it was at the end of Lynch Street. As time went on, I found it wasn't irony at all. It was their reality. I had stepped into a time warp is how is seemed.

I got in, registered, and received my dorm room where I met my roommate, Victor from Marrero, Louisiana, which was considered a suburban area of New Orleans. He was cool until he got around other people. That's when he tried to portray to be someone he was wasn't, being boastful and standoffish, but one on one, he was really friendly. I met a bunch of other guys also, some from Chicago, South Carolina, Philly, and Mississippi, but those that became my flock were mostly from the west coast.

Two of my main boys were Jerry and Ron from Las Vegas, Nevada. We kept each other from adapting to that Southern drawl by keeping that west coast slang going. When I first got there, I asked a guy where the store was, and I had to get someone to translate southern English into Standard English. The accents were thick! Also, when I first got there, I called home and found out that my mother's stepmom, the woman I knew as Grandmama, had passed away from a stroke. My mother sent me an obituary in the mail.

My classes weren't too hard. I just had to stay focused and discipline myself to study and do my homework. Oh yeah, college was a constant party! From get-togethers in the dorms to campus dances to frat parties to large dice games of "4, 5, 6" to college football games, it was real easy to toss the textbook to the side. Football games were the best! At a Black college football game, the halftime marching band show was the main event! JSU being number one in the SWAC with The Sonic Boom of the south always rocked the house! Where the ladies, oh, the ladies where always on point! When Ben got there, he even took me to some high school games, and I spent Thanksgiving with him and his family.

One day on the way back from IHOP with the west coast crew, my roommate was talking crazy in the car like he was the boss of everybody. I got tired of his mouth and told him to wait until we got back to campus, and I was going to put hands on him. He thought I was playing... We got back to the dorms, and I let him come into the hallway before I socked him up real good. After that, I moved upstairs with Jerry and Ron from Las Vegas. Ben and his brother came to the campus to make sure everything was all right. He wanted to smash him, but I told him that wasn't necessary.

As the end of the year drew closer, I ended up contacting Rose. She began to tell me she had a daughter by a guy she had known for a moment, but he wasn't involved in her life any longer. When I went home for the holidays, I spent Christmas with her. She later called me and said she didn't want to continue to build our relationship back again because I no longer loved her with the same affection I used to. She was right. It wasn't the same anymore. Life had happened, and time went by. It was time to turn the page and move on.

During the second semester, I got a little wiser. I saved some of my money by catching the Greyhound bus to Mississippi that time. It took two days to get there though, with a whole day just driving across Texas. Once I got back to campus, I got a call from my mother telling me Lil KB was in a car accident and had broken nearly every bone in his skull by going through the windshield. He was in the hospital, and the doctors were taking precautions, so his brain didn't swell.

"Okay, but he's going to be alright, right?" I asked. "Is he going to be okay?"

"Yeah, son," she said sadly. "He's going to be okay. Don't worry."

"Alright, keep me posted," I said. "Love you, bye." I didn't want to stress out about it. That was my Dogg through thick and thin! So, I didn't want to accept what was happening. A few days went by, and my mother called again.

"Ray, Lil KB is gone," she said. "He's gone, Ray."

"NOOOO!" I lost all composure and wept like a baby. Too many friends gone too soon. It had gotten to the point where I sat back and wondered, *Who's next? Will it be me?* One day, my mother asked me very casually what I wanted to wear at my funeral, as though it was inevitable that she was going to bury me. Funerals had become so common in our lives that we were desensitized. Parents are not supposed to bury their children. Children are supposed to bury their parents at a nice old age. Unfortunately, that is not the norm in today's society, but I was getting tired of it.

I decided to go out to a club and hang out with my roommates and a few others to take my mind off everything. The club was jumping. They had been handing out flyers around campus to promote the night's event, so the college crowd was heavy. I was trying to get as faded as I could be off their watered-down drinks. I noticed their security were actually off-duty police officers. The drinks started to catch up with me, both in my bladder and in my brain. As I made my way to the restroom, two black cops came in after me. I used it and went to wash my hands, while one of the officers observed me spitting in the sink.

"You do that at home?" the officer shouted. That dude didn't have anything better to do, but come and bother me. I was already upset and almost drunk.

So, I responded, "Yeah, I do that at home!"

"You just bought yourself a ticket up out of here," he said.

The two officers escorted me outside to the front of the club, as the other cop who hadn't said anything yet started to tell me, "Just stay out here about fifteen minutes until things calm down, and then, you can come back inside," he said.

That was nonsense, but they had the control, so I had to follow their instructions. I had my non-filtered Camel cigarettes in my pocket, so I figured it would take me about fifteen minutes to smoke one, so I did before going back inside and posting up with my roommates. All of a sudden, the same cops came with their flashlights in my face shouting, "Didn't I tell you that you weren't allowed in here?"

They grabbed me and dragged me outside where they slammed me on the ground and handcuffed me. Then, they proceeded to body slam me with handcuffs on a few times onto the ground. I was thrown into the back of a patrol car where I received more blows to the face on the way to the police station. At the station, they took all my property, put it in a bag, and placed me in a holding tank with about thirty other dudes who were arguing over five burlap blankets. I found a spot on the concrete bench along the wall and sat down. I was transformed and lumped up, looking like the Elephant Man! All I could do was try to nurse my wounds the best way I could.

"Aye, where you from?" one of the younger dudes asked me.

"I'm from L.A.," I said.

"You from L.A.?" He got excited.

"Aye, man! Leave him alone," said one of the older dudes. "Can't you see he's already beat up?"

The next day, I started banging on the door to ask the guard why I was there, what I was being charged with, and when I was supposed to go to court. He told me to fill out a request form that he slid through the slot in the door and said they would get to me in the order it was received. I asked every day if I was being reviewed, but no information was given to me, day after day. In the mornings, they gave us two boiled eggs, and we drank water from the sink. Every day at lunchtime, we received a grated cheese sandwich and drank the water out of the sink. Then, dinner was a frozen burrito, and we drank the water out of the sink. I had a cassette tape in my property of Outcast's record "SouthernPlayalisticadillacmuzik" that I kept singing in my head. One week, two weeks, three weeks. I spent almost all of January 1995, in a holding tank with about thirty dudes, arguing over five burlap blankets. Until one day, my name was called, and I was told that I made bail.

"Bail? What bail? I didn't even know I had a bail!" I said.

I was released with my property and nothing else. No paperwork, no court date, no nothing. They just left me in there to heal. Had I not been bailed out, it's no telling how long I would've been in there.

Nevertheless, I was definitely glad to be leaving. As I got into the car with Jerry and Ron, they were telling me how they took up a collection around campus to bail me out. I was greatly appreciative! Then, I handed Jerry the Outcast tape that I had in my property.

"Man, put that in the tape deck," I said.

Somehow, I managed to resume my classes and tried to catch up with the assignments. The campus gave me a job in the cafeteria washing dishes, but they fired me for being late too many times. Then, I got a job at Shoney's Restaurant, and I was getting dropped off by Jerry until one day he had a class to attend when it was time for me to go to work, so I started walking. By the time I got there, I tried to explain to the boss, but he simply replied, "It's okay. You people are always late. You're fired." The walk back to campus was even longer.

My roommates took a ride downtown one day and quickly headed back to campus because they said they actually saw the Ku Klux Klan marching with sheets on, holding picket signs with Buckwheat's picture on them with his face whacked out. They weren't playing in Mississippi, and I was getting home sick real fast.

Well, summer time came right on time, and I immediately went back to what I thought was normal: selling crack, smoking sherm, and gangbanging. However, there were a couple of things that had changed since I left. No one shared a 40oz. beer any more. Instead, everybody had their own individual tall cans. I missed the transition, but I was curious how it had happened. The second thing was I found out that my other road dogg, Baby NoGood had turned 20s while he was in jail. That definitely changed my normality.

I started serving in the dope spot with the homie on Walton and smoking way too much sherm. I would buy a stick and put it into my pack of cigarettes, and it would light up the entire pack of cigarettes. So every day, I was smoking at least twenty sticks of PCP! Before I knew it, I was walking around like a zombie. Then, I had a nightmare that I'll never forget of Jack Nicholson, as he was in the movie "Shining," chasing me down Jefferson Boulevard trying to kill me. The homies threw a party, and I thought it was to lure me there in order to kill me. I was paranoid!

I went home and got on top of my mother's roof. She came outside and asked what I was doing up there, and I told her I was looking for my keys. I jumped down and hopped the back fence, running through the alley to find myself sitting in the back of a Hispanic church on Normandie. I didn't know what they were saying, but I felt safe. Yet and still, I continued to smoke sherm and run the streets. Before I left back to college, I got TGB tatted on my back for the Tiny Gangsta Brim generation, but I was high as a kite.

Upon returning to school, my double life began to catch up to me. There was entirely too much PCP in my system to jump back into the books and quit cold turkey. Jerry saw me and started laughing at my pitiful sight. I had lost about thirty pounds and was looking just like the smokers I was selling crack to. He said Rod had transferred to UNLV. He had gotten tired of the South. We were then sophomores and had to move out of the freshmen dorms and into the upperclassmen dorms, but I wasn't feeling social at all. I was going through withdrawals and needed help, but I didn't know where to turn.

One of my professors from the year before, a young chocolate coal black beautiful sister pulled up in her car alongside me, as I was walking to class and told me if I needed to talk to anyone I could come down the street to her office, but I never went. Pride and shame kept me from it. I must've looked awful! No way! I couldn't tell her my issues. I heard a rapper say, "If you are feeling down, read Proverbs."

So, I started reading Proverbs in the Bible, which didn't help too much because I didn't understand the Bible. I began to get a misconception of the Word of God and actually started to think that

that just maybe, I was Jesus. Maybe, I was Christ returning to the world and the people were going to kill me again. Maybe, that's why I was going through that. I began to walk around campus telling people. "Jesus loves you." My rationale told me that was my destiny. I was losing it. I didn't really know what a nervous breakdown was, but that was probably it.

After I finally came back down to Earth and realized I wasn't Jesus after all, I started to think more clearly and focus back on my classes. The PCP was out of my system, and my weight started to pick back up. That was a blessing. There was one friend who remained my friend through it all and never changed up. That was Michael from Philadelphia or Philly Mike for short. He actually helped me stay grounded by walking and talking with me around campus. I appreciated that.

Chapter 33
Married Life

I soon decided that I no longer wanted to be far away from home, so I put in a transfer to USC. Unfortunately, JSU wouldn't release my transcripts until my student loan was paid off. They were trying to keep me out there with minimal resources. So, after I went home for Christmas 1995, and when it was time to go back to school, I just didn't go. No one said anything or asked why. I just went back to the hood with no plan. Until one day I was talking to Sharol, and she told me about the California Conservation Corps. She said they hired at-risk youth from the inner city from the ages of eighteen to twenty-three years old. *Why not?* I thought to myself, *I'll check it out.*

Turns out, it was a very good idea! I went for an orientation at the L.A. Center on Vernon and Main, and they told me all about it. The job was geared to prepare the youth for the working world, learning skills while fighting all natural disasters, including wild land forest fires, floods, and earthquakes, or better called Emergencies.

When not dispatched to an emergency, your crew could be doing a number of things, such as fire reduction, construction and rehab of horse and hiking trails at California State Parks, assisting Caltrans on the freeways, planting trees, etc. The motto was "Hard work, low pay, miserable conditions, and more." Each corps member was given a year's time in the program unless they promoted. Then, they would get extensions on their rime, but after the initial year, they should be qualified for all state jobs. The Corps also helped them get their diploma or GED while they worked. They told me that the L.A. Center was non-residential, but if I wanted to live there, they had residential centers all throughout California that I could go to. That was right up my alley because I needed to get back out of my mother's house. The soonest opening they had was about an hour and a half up North in Camarillo, CA. I jumped on it. They scheduled me a Greyhound bus ticket to leave in two weeks.

Things were starting to look up again! The skinny girl, Kara, had even gotten back in touch with me. She told me that she had gotten with a guy and had a baby boy, but she wasn't happy. I invited her over to catch up on things, and to my surprise, she wasn't skinny at all anymore! She was as thick as Sharol was. She looked incredible! She was playing hookie from a Jehovah's Witness meeting to come and see me. So, I led her to my room and took her down. Quit playing!

I left to Camarillo and liked it very much. They paired me with a roommate who was from Czechoslovakia named Remy. He was cool. One evening, we were hanging out with the two guys across the hall from us, Ron and Dwight. They came to our room talking about Ouija boards, telling wild stories of crazy stuff happening.

"That stuff is real, man!" Dwight said. "You can talk to your dead homeboys."

"No, you can't," Ron interrupted. "It's always a demon, never your friend or family member."

"Yeah, that's right," I said. "Those demons are trying to trick you."

"We should play with it," Ron said.

"Cool," I said. "But, we don't have a board." I didn't care. I was already hearing voices in my head. What was one more going to do?

"It's better to make one anyway," Ron said. "It's more powerful, because you put effort into making it. It's also stronger when you have the same amount of female players as you do male."

"Alright, Mr. Expert. Let's quit talking about it and make one and play it," Remy said.

"Wait a minute, bro," Ron demanded. "You have to know this stuff before you play. It's very important. Everyone has to keep their hands on the marker until the spirit says goodbye. If you take your hands off before, you run the risk of getting possessed by the spirit."

"Alright, we got it," Dwight said. "Let's make it."

Ron made the board and the marker and drew the symbols and letters on it. It looked weird, but close enough. We put the board on a small desk in between the two beds. I sat on one, and Remy and Dwight sat on the other bed, and Ron sat in a chair on the opposite side of the desk.

"I want to go first," Dwight said. "I want to talk to my cousin that died last year."

"Alright, but it won't be your cousin," Ron said.

"Whatever," Dwight brushed him off.

We began to put the tips of our fingers on the marker and let it move around as Ron instructed us. It felt like we all were just pushing it around until Dwight started asking questions.

"I'd like to speak to my cousin Brian," Dwight asked. "He died last year in a car accident." The marker kept circling around slowly, so Dwight asked again. That time the marker went to the top of the board and paused over the word "Hello" for a second before circling around again. We were shocked, but at the same time excited that we'd gotten a connection.

"Is this my cousin, Brian?" Dwight asked looking unsure. The marker briefly paused on "Yes."

"Are you here in the room with us?" Dwight asked.

"Yes," it paused.

"Are you sitting in the empty chair?" Dwight asked.

"No," it paused.

"Are you sitting on the bed by the window?" Dwight asked.

"No," it paused.

"Are you sitting next to me on the bed that I'm on?" Dwight asked.

"Yes," it paused.

"Okay, so if you're really my cousin and you're sitting next to me, then give me a hug," Dwight said.

All of a sudden, a voice shouted out from what seemed like it came from down the hallway,

"NO!! YOU'RE NOT SUPPOSED TO HUG THEM!"

We got spooked! How did this guy hear us from down the hallway with the door and window closed? Dwight got even more spooked and took his hands off the marker! As soon as he did that, a gust of wind blew through the room straight onto Dwight and made his clothes ruffle! Then, we were all freaking out, because like I said, the door and window was closed! The marker began to go wild all over the board!

"You guys, don't take your hands off!" Ron shouted.

Dwight got off the bed and backed into a corner and sat on the floor Indian style with his teeth chattering as if he was in 30° below zero freezing weather! He sat and rocked back and forth calling out to Jesus!

"Jesus!!! Please help me! I'm sorry! Jesus!!!" he shouted.

"Goodbye! Goodbye! Goodbye!" We all started shouting, but the marker continued to go crazy all over the board!

"Goodbye!" We continued.

"No," the marker paused.

"Goodbye! Goodbye!" We shouted.

"No," the marker paused.

"Goodbye! We don't want to talk no more!" Ron shouted. Then, the marker spelled out H-E-L-L-N-O! We were terrified! Plus, Dwight was still going off in the corner! After what seemed like forever, the marker finally went to goodbye and stopped. Dwight calmed down, and his teeth stopped chattering.

"Man! Let's throw this thing in the trash, right now!" I said as we cautiously took our hands off the marker. Everyone agreed, and we all walked outside to the trash dumpster and threw it away together!

"I'm cool on that stuff, man!" I said.

Everyone agreed, and we all went to our rooms and went to bed. I asked God to forgive me about fifty times! The next morning, I woke up and went to the closet to grab my toothbrush off the shelf and low and behold, the Ouija board was on the shelf!! Marker and all!

"Remy!! Get up!" I shook my roommate as he woke up in shock. "Look! This thing was in the closet just now on the top shelf!"

"WHAT?! Remy shouted. We both couldn't believe it!

"Come on," I said. "Let's see what Ron has to say about this one!" We went across the hall and told Ron what happened.

"Oh yeah, I forgot!" Ron said. "You can't just throw it away if you don't want it anymore. You have to either burn it or give it to someone who wants it."

"Fine time to tell us, bro!" Remy said to Ron.

"Well, we can't burn it. We'll definitely get sent home for arson." I said. "Come on. Let's see if somebody wants it!"

We walked through the hallway, asking everybody we ran into if they wanted it, but everybody said no. We went upstairs to the second floor and caught Terry coming out of his room.

"Aye, Terry! What's up?" we said.

"What's up?" He looked at us puzzled.

"Do you want this Ouija board? It works!" I said.

"Yeah," he said, as he took it out of my hands.

"Cool," I said, as I gladly gave it to him. We were all relieved it was over!

Everything went back to normal, but I had the same street mentality of doing things the way I wanted to and soon found myself fired. Fortunately, the program is set up for kids with my kind of logic, so if you get fired the first time, they give a chance to get your priorities straight, and if you're serious about the job, you can write them a letter and go back as a second chancer.

So, that's what I did. I went back and took full advantage of what the program had to offer. I learned a lot about power tools, especially the chainsaw. Come to find out, I was pretty surgical like a doctor. That was something I never would've known about myself had I stayed in college. I met a lot of great people, and some became good friends, like my C-1 John Shashino-Cruz, who taught me everything I know about power tools and helped bring my skills to the surface. Plus, JJ and Knievel from Lime Hood Piru, out in Compton, CA, who I am still friends with today.

As my one-year time started to come to a close, I decided to transfer to the LACIMA Fire Center in Julian, which is in the San Diego mountains. At the Fire Center, you actually became a Type I Wild Land Firefighter on a hand crew, working with CDF captains. You were also automatically granted a two-year extension after you passed the exams. I was all in, passing the exams and was placed at Second Brush Hook behind the Second Chainsaw Vets.

Everything was going real good! I had the best job that I had ever had in my life because I loved what I was doing, so it was more fun than work. Kara had just had another baby boy, but because she was dealing with her baby's daddy, she told him that the baby was his and gave the baby his last name Roland Butler. When I came home to visit in L.A., I saw the baby boy, and he was my twin. I knew and her baby's daddy knew that he was my son. Later, his name was changed to mine Roland Watkins.

The following year, Kara hit me with an ultimatum in 1998. She was still struggling to be a Jehovah's Witness, and she wanted to do it right and told me she had to get married or stop having sex with me. At that time, Kara was the one I was going to see whenever I went down from the mountains for a weekend in L.A. So, I figured, why not. The only thing I was missing was a wife. Plus, income tax season was coming up, so I suggested we go to Las Vegas and get it done.

So, we did. On our way driving to Las Vegas, we were having a conversation about arguments and getting upset when she mentioned that one time she got upset with her oldest son's dad, Big Ronson, while he was sitting on the couch, and she threw a full can of soda and hit him in the head with it, making him immediately jump up and knock her out cold! *What?* I thought to myself, *This girl might be crazy!* Of course, it doesn't give him an excuse to knock her out, but even the doctor gets kicked sometimes when he tests your reflexes.

My first mind was telling me to bust a hook slide and head back to L.A., but I brushed it off as being an isolated incident and went along with the plan. Then, what do you know? The very night of the wedding, she conceived our daughter, Kayla Watkins.

We got an apartment in El Cajon, so she would be close to me in San Diego, but Kara soon got fed up and wanted to move back to L.A. because there was so much racism in El Cajon.

"Every time I walk to the store, people drive by and holler racial slurs out of their cars!" Kara said.

So, she moved back to L.A. In turn, there was so much going on and things to take care of that I had to be home for more than a weekend. So, I made the decision to transfer to the L.A. Center for non-residential status. The only thing is the L.A. Center crews didn't actually fight the fires. They were only incident command camp support, but for earthquakes and floods, they were hands-on first responders. At least, I got my chance to live my childhood dream for a little while. When the teacher would ask what I wanted to be when I grow up, my answer was either a firefighter or a lawyer. Becoming a firefighter was a blessing, but it was time to see what else God had in store for my life.

That same year, Kayla was born two months early with a hole in her intestines and weighing 2 lbs. 13 oz. She had to stay in the hospital for two months inside of an incubator, so her body could finish maturing to a healthy level. The doctors put a colostomy bag on her stomach, after bringing the undeveloped section of her intestines to the outside of her body. I was asking everyone who knew how to pray to pray for her. I would be there with her every day after work, reading children's books to her, talking to her, and touching her. The nurses said it helped her grow a lot faster than the other babies whose parents came every now and then. The bag was finally able to come off, and Kayla was able to go home with us. God is good! He helped her fight for her life right from the beginning!

I soon worked my way up to crew leader at work, extending my time another year, but I didn't need the time because in 1999, I was hired with Caltrans Department of Transportation, making three times as much that I was making before! It was a blessing! At the time, Kara had persuaded me to study the doctrine of Jehovah's Witnesses with an elder from their Kingdom Hall. I agreed, but I knew that something was wrong with their belief.

For instance, you couldn't be a witness or even get baptized and be considered saved until you finished your numerous weeks of studies and then met with the board of elders to be approved by men that you were qualified. So, if you died before all that happened, you wouldn't be considered a Christian yet? It was weird, plus a whole lot of other stuff that was not in the Bible, but I studied to please my wife. Go figure.

One thing the elder did help us with though was when all of a sudden the children started using curse words when they were not going outside or anything, and my wife and I were not using them around the children. Plus, arguments were occurring more and more between us. The elder told us there was something demonic in our apartment. The first thing I could think of was my gargoyle demon face mask that I brought back from Japan in '92. I had it hanging on the bedroom wall. I also started to get sleep paralysis when waking up. At first, I didn't want to get rid of the mask because it was an expensive souvenir, but when I finally decided to throw it away, the children immediately stop cursing and the arguments died down.

It was time to move to a bigger place and get out of the one bedroom we had. So, we ended up moving to the Jungles on the west side of Crenshaw Boulevard. I began to hang out in the hood more and also started back smoking sherm again. With smoking sherm came infidelity to please my own self. It was a cycle that once started, it had to be followed through especially when I was denied at home. Alcohol, PCP, and a woman, in that order. Those bad seeds that I planted began to quickly grow fruit that was not sweet to the taste.

One night, I drove home by the grace of God high out of my mind and drank in my '87 Cutlass Supreme, with the music banging the oldies. I pulled the car into the garage and continued listening to my music and enjoying my buzz. The next thing I knew, three guys had come into the garage and closed the door down behind them. I had the car still running with the lights on and the music blasting, but I could still faintly hear them talking as the first guy who entered pointed a gun in my face.

"Yeah, cuzz. Go on and get out the car!" he said.

My vision was kind of blurry, but I knew those dudes were not Crips. They were too familiar. I slowly got out of the car even more cautious than following the directions of the police. I had the music blasting, and we were inside a closed garage. They could have easily killed me, and no one would have heard the shot. I slowly lay down in the semi-dry puddle of oil next to my car and closed my eyes. All muscles relaxed and water released, as I prepared to expire. They went through my pockets and took off my shoes, finding the $900 I had in my sock. I heard the voice of one of the other two say, "Let's kill him! We should kill him!"

But, the one that put the gun in my face said, "Naw!"

I thank God he was the one in charge… They opened the garage door, and the three of them took off in my car. I got up and went upstairs, looking a mess, while my wife sat in the bedroom doing something with her hair.

"Man! They just robbed me downstairs!" I shouted.

"Noooo!" Kara got hysterical.

I called G-Nutt who was fresh out of the pen again, but I really didn't want to get him involved because he was really trying to do good that time. I just needed to tell him what had just happened. I got the car back through the word on the street, but I didn't want it anymore. The best decision was to trade it in for a '91 Cutlass, and I kept the line moving. Oh, but the seeds were still growing, and the fruit blossomed, even in wintertime.

I took the children to the movies one day to see the latest cartoon, and Lil Ronson said, "Oh, I seen this movie already!"

"Oh yeah?" I asked.

"Yeah, with my mama and this man," he said. "We went over another man's house before too, and I was playing with his son outside while they were in the house. His son got blue eyes, but he not white."

"Is that right?" I asked.

I started checking Kara's voicemail messages and got the shock of the century. Different guys back to back were trying to put their bid in.

"Aye, what's up with you…"

"Aye, this is the dude you met at the Slauson swap meet…"

"Aye, call me back…"

"Aye..."

I was sick! I confronted her about it, and of course, she denied it. I kept pushing the issue. "Lil Ronson wouldn't make up a story like that," I said.

Then finally, she admitted it. We sat down at the dining room table, and she went on about how she wanted to be with other men and that is what she wanted to do. So, we came to an agreement that she would save up enough money and move out. Until then, we both would do whatever we wanted as if we were single. That was the plan. The only problem was, she could give out her number quicker than I could collect them. She would cook dinner in the evening, give the children a bath, and leave until the morning, passing me, coming in as I left for work. I was super sick!

One day, I got too high again, and the devil started talking in my ear saying, "You got four bullets in your gun. Enough for all of them. You should do it. Why not? She gotta go!"

I went back home drunk and high and found her sleeping on one couch and Roland on the other. Kayla and Lil Ronson were in the bedroom asleep. I woke her up and told her it was time for her to go. As I cocked the gun back, she jumped up, grabbed my son, and ran out of the house. Soon after, the police were there to get me. I went to jail and took a deal to do four months in a halfway house. That way, I could keep my job. That was the beginning of 2001. While I was locked up, we lost four homies within two months: Big Chub, Denny Ray, Lil Sugar Bear, and Lil Killa Jess.

After I got out, I told Kara I was not dealing with her anymore, but she was expecting me to come back home. She left a message on my voicemail saying, "If you don't be with me, you deserve to be in jail." I didn't pay it any mind until I had to go to court and turn in a progress report for my parenting and anger management classes.

The bailiff pulled me to the side and said, "You have a warrant for your arrest. Assault with a firearm and terrorist threat."

"What?" I said.

"Yeah, take off your belt, empty your pockets, and take out your shoestrings," he said.

I couldn't believe it! I spent four more months fighting a case I didn't do because she wanted to lie and put me back in jail. Going through riots, fights, and the whole nine, but I was not taking a deal that time because I knew I was innocent. Plus, they were trying to give me sixteen years because the first case would give me a prior for the same charges. Eight counts in all, run consecutively. They were trying to hold me for a while, but the jury saw she was lying and found me 'not guilty'! I was the happiest man with used underwear on!

As I went back to the holding tank, I ran into Terry who I knew from Camarillo in the Conservation Corps. I spoke to him, but he was wide eyed and had a constant smile on his face, looking spaced out. He was wearing the medical ding ward jumpsuit, so I knew he was on some serious psychiatric medication. I wondered what had happened to him. He was a normal guy when I knew him five years before. Later, it clicked! I remembered I was the one that gave him the Ouija board five years ago! My goodness! I felt really bad...

After I went home, the detectives called me asking if I wanted to press charges on my wife for falsely accusing me, and I said, "Man, I'm trying to get as far away from y'all and her as possible right now! I am cool!"

Chapter 34

New Life

As soon as I got free, I went and cashed the checks that were waiting on me from my job. There was no sense in waiting until they were null and void. It had already been four months, and I didn't want the hassle of having to get new checks issued. I was very grateful and appreciative for my coworkers who came to my trial and testified on my behalf, but to be truthful, it would have really been painful to see their faces knowing I couldn't put my orange shirt on again. Since my car had been repossessed while I had been locked up, I needed another vehicle ASAP!

Joseph Jr. said he knew of a good auction out in Orange County that he could take me to. I ended up getting an '87 Ford Taurus wagon for $500 on the nose! It ran pretty good, so I was satisfied. Plus, it was big enough for me to pick up my kids and some more people's kids.

The next goal to reach on my agenda was finding another job before I spend all of my reserves. Plus, I already had made the decision I wasn't selling crack anymore. In my opinion, crack was the worst culprit of Black economic demise since the massacres of Black Wall Street in 1921, in Tulsa, Oklahoma. It was time to stop being a part of the problem and help the solution. The job scene was my best hustle, and the hunt was on! I didn't waste any time putting in applications left and right. Until I found a job, looking for a job was my job.

Just as I was dropping off an application in the Nickerson Garden Projects for a position as a maintenance worker, one of the secretaries for Caltrans paged me. When I called her back, she said it was okay for me to come back to work! She went on to say that she was instructed to send my file to Sacramento for termination a while ago, but she held onto it because she knew my situation. I don't even know how she knew I was out, but I thanked God and her for looking out for me!

It seemed like I had missed a whole lot when I was gone. Maybe, I just didn't notice because I wasn't hanging around my mother's house too much when I was living with my wife. My sister Ashley had a pretty little nineteen-year-old friend who was hanging with her a lot lately. Come to find out Vooshia knew the whole family. She fell asleep on the couch one day, and I kissed her like Sleeping Beauty on the cheek with my mother and Ashley standing there.

Of course, later they told her the get down, and she started to have an infatuation for me. We hit it off and started dating and getting to know one another on every level. I was already working on getting an apartment that my uncle and aunt owned, but it was taking a while to be ready to move in. As a matter of fact, it was the same one-bedroom apartment my mother and father was living in on 64th Street when I was born. When the apartment was finally ready, I took Vooshia to move in with me.

January 9, 2002 was a blessing for me! It was my birthday, and I wasn't in nobody's jail. Freedom can be taken for granted until you lose it. As for me, there were two things that became precious to me like a rare jewel. First was the watch on my wrist. It didn't have to be an expensive watch, just as long as I knew what time it was and didn't have to ask or wait for someone else to tell me. The other thing was keys in my possession to open doors, allowing me to come and go as I pleased. Like I said before, it was my birthday! Beating another statistic of young Black men dying or getting killed by the age of twenty-five, I had just made twenty-six!

To celebrate, Vooshia and I went out to Hollywood to the House of Blues for the Mack 10 concert. It was off the hook! Best birthday I had in a long time! There was even a fight that broke out in the audience near the stage, and Mack 10 immediately had the music cut off and told everybody to stand back and let 'em get down. After the two young men were done fighting, Mack 10 asked, "Alright, y'all straight? It's a Gangsta Party, ain't it?"

"YEAH!" everybody shouted. Then, he continued with the show. Classic!

Although I was back to work, I was also back to the streets and back to my old habits. It was an everyday thing for me, drinking alcohol, smoking sherm, and Black & Mild cigars. My only reserve was not getting high or drunk at work, but as soon as the workday was done, altering my mind state was the number one goal, and that was just the beginning.

One day, I was flossin' in my relative's ride, a 1975 convertible rag top, Glasshouse Caprice Classic on Dayton wire 13" wheels. Yeah, I was lying big time! Everybody thought it was mine. I drove it to Lil T-Bone's house because he was having a small function with the homies. Always gambling, you could find me in the basement in a one-on-one Domino game with DG. There was a cup of Hennessy on my left and a can of Olde English 800 on my right, and I was sipping on them both with refills, not a few.

It wasn't until I stood up and started walking outside that it all hit me! I was faded! I was ready to leave, so I jumped in the ride with the top down and drove to the corner of 11th Street and Vermont Avenue when I blacked out. When I came to my senses, I was standing at the front of the car, which was wrapped around a light pole on 60th Street and Vermont, with blood all over my face. Apparently, I had been driving on the sidewalk on autopilot. I had torn down the street sign and the stop sign, and I had a small city tree in the backseat of the car.

I had side swiped two storefronts, tearing off the bar gates, and the car was stopped by a light pole that didn't move when I ran into it. There was a six-pack of Olde English 800 beer in the passenger seat. So, that means I had made a stop along the way, in between 11th Street and 60th Street, and unknowingly made money transactions before continuing to drive beyond intoxicated. While standing in front of the car, I blacked out again. The next time, I came to my senses, I was handcuffed in the backseat of a patrol car, and my mother was tapping on the window hollering, "LOOK WHAT YOU DID! LOOK WHAT YOU DID!"

"I CAN'T CHANGE IT NOW!" I hollered back before blacking out again. I later found out that Keeta Boo saw me and went and got my mother.

I woke up again, and that time I was handcuffed to a hospital bed with two officers sitting on a bench across from me. A doctor came in and started poking at my face while asking, "Does this hurt?"

"Yeah, it hurts, man! I told you it hurts! How many times do I have to tell you?" I was going off on the doctor.

"You're a lucky man," the doctor said. "Giving what you have been through, you only broke a bone in your right eye socket." After the doctor was done, the police officers walked over to me.

"Now, you talked to him how you wanted, but you're not going to talk to us like that," one of the officers explained. They took me to jail for driving under the influence and for reckless endangerment. Even after I got out, I still hadn't learned my lesson. I was just a little more careful while driving.

On July 12, 2003, Amari Watkins was born, my third child and second daughter! I thought to myself, *Now this time, I'll get to live with my child and raise her from birth until adult.* What more could a father ask? As I kept running the streets, trying my best to ruin my life by continuing to go to jail, getting DUIs, and doing what gang members do, it was clear that my priorities were not yet in order. Plus, I was still full of demons that were always talking to me and telling me to do stuff. When I was high and drunk, I would start to listen to them and sometimes do what they were suggesting. That's why most of the time, I would give my guns to the homie Insane Dre.

Working on the freeways, I would find guns left and right. We were supposed to turn them in to the highway patrol whenever we found guns and drugs, but I was a gang member first, and gang members didn't get rid of guns unless it was necessary. The only problem was every time I seemed to hold on to one, an opportunity to use it would come right along and present itself. So, if no firearms were around, the trouble I did get into wasn't so bad, like waking up in hospitals handcuffed in restraints to the bed because I had blacked out from too much sherm and the demons had taken over my body. Some people woke up in a jail cell, asking the guard why they were in there only to find out they were there for murder while under the influence of PCP. I didn't want to become that dude…

One day, Vooshia was talking smack to me like she was crazy, and the demons started talking loud in my head saying, "Who she think she is, talking CRAZY? The next time she talks crazy like that, you should whoop her with a belt! Yeah, give her a whopping!"

Sure enough, the next time she said something crazy, I started whopping her with a belt like she was seven years old. That very same day, she took Amari and moved out. I came home the next day and all of her stuff was gone, leaving me alone with my demons of deception. Yeah, deceived I was, thinking that now it was really time to live, bachelor style. Hanging with the homie CK or S-Gee and Lil Buck. I even had a Lil Spike named after me. Pretty much, the blind leading the blind. Don't forget Baby Boy, Slim, and Lil Gooch.

My life started to spiral even more downhill than it was before. There were different women every week, but they were never satisfying. I was free to live how I pleased, but I was ruining myself with drugs and alcohol. I started having fights with my homeboys, which I hated to do. Even my own family started to not like seeing me coming, because I was a different person when I was high.

Despite what happened, Vooshia still allowed me to spend time with her and Amari on the weekends. Sometimes, I spent the night at her duplex in Inglewood. I was grateful for that, but I could no longer fake it or hide my addictions. Going to the movie theatre was also a task. I started sneaking in two 24 oz. cans of beer inside just to sit through a movie. I had noticed the changes, and I didn't like it.

I was getting tired of being a slave to all of the addictions that controlled my life. I drank alcohol every day and even on Sunday. I was addicted to PCP, which I had tried to stop before on my own, but that didn't last. One time, the homie Lil Rat said that old saying, "Once a sherm head, always a sherm head," and I couldn't even get mad because it was proven to be true in my life. I was also addicted to sex. I had to have it. No feelings involved, just pleasure. No names, just faces. No description, just a body. I was sick! Sick of myself. I was even sick of being a hood rat. Most of my spare time was spent in the hood. Even if there was nothing going on, I just had to be over there.

Although I was far from living like a Christian, I knew that in my heart of hearts I needed prayer. That was the first thing I could think of, not a counselor or a 12-step program. I did those for the courts, and they were just that, for the courts. Vooshia went to church every Sunday, Tuesday, and Thursday. Her grandparents were the pastor and first lady of the church. It was a Tuesday night, so I knew she would be going, so I gave her a call to pick me up along the way. She was shocked at my request, but at the same time, she was more than glad to pick me up for church.

Vooshia picked me up while I was smelling like a little bit of this and a little bit of that. I didn't care at all! Jesus said to come as you are, so I did just that, with all of my problems. We went inside the church and sat right in the back while her granddad was preaching up a storm. I wasn't really paying attention to what he was saying. I was waiting for him to be done and to call for the alter call, so I could get a prayer. He finally wrapped up his message, and I was getting ready to walk to the front for prayer, but to my surprise, there was no altar call made. I sat there for a moment, wondering maybe he was waiting for something before he made the call, but nope. He had already said, "You are now dismissed."

So, Vooshia, Amari, and I got up and started making our way out of the church. Very disappointed, I knew I wasn't the most favorite guy on the block for the way I had treated Vooshia in the past, but my goodness. Before I could reach the door, another preacher was coming down the aisle, calling after me and trying to get my attention.

"Excuse me, young man?" he asked. I later found out he was a brother of the pastor and also a pastor himself.

"Yes, sir," I responded as I turned back around.

"Did you want prayer?" he asked.

"Yes, I did," I said.

"Well, we could pray right now if you don't mind." The preacher stood there, seemingly wanting to pray just as badly as I did.

"Alright," I said.

He took both my hands into his hands and looked me straight in the eyes and said, "After this prayer, you will never be the same… Repeat this prayer after me 'Dear Heavenly Father, I come to you as a sinner, asking that you forgive me for all my sins. I'm sorry for the wrong things I have done against you. I know that Jesus Christ is Lord, and He died for my sins, and you raised Him from the dead on the third day. I ask that you come into my heart and be my Lord and Savior, because I can't do it on my own. I thank you for forgiving me. I thank you for saving me. In Jesus' name, I pray. Amen!' Welcome to the family of God!"

"Amen! Thank you," I said.

I left the church feeling much better than before. Vooshia dropped me back off at my apartment, and I went to bed as usual. I was grateful for the prayer, but I didn't fully understand what had just happened. The next morning, I woke up and went to work, but after work, I drove straight home without any urge to drink any alcohol. It was weird. A few days went by of the same thing, so I went and bought two beers out of habit. Going from drinking every day to not drinking at all was a big change! I didn't know how to act. With the two beers in hand, I walked to the back of my apartment building and sat down on a turned over bucket to get ready to drink. As I cracked open the first beer and took a sip, it was disgusting! As if I had never had a drink in my life! I took that beer and the unopened one and threw them both in the trash.

Wow! I thought to myself, God has taken the taste out of my mouth! I went to Vooshia's place for the weekend as usual and was playing with Amari. As it started to get late, I went inside Vooshia's bedroom alone as I felt a need to pray. Down on my knees on the side of the bed not a word was said, but I felt a strong conviction come over me, and somehow, I knew that it was because of fornication in my life. Vooshia came into the room and saw me weeping and asked, "What's wrong?"

"I can't do this anymore," I said. "We have to get married."

I couldn't explain what I was going through, but I knew it was God doing it. Every day it seemed that something negative was being worked out of my character, and I felt the need to attend church. Upon telling my mother and siblings that I was going to church, they began to take notice. I even called the homie S-Gee and told him I was going through some changes, but he explained everybody goes through changes. That was true, but those were not ordinary changes. It was a supernatural thing happening to me at thirty-one years of age in the springtime of 2007.

Next, the Lord took my mind back to the third grade when I said the first curse word with my buddy Ben and how I subsequently began using those words on a regular basis. I was like, "Wow, Lord! I want to go back to before I said that word!" And immediately after I agreed with God, no foul word proceeded from my mouth. Then, He took PCP away, after I felt a vibration go through me as I took a hit off a stick. It was then that I knew that I was offending the Holy Spirit, and I no longer wanted the poison in my system. At church, the pastor said a scripture that stuck with me, *"Therefore, if any man be in Christ, he is a new creature: old things are passed away; behold, all things are become new"* (II Corinthians 5:17).

The scripture was definitely true because it was currently happening in my life! The air seemed a little fresher and every color seemed a little brighter! Even the song that the birds chirped was now a beautiful praise unto God! There was evidence in my life personally that I could honestly say that God is real! I know it because He showed up in my life at a time when I wasn't loving or honoring Him in any way. Yet and still, He chose me! He says in His Word, *"Before I formed thee in the belly I knew thee; and before thou camest forth out of the womb I sanctified thee, and I ordained thee a prophet unto the nations"* (Jeremiah 1:5).

The Bible further explains that this gift of salvation is for everybody who makes a decision to accept Jesus Christ into their heart to be their Lord and Savior and that God doesn't wish that any should die, but that all would come to repentance (II Peter 3:9).

"For God so loved the world, that he gave his only begotten Son, that whosoever believeth in him should not perish, but have everlasting

life. For God sent not his Son into the world to condemn the world; but that the world through him might be saved" (John 3:16-17).

The Lord began to take me from glory to glory as He matured me in the things of God! Accepting Christ into my life had proven to be the most important thing I had ever done in my life, and I would highly recommend that everyone did the same. As I continued to grow in the Lord, two years later in 2009, I was proven and ordained as a deacon in the church and in the body of Christ. Social media became a wonderful tool for me to reach God's people with His Word in parts of the world that I never would have been able to at such a fast pace.

One day, Mrs. Jackson's daughter Lady 'liked' one of my posts. She then sent me a message, stating her mother had already gone home to be with the Lord. I was very saddened by the news.

"If only Mrs. Jackson could see you now," she said. When she said that, her comment jolted my memory of how she used to always call me Deacon Ray, even when I was banged out and smoking sherm.

And all I could say was, "Wow! To God be the glory!"

www.ingramcontent.com/pod-product-compliance
Lightning Source LLC
Chambersburg PA
CBHW062153080426
42734CB00010B/1675